D1590465

Dante Gabriel Rossetti and Jane Morris

Their Correspondence

Janey—posed by Rossetti in his garden at 16 Cheyne Walk

DANTE GABRIEL ROSSETTI AND JANE MORRIS

Their Correspondence

edited with an Introduction by
JOHN BRYSON

in association with
JANET CAMP TROXELL

CLARENDON PRESS · OXFORD
1976

Oxford University Press, Ely House, London W.1

GLASGOW   NEW YORK   TORONTO   MELBOURNE   WELLINGTON
CAPE TOWN   IBADAN   NAIROBI   DAR ES SALAAM   LUSAKA   ADDIS ABABA
DELHI   BOMBAY   CALCUTTA   MADRAS   KARACHI   LAHORE   DACCA
KUALA LUMPUR   SINGAPORE   HONG KONG   TOKYO

ISBN 0 19 812464 3

Filmset and printed in Great Britain by
BAS Printers Limited, Wallop, Hampshire

Preface

THE letters from Rossetti to Mrs. Morris were given to the British Museum (Add. MSS, 52332 A. and B. and 52333 A. and B.) by the executor of May Morris after her death in 1939, and were placed on reserve for a period of fifty years dating from her mother's death in 1914. They became available for consultation in 1964 and are now printed in full for the first time. There are one hundred and fourteen letters to Janey, one to William Morris, and one sent with a present of dormice to the daughters, Jenny and May. A detailed account of the letters and their content was given by R. C. H. Briggs in the *Journal of the William Morris Society*, Vol. I, No. 4, Summer 1964. Four late letters that have strayed from the series are to be found in the *Letters of Dante Gabriel Rossetti* edited by Oswald Doughty and J. R. Wahl; these are included.

Mrs. J. C. Troxell has contributed the thirty-seven letters from Janey. These she acquired from the Rossetti family and they have now passed from her to the library of Princeton University. An additional letter from Janey comes from the British Library (Ashley MS. 5755, fol. 107). Two letters in the Troxell collection that Janey wrote to Ford Madox Brown and to William Michael Rossetti during Dante Gabriel's illness in 1872 are printed in an Appendix.

Rossetti's letters begin in March 1868 and end in October 1881, when he was on his visit to the Lake District with Hall Caine six months before his death. Janey's start just before the Morrises moved from Turnham Green to the house on Hammersmith Mall in the autumn of 1878, and cover only the three years till 1881. Earlier letters of hers have clearly been destroyed. The correspondence is not continuous, and only occasionally is the interchange consecutive. On the Rossetti side there are two major breaks—an interval of fourteen months from May 1868 till July 1869, and another of seven years between 1870 and 1877. There are no letters from him during the period of mental breakdown and collapse in the summer of 1872, and naturally none from the time of his return to Kelmscott on recovery till he left it finally in 1874.

In the case of both writers there is little to explain why some letters have survived and others not. Janey tells him, when she is hunting for an address he had sent, that to wade through a drawerful of his letters to find it would be the work of a day for her. It is clear that much has been lost. Rosssetti left instructions that letters in his possession were to be destroyed after his death.

Only rarely does either writer give anything but the day of the week as indication of date. The envelopes of most of the Rossetti letters have been preserved, and from the postmarks a tentative order can be established (provided that the envelope accompanies the right letter, which is not always the case in the British Museum arrangement). Janey's letters sort themselves into a number of groups that can be dated—e.g. the move to Hammersmith, her visit to the Howards at Naworth, and the letters written from Bordighera. Others depend on context or internal clues for their placing, and a few are unplaceable in sequence. Rossetti's punctuation is colloquial and informal; this is retained, though occasionally where sense demands it has been brought into line with modern usage. In the matter of punctuation Janey is a law unto herself and it has been thought best not to interfere with her style.

In the notes the editor attempts to identify persons, to explain allusions to contemporary events, and, with the indispensable help of Virginia Surtees's *catalogue raisonné*, to give some account of the pictures mentioned. Where he has failed to solve a problem or trace a reference he hopes the reader may be more successful in finding an answer.

Illustrations have been chosen to show the pictures discussed in the letters and to give portrait-drawings of some of the friends mentioned. These are by Rossetti unless another artist is indicated.

Books referred to are not listed separately but are mentioned in the notes.

Acknowledgements

I had the privilege of knowing Mrs. Rossetti Angeli, Rossetti's niece, and in conversations with her I learned much about the artist at first hand. She gave me her permission to edit his unpublished letters to Mrs. Morris, and her daughter, Mrs. Imogen Dennis, now owner of the copyright, has kindly consented to publication. Mrs. Janet Camp Troxell has made the edition possible by contributing her group of Janey's letters.

To three friends who have helped in the preparation of the book I am deeply indebted. Mrs. Virginia Surtees with the authority of her *catalogue raisonné* and her invaluable knowledge of Rossetti's paintings has been able to solve many of my problems, and she has given constant encouragement and help. Mr. John Gere has discussed the work with me and has kindly read my comments and notes, which have benefited greatly from his criticism and knowledge. Mr. Vincent Quinn with patience and skill has helped in the process of transcribing the letters and in the attempt to settle their chronological order. I am grateful to all three for the assistance they have given.

For information on various points I am obliged to Miss Mary Bennett, Mr. John Sparrow, the late Mr. Philip James, Mr. C. G. Christian, Prof. W. E. Fredeman, and others unmentioned. My thanks are due to Lady Gibson, Mr. David Rust, Mr. R. M. Ritchie, and Mr. and Mrs. Richard Ormond for permission to reproduce pictures in their possession. During the preparation for printing Mr. Jon Stallworthy, Mr. Anthony Hobbs, and the skilful staff of the Clarendon Press have been most helpful.

I am grateful to the many galleries and institutions that have helped with the illustrations. Their contribution is acknowledged in the List of Illustrations.

JOHN BRYSON

Contents

List of Illustrations   x

Abbreviations   xii

Introduction   xiii

THE CORRESPONDENCE   1

Appendices:

I.   Letters of Mrs. Morris unplaced in the Rossetti Series   189

II.   A Fragment   192

III.   Two letters from Mrs. Morris to Ford Madox Brown and to William Michael Rossetti written at the time of D. G. Rossetti's breakdown in 1872, from the Troxell collection   193

Index   209

List of Illustrations

Janey—posed by Rossetti in his garden at 16 Cheyne Walk   *Frontispiece*

LETTERS

3 Portrait of Mrs. Morris in blue dress. *Society of Antiquaries*
   (Kelmscott Manor)   *page* 3
5 Pandora. *Private Collection*   6
5 Sibylla Palmifera. *Trustees of the Lady Lever Art Gallery, Port Sunlight*   7
5 The M's at Ems. *By Courtesy of the Trustees of the British Museum*   16
7 Beatrice (by Burne-Jones). *Private Collection*   13
8 The German Lesson. *British Museum*   16
10 Resolution; or, The Infant Hercules. *British Museum*   22
14 Wombat Drawings (by Treffry Dunn). *British Museum*   32
14 Death of a Wombat. *British Museum*   32
20 The Sphinx; or, The Question. *By Permission of the City of*
   Birmingham Museum and Art Gallery   38
22 A Vision of Fiammetta. *David Rust Esq.*   41
23 Proserpine. *The Tate Gallery, London*   44
23 Water Willow. *Samuel and Mary R. Bancroft Collection—Delaware*
   Art Museum, Wilmington, Del. U.S.A.   46
25 The Blessed Damozel. *Courtesy of the Fogg Art Museum, Harvard*
   University. Greville L. Winthrop bequest   51
30 Dante's Dream. *Walker Art Gallery, Liverpool*   65
30 Astarte Syriaca. *By Courtesy of the City of Manchester Art Galleries* 66
33 Perlascura. *Ashmolean Museum, Oxford*   70
34 Silence. *Ashmolean Museum, Oxford*   72
35 Reverie. *Ashmolean Museum, Oxford*   73
50 St. Edith cartoons (by F. Madox Brown). *Whitworth Art Gallery,*
   University of Manchester   87
57 & 58 Predellas for Dante's Dream. *Fogg Art Museum. Greville*
   L. Winthrop bequest   94
62 The Story of Nastasio degli Onesti (by Botticelli). *Prado Museum,*
   Madrid, and Pucci Collection, Florence   98
63 La Donna della Finestra. *Fogg Art Museum. Greville L. Winthrop*
   bequest   101
68 La Bella Mano. *Samuel and Mary R. Bancroft Collection, Delaware Art*
   Museum   106
71 Phyllis and Demophoon (by Burne-Jones). *No. 1, City of Birmingham*
   Museum and Art Gallery. No. 2, Trustees of the Lady Lever Art Gallery,
   Port Sunlight   111
78 Found. *Samuel and Mary R. Bancroft Collection, Delaware Art Museum*   119
79 The Day Dream. *Victoria and Albert Museum, London*   121

page

106 Veronica Veronese. *Samuel and Mary R. Bancroft Collection, Delaware Art Museum* 144
111 A Birthday Sonnet. *Private Collection* 151
117 La Pia de' Tolomei. *University of Kansas Museum of Art* 157
118 Salutation of Beatrice. *Toledo Museum of Art, Toledo, Ohio. Gift of Edward Drummond Libbey* 177
133 Mnemosyne. *Samuel and Mary R. Bancroft Collection, Delaware Art Museum* 177
140 Desdemona's Death Song. *Janet Camp Troxell* 183

ROSSETTI AND MORRIS GROUP

D. G. Rossetti, self-portrait, 1870. *National Portrait Gallery, London* 195
D. G. Rossetti by Charles Keene *c.* 1880. *Ashmolean Museum, Oxford* 195
William Morris, attrib. C. Fairfax-Murray, *c.* 1870. *National Portrait Gallery, London* 195
Mrs. Morris by Burne-Jones. *Private Collection* 195
Janey reading, Scalands, 1870. *Private Collection* 196
Janey in old age at Kelmscott Manor. *St. Bride's Printing Library, London* 197

SITTERS AND FRIENDS

Maria Zambaco. *Mr. and Mrs. Richard Ormond* 198
Marie Spartali (Mrs. Stillman). *R. M. Ritchie Esq.* 198
Aglaia Coronio. *Victoria and Albert Museum, London* 199
Mrs. Crabbe (Ruth Herbert). *Ashmolean Museum, Oxford* 199
James Smetham, self-portrait. *Ashmolean Museum, Oxford* 200
Charles Augustus Howell by Frederick Sandys. *Ashmolean Museum, Oxford* 201
Theodore Watts-Dunton. *National Portrait Gallery, London* 201
Rosa Corder by Whistler. *Copyright The Frick Collection, New York* 202
Frederick R. Leyland by Whistler. *Courtesy of the Smithsonian Institution, Freer Gallery of Art, Washington D.C.* 202

SETTINGS

The sitting room at 16 Cheyne Walk by Treffry Dunn. *National Portrait Gallery, London* 203
The drawing room, Kelmscott House, Hammersmith Mall 204
Cabinet painted by Burne-Jones in the drawing room (Kelmscott House). *Victoria and Albert Museum, London* 204
The library at Kelmscott House 205
Mrs. Morris's room at Kelmscott House 205
Mrs. Morris's bedroom at Kelmscott House 206
Hammersmith Mall from the river 207
Kelmscott Manor, Oxon. 207

Abbreviations

S. *The Paintings and Drawings of Dante Gabriel Rossetti (1828–1882).* A Catalogue Raisonné, by Virginia Surtees, 2 vols., 1971.

D. and W. *Letters of Dante Gabriel Rossetti*, edited by Oswald Doughty and J. R. Wahl, 4 vols., 1965.

M. *Dante Gabriel Rossetti.* An illustrated memorial of his art and life, by H. C. Marillier, 1899.

Introduction

WHAT is the interest of these unpublished letters of Rossetti and Mrs. Morris? Do they throw new light on their relationship? Are they in fact love-letters? Inevitably the correspondence invites these questions. The answer it gives is that his enduring devotion to her is clear, but that her feeling for him, at this stage of the relationship, was more than a valued friendship there is no evidence. It may have been different once, but proof of that must be sought elsewhere. One must remember that these letters from Janey are late letters relating only to the last three years of Rossetti's life, and that the correspondence is neither continuous nor complete. There are unbridgeable gaps on both sides. Many letters have been lost or destroyed. The Janey letters are few in number but interesting as giving fresh glimpses of a figure about whose personality we know little.

Rossetti leaves us in no doubt about his feelings. A renewed intimacy started about 1867, and in an early letter he tells Janey that since they have come together again there has been a clearing away of the chilling numbness that surrounded him in the utter want of her. No one else seems alive to him now, and places empty of her are empty of life. She is the noblest and dearest thing the world has to show him. If he still wishes to do any work it is that he may not sink into unworthiness and deserve nothing but her contempt. How she replied we do not know, for none of her early letters has survived. When hers do begin, some ten years later in 1878, their tone is that of affectionate, practical, common-sense. She will sit to him whenever her state of health and her ailing back allow; she reproaches him for his reluctance to exhibit with other artists at the Grosvenor Gallery; she will not let him off so lightly if he sends her another Jeremiad in depression. He thanks her for gentle kindliness in his dullard state. His feelings remain unchanged, and in a late letter there is a significant passage when he is referring to a sonnet he has sent:

The deep-seated basis of feeling, as expressed in that Sonnet, is as fresh and unchanged towards you as ever, though all else is withered and gone. This you wd. never believe, but if life and fate had willed to link us together you wd. have found true what you cannot think to be truth when alas! untried.

It is not then as a record of mutual passion that the letters are of interest, but rather for what they tell of the everyday life and pursuits of the pair. There is much to be learned from them about Rossetti's painting and writing during the latter part of his career, information about the many pictures and poems she inspired—much, too, about patrons, friends and enemies, and about the contemporary scene. They were both great readers, and they exchange opinions on what they have read. Their health is a matter of deep concern with both.

While Janey, accompanied by William Morris, was taking the cure at Bad Ems in the summer of 1869, Rossetti stayed twice at Penkill in Ayrshire as the guest of Alice Boyd. He writes of life there with her and Bell Scott. It is to these Bad Ems letters that the often reproduced comic drawings—*The M's at Ems* and *The German Lesson*—belong. They were sent to amuse her and they earned some reproof for their freedom. Since she is benefiting from the baths, he says, Ems must henceforth change its name from Bad to Good Ems. At Penkill there is a cave on a slope overhanging a stream, the very place for Top to spin his endless poetry in and for her to listen to the curious urgent whisper of the stream. Rossetti himself had tried to catch that stream's secret:

> What thing unto mine ear.
> Would'st thou convey,—what secret thing,
> O wandering water ever whispering?
> Surely thy speech shall be of her,
> Thou water, O thou whispering wanderer,
> What message did'st thou bring?

With the aid of 'trial-books' he was preparing the 1870 *Poems* for the press, and he makes a comparison of his method of work with Topsy's. Topsy, busy with 'The Earthly Paradise', will be roaring and screaming through the Parnassian tunnels and junctions in his usual style, while his own proofs have hung on hand very much with the tattooings he has given them. Topsy's mountain will indeed view his poor mouse with scorn:

I have been working on what may be called the flea-bite principle, however, at my poetry going through the press, and I find that correction, when one suffers from the vain longing of perfectibility, is an endless task—and Topsy will I fear look with utter scorn on this fidgetty fretting over old ground. He is in the right for himself, I know: but I have nothing of his abundance in production: and to attain confidence first in the plan of any work, however small, and afterwards to aim at rendering it faultless by repeated condensation and revision is the only system that gives me a chance.

It is a revealing statement about his work, which anticipates what he was to say years later to Hall Caine—'Fundamental brainwork, that is what makes the difference in all art.'

Not only does Rossetti tell Janey how he is planning the 1870 *Poems*, but in later letters he lets her know how the 1881 *Ballads and Sonnets* are shaping. There are the 'Beryl Songs' he is adding to 'Rose Mary', and his new historical ballads 'The White Ship' and 'The King's Tragedy'. From time to time he sends her sonnets he has written for 'The House of Life', and the tone of some of these caused misunderstanding. Apologizing for   stupidity over one of them she writes: 'Do send the songs you speak of for the Rose Mary poems, and anything else you are doing. You must feel sure how welcome your work always is to me—and there is little pleasure left one in this world.'

The good-humoured mockery of Topsy in the Ems letters and cartoons changes gradually to something less friendly as Morris's Nordic interests increase and his socialist career advances. When Janey is at Oneglia in the winter of 1877 with her children Rossetti asks ironically what progress Jenny and May are making with their Italian—but he supposes they think Icelandic ought to be the civilized language of Europe and are not bothering. Top, he goes on, is the Odger, the Trade Union champion, of the future—depend on it he'll be in parliament yet. 'O! for that final Cabinet Ministry which is to succeed the 'Cabinet d'Aisance' of his early years.' Has he thrown trade after poetry and does he now execute none but whole-sale orders in philanthropy—the retail trade being beneath a true humanitarian? Has he indeed subscribed a penny to the fund in aid of Keats's sister? When the original partnership was dissolved in 1875 and the 'Firm' came under Morris's sole control the break was complete; all communication ceased between the one-time friends. It is noteworthy that apart from the early study for the head of King David in the Llandaff altar-piece Rossetti never made a portrait of Morris.

The books they are reading and exchanging are a constant topic of interest. We know nothing of Janey's literary education, but clearly she liked books and was by nature a curious reader. There is the pleasant story told by Val Prinsep of how Morris pursued his courtship at Oxford by reading *Barnaby Rudge* to her. She asks for the source of an engraving Rossetti has cut from some journal and sent her. She has found an intensely sensational story on the back of it, for she still keeps up her old habit of reading every scrap that comes her way. She can make intelligent comments on what she has read, and Rossetti's critical remarks are always forceful and pointed. It is a lively exchange.

Their long and varied book list throws light on the tastes and temperament of both readers. Dante heads the list with Gabriel's gift of a copy of the *Vita Nuova*, though Janey confesses elsewhere that she is having difficulty with Christina's Italian versions of the 'Sing Song' poems. They read the historians of Italian art, Vasari, Baldinucci, Crowe and Cavalcaselle—the latter pair being 'the worst of writers and most valuable of authorities'. There is an admirable appreciation of Donne by Gabriel which is a useful reminder that, with tributes from Coleridge, Rossetti, and Browning, Donne did not have to wait till our own age for admirers. When they are both reading Coleridge Janey remarks on how 'his incompleteness annoys', and Rossetti then lends her Cottle on Coleridge and Gillman's Life of the poet. He has discovered the curious fact that Buchanan's attack on him years ago was plagiarized from a passage in Cottle. From the detached tone of his remark it is clear that he can now look back calmly and with detachment on that 'old unhappy far-off' attack. In another letter Janey asks if he knew the author of *Erewhon*: he has not read the book and what he chiefly remembers about Butler, who was a great friend of Nolly Brown, is that he had eyebrows exactly like two leeches stuck on his face. Of FitzGerald she knows only the *Omar Khayyam*, so Gabriel introduces her to the translations of Calderon, a dramatist whom he thinks in some respects the equal of Shakespeare. She enjoys the Calderon plays immensely and is slow to return the book. Chatterton is one of Rossetti's late enthusiasms: he devoted a sonnet to him and has an apt phrase about his text—'a teaser, so much older than antiquity'. There is another happy remark when, during his stay in the Lake District, he is re-reading Boswell—'the ponderous Boswell which however never flags'. The last remark in Rossetti's last letter is about a young writer, and it is not kind. He has glanced at 'the wretched Oscar Wilde book', which the Burne-Joneses so admired—'enough to see what trash it is'. Poor Oscar! It was not *Salome*, which might have shocked, but only his first book, the *Poems*, 1881.

Pictures are of course the other major topic. Rossetti's letters are indeed a journal of 'work in progress', from the 1868 portrait of Janey in the blue dress which is now at Kelmscott to the *Desdemona* left unfinished at his death. *Pandora, Proserpine, Fiammetta, La Pia, La*

Donna della Finestra, and *The Day Dream*, all the attempts to immortalize her which failed to satisfy him: 'How nice it would be if I could feel sure I had painted you once for all so as to let the world know what you were—but everything I do from you is a disappointment.' 'Denique pictura clara sit illa mea' is the motto on the Kelmscott portrait—'May my picture add to her fame'. The letters are also a record of his patrons and of other models when Janey was abroad or not well enough to sit. Then Alexa Wilding or Marie Spartali (Mrs. Stillman) takes her place, and Rossetti speaks of the latter's gracious and inexhaustible good nature. 'Who would have thought a year back,' replies Janey, 'when I appeared so much the stronger woman of the two, that she would be sitting to you when I am becoming a mummy?' Mrs. Stillman introduced a Miss Florence Moore, a friend of hers who wished to do a little sitting on the usual terms. She was said to be of a refined order of beauty and recommended for 'Dante subjects'. 'Poor little Miss Moore,' he remarks, 'if she does not pick and choose her artists, she will find it no lady's vocation.'

Rossetti was always reluctant to exhibit his work in public so the private patron plays an important part in his career. The buyers of his early work like Rae, Leathart, Plint, and others were gone and their successors now were William Graham, M.P. for Glasgow, Frederick Leyland, the Liverpool shipowner (better remembered for his quarrel with Whistler over the Peacock Room than for his friendship with Rossetti), Constantine Ionides, the Greek financier, and the troublesome lawyer 'Valpy the vampire' who hated nudity. The patrons often had difficulty in getting the artist to complete the work they had commissioned. Working from old studio drawings and with the help of the studio assistant he was always ready to repeat a success if there was a new buyer in view. Even the *Beata Beatrix*, his memorial tribute to Elizabeth Siddal, did not escape repetition. One picture which looms large in the letters in every sense is the huge *Dante's Dream*. Painted for William Graham it proved to be too large for his house, and was exchanged for a smaller version to be painted with the addition of predellas. The large picture was then acquired by Valpy but came back once more when the lawyer retired to Bath. He had struck an exorbitant bargain for smaller works in exchange—a bargain which was to give Rossetti never-ending trouble. Finally through the efforts of Hall Caine it came to rest in the Walker Art Gallery, Liverpool. In the later letters much is told about the progress of another picture, *The Day Dream*, or *Monna Primavera* as it was first called. This was commissioned by Constantine Ionides from a drawing of Janey seated in a sycamore tree, which hung over the mantelpiece in the studio and is now in the Ashmolean Museum, Oxford. Rossetti thought this portrait equal to anything he had done, and he tells her of the infinite trouble he took to get it right and to find the spring flowers for it.

Old Masters appear as well as his own work. He sends Janey a comprehensive comic rhyme listing the Italian painters of the Renaissance, and he tells her about Leyland's purchase of the Pucci family Botticellis. He himself owned a portrait attributed to Botticelli which he later sold to Constantine Ionides. Apart from the work of a few friends like Shields and Smetham he does not say very much about contemporary artists. He praises an early Burne-Jones *Beatrix*, and makes a mocking reference to the nudity of that artist's *Phyllis and Demophoon* which caused scandal at the Old Water Colour Society. He cannot resist a good-natured laugh at 'old Brown's' cartoons for church windows. About Whistler there are stories in plenty, but not a single word about any of his pictures. We get the feeling that Rossetti's interest in contemporary art did not extend far beyond the walls of his own studio. When staying with the Howards at Naworth, Janey wrote to ask about Signor Costa, an Italian artist she had met there. Rossetti had not heard of Costa, though he was a landscape painter who exhibited at the Grosvenor and elsewhere in London, and whose sensitive work was popular in England. The comments on Manet echo what he had said about contemporary French painting in a letter to his mother when he visited Paris as a young man. His views have not changed. Here he is writing about Manet's illustrations to Mallarmé's translation of Poe's poem 'The Raven'—a book which Arthur O'Shaughnessy had left him as a legacy: 'A French idiot named Manet who certainly must be the greatest and most conceited ass that ever lived . . . To view it without a guffaw is impossible'. True, these lithographs are not Manet at his best, but at the back of Rossetti's mind there lay, perhaps, a sense of intrusion. Long ago he had illustrated that poem himself.

After the Morrises moved in the autumn of 1878 from Turnham Green into the Macdonald house on Hammersmith Mall we get glimpses of domestic life there and in Chelsea. Noise from the river, the search for servants, the return of his belongings from Kelmscott Manor, and the neglected garden at Cheyne Walk. Health and the state of the weather are important themes. 'Dear suffering Janey' he writes, and is always ready to recommend any medicine he has tried or even heard of. He copies a prescription for an iron tonic ordered by Marshall, his own doctor, but with the warning that unless taken with care it may loosen her teeth. Or would she rather try a bottle that has helped his friend Shields's neuralgia? He will send it by post. He advises cod-liver oil as she is getting too thin, and there are those sneeze-powders—has she heard of them? With the practical commonsense which was a feature of her character she accepted his nostrums, while mentally labelling them 'Use with Caution'. He suspected it: 'You don't tell me if you tried the bottle I sent. I suppose you sniffed it and scorned it.'

In lighter mood they exchange gossip and stories about acquaintances. There is even a passing note of jealousy over her friendship with Theo. Marzials, 'the gentleman turned singer'. Gabriel wishes he had more stories of Howell for her, for there is nothing to match them except his lies:

> The Portuguese fellow called Howell
> Who lays on his lies with a trowel.

When protesting about forgeries of his drawings, which were appearing on the market, Rossetti names no names: but we know how the ever-observant Max Beerbohm with a backward glance into the Rossetti circle caught Howell and Rosa Corder 'perpetuating the touch of a vanished hand'. Howell and Whistler make a fine pair. When the bailiff is at Whistler's door ready to serve a writ boastful Howell goes down to deal with him—only to be recognized and dunned for his own outstanding debts. Little Fairfax Murray, who was to make a notable collection of Rossetti works, is a source of amusement; he had equal pride in his bandy legs and in his knowledge of Italian art. Holman Hunt, with William Morris and William Michael Rossetti, goes off to St. James's Hall to attend one of the many meetings in support of the Deceased Wife's Sister Marriage Bill which did not become law till 1907. Hunt had a personal interest in the matter since, before the Bill was passed, his own marriage to his first wife's sister had to take place abroad. The generous side of Rossetti's nature shows itself in his efforts to help Smetham's family when the artist suffered a mental breakdown. His affection for his own family is hinted at in the group photograph taken by Lewis Carroll in the garden at 16 Cheyne Walk. It is displayed, too, in the sonnet he designed as a tribute for his mother's eightieth birthday.

During these years three men had made life possible for Rossetti at Tudor House. Treffry Dunn the Cornishman from Truro who, starting as art assistant, soon found himself combining with this the functions of secretary, and general factotum. He has told us what life with Rossetti was like, and in a water-colour has shown us the studio. Theodore Watts, who was not yet devoting all his care to Swinburne nor had yet added Dunton to his name, came as a loyal friend and guide in legal affairs. Lastly Hall Caine enters, a young enthusiast from Liverpool. Soon, with Janey's approval, he settled in as house-mate and gave Rossetti companionship when he most needed it in his last gloomy years. In the background was Fanny Cornforth, ex-model and mistress, who was there looking after her own interests. Fanny is never mentioned in a letter to Janey.

While Janey was staying with the Howards at Bordighera in the winter of 1881 Henry James, who was then at San Remo, came to call. Writing to Fanny Kemble he gave an account of his visit, telling her that he quite fell in love with the Howard's eldest daughter, 'a most delightful little maid of about 15' (in later life the formidable Lady Mary Murray). But he did not fall in love with Mrs. Morris:

the strange, pale, livid, gaunt, silent, and yet in a manner graceful and picturesque, wife of the poet and paper-maker, who is spending the winter with the Howards; though doubtless she too has her merits. She has, for instance, wonderful aesthetic hair.

Did he remember, one wonders, how much ill-health she had suffered?

When Janey came home in the spring of 1881 the exchange of letters continued, and Gabriel tells her yet again that the removal of her long interest in him would be the only thing he could not bear. In the autumn in ill-health and depression he went with Caine and Fanny for a month to the Lake District. Before returning to London he wrote to her from Keswick on October 1st and then the correspondence ends. There is a silence during the six months that remained until he died at Birchington on Easter Sunday 1882, with family and close friends around him. Janey was not there. In his will made on the day before he died she was remembered in a bequest of three of the best of the chalk drawings for which she sat and the profile head hanging in the studio. Janey lived on into dignified old age at Kelmscott, retaining much of her beauty. She died in 1914, age seventy-five.

Their Correspondence

6 March 1868

My dear Janey,

Next Wednesday was the day I hoped to see you, but I think perhaps to secure my finishing something I am about before-hand, I had better say Friday—i.e. 2 days later. On Friday next then I will expect your kind visit, and if you can come early enough to sit that day—i.e. about one o'clock, my gratitude will commence at that hour.

All is ready for the picture, as I have already made some studies and know exactly what I have to do as to the action of the figure, which, my dear Janey, is a very easy one, so you shall be punished as little as possible for your kindness. The drawing of your head will take I expect two days, and then straight to the picture.

If you find it more convenient to come only in time for dinner on Friday, and so have a rest after the journey that night before you sit, that plan will of course do perfectly for me, but if I do not hear to the contrary, I will expect you in time to sit on Friday, and Morris at dinner time. It strikes me as probable that you and Bessie[1] might like to come together, as otherwise she would be left very dull at home, unless she thinks it necessary for the safety of the establishment to stay behind. If she can come, it would give me much pleasure, and there will be no difficulty as to an extra bed-room, as there are several in the house.

So on this point perhaps you would in any case write me a line again when you have settled your plans.

Yours affectionately,
D. G. Rossetti

[1] Elizabeth Burden, Jane's sister, who lived with the Morrises. She helped in the firm and taught needlework at the Royal School of Art.

Dear Jenny and May,

Here come 2 little dormice to live with you—I know you will take great care of them and always give them everything they are fond of—that is, nuts, apples and hard biscuits. If you love them very much I dare say they will get much bigger and fatter and remind you of Papa and me.

Your affectionate
D. G. Rossetti

The Misses Morris
26 Queen Square
Bloomsbury
(by hand)

16 Cheyne Walk, Chelsea
5 May 1868

3 My dear Janey,

About the blue silk dress it occurs to me to say that I think the sleeves should be as full at the top as is consistent with simplicity of outline, and perhaps would gain by being lined with some soft material, but of this you will be the best judge. The pieces of gold embroidery in front might (if you have time to make it) be some-

thing like this, unless as is very possible a better idea strikes you. However it is a great pity that the last portrait[1] (which I fancy is the one you will choose) is in such a position that both this and the embroidery which you propose to put at the back will be hidden. In the other front view portrait these will show to great advantage. Every one seems to like the last picture of you the best, including Leys[2] who was here the other day and recognized it at once. I am most desirous to get to it again, and make no doubt of being quite ready by the time you told me you expect to be in town again, as the *Venus*[3] gets on rapidly and I hope will soon leave me.

I am very glad little Jenny and May[4] liked the dormice. When I chose them they both seemed all right, and I hope the 'downy cove' who sells them did not substitute an invalid. I fancied you had left London before, or should probably have brought them down myself.

What do you think? Yesterday the stray dormouse was caught at last. I had heard a scratching constantly in the room for a day or two, but never guessed what it was or thought of looking in the trap till yesterday afternoon, when I found the poor little chap in it almost dead, hardly thicker than his tail and with his eyes nearly shut, but still gnawing at the wires. His bones were almost through his back,

Portrait of Mrs. Morris in blue dress

and his hair had got stuck together in little spikes which made him look like a porcupine. At first he was almost too exhausted to eat, famished as he was, but is now coming round again.

I hope Leyton[5] will agree with you as well as Chelsea and trust to show you some improvements in the garden when you come here again. Meanwhile please give my love to Morris and believe me

Yours affectionately

D. Gabriel R.

P.S. I hope you will wear the dress to take away the stiffness.

[1] Probably the portrait of Mrs. Morris in blue silk dress seated at table with glass of flowers. Painted 1867–8. Given to Mrs. Morris and now at Kelmscott (S.372). Another portrait in blue silk dress entitled *Mariana* was commissioned by Wm. Graham and painted during 1868 (S.213). See letter to Alice Boyd, 24 July 1868 (D. and W. 782).
[2] Jean Auguste Henri Leys, 1814–69. Belgian historical and genre painter. Created baron 1862. Alma Tadema was one of his pupils. Known for his decoration of the Hôtel-de-Ville at Antwerp with a series of pictures illustrating the history of the city.
[3] Watercolour replica of *Venus Verticordia* done for Wm. Graham 1868 (S.173F). Rossetti made several versions of the original which was begun in 1864.
[4] The Morris daughters.
[5] Near Walthamstow in Essex, where Wm. Morris's mother was then living.

16 Cheyne Walk, Chelsea

7 May 1868

4 My dear Janey,

The silk is just the thing, and the idea delightful. I re-enclose the pattern in case you should need it. I suppose, in order to be thoroughly useful, it ought to be as much as 20 inches square, in which case it could be slipped over one of my sofa cushions but only one side of the cushion-case need be embroidered. Between this and the dress I shall be giving you an awful lot of work.

On reading your letter I took out the little mouse to report on his condition. He is wonderfully improved and is getting quite plumped out and sleek again—only a place he had worn bare on his nose by gnawing at the trap does not fill up yet.

Will you tell Morris that I have not got any Earthly Paradise[1] whatever at present though I understand one is being offered to a lethargic world no further from Chelsea than Covent Garden. Meanwhile I have attempted some approach to a private Eden by sticking up a big tent[2] in my garden. Would you also tell the Bard and P.J.[3] (I will not indulge him with his favourite title in full) that I think the little chimney glass and shelf I am to have had better be in ebony if not a monstrous addition to expense.

Affectionately yours
D. Gabriel R.

Mrs William Morris
Leyton House
Leyton

[1] Parts I and II published April 1868, by F. S. Ellis, Covent Garden.
[2] A dinner in the tent is described in Letter 7, and G. P. Boyce in his Diary, 1 June 1868, mentions a party attended by Janey and Wm. Morris, Burne-Jones, Howell, and others.
[3] Unidentified.

Wednesday [21 July 1869]   5

Dear Good Janey,

I was so glad to hear from you and know that you had had a pretty good passage. From what you say I judge you were not absolutely ill. And it delights me to know that the cloaks prove of service to you, and that you will be always wearing one of them. I hope you are able to get out a little, at the different places you stop at but indeed I suppose that it is necessary for you to husband your strength as long as the journey lasts.

I went on Sunday to Little Holland House to lay Mrs Prinsep's[1] *unquiet* spirit. You may imagine the outpourings, but she is really *very* nice and kind. We dined in the open air in the garden which was very pleasant and I hoped you were as pleasantly situated to enjoy the fine weather. On the whole I am glad that the heat has decreased now, and suppose it is probably the same where you are. I think it is a very good thing you were not deterred from starting. I think I told you that Nettleship's[2] drawings had been rejected at the R.A. I enquired of Watts and Leighton about this, and found them expressing the greatest astonishment, as they had never seen the drawings at all! nor was Nettleship's name even on the list of candidates. Some blunder has occurred—whether through his not feeing the porters or what, I cannot tell yet; but an enquiry will be made, and let us hope he will get in.

Pandora

5. 21 JULY 1869

I did not see Ned[3] on Saturday night, as he never came round, and wrote to me since, that he had been too unwell. I shall go round to the Greeks[4] tonight and probably see him there.

My going out more lately has had the result which has always stopped such proceedings with me,—that is, an influx of visitors taking up my time. I have not done much work for some days past, but must remedy this and avert your wrath when you return. Graham[5] saw the Pandora[6] yesterday and was so delighted with it that I shall certainly make this one do for his uncle and begin the

Sibylla Palmifera

full-length one on my own hook when you can sit again. I want very much to do this full length, as it is a very favourite design of mine. I also want beyond everything to paint another portrait picture of you: a little more severe in arrangement than the first—as I am sure I can do something more worthy of you than I have yet managed. But I shall get ahead with all the other things now, and really get them out of hand I trust and the big picture begun.

I expect probably to leave for Penkill[7] in about 3 weeks or less now. I shall take some work to do there in the shape probably of a duplicate of the Sibyl[8] which I have promised to do for Leyland.[9] I want much to get the little Beatrice[10] I was doing from you finished, but the hands are in the way as I think I *must* alter them and all the models have such vile hands. I have an idea I may ask Mary Spartali[11] to sit for them.

The accompanying cartoon[12] will prepare you for the worst,— which ever that may be, the seven tumblers or the 7 volumes. I hope the weather at Ems will not be so severe as the French Doctor anticipated and shall be anxious to know whether there, as here, the heat has greatly abated.

I have given Ellis[13] the printer a number of scrappy poems and sonnets to print that I may keep them by me in an available form and perhaps be induced to do more. When I get them, I will send you some.

I suppose Bessie and Lucy[14] are enjoying themselves vastly. Love to them as well as to dear Top and to your dear self. Yesterday Macmillan rushed in with Field the American publisher who seemed put out because he could not see Top again at present as he seemed to wish. He told me that the news of Norton[15] is not very good. He has been less well since leaving England. That the contrary may be signally your case, and that you may return ere long strengthened and happy is the warmest of all wishes on the part of

Your affectionate
Gabriel

Mrs W. Morris
Poste Restante
Cologne

5. 21 JULY 1869

[1] One of the seven Pattle sisters, wife of Henry Thoby Prinsep, Indian Civil Servant, and mother of Val Prinsep the artist. The Prinseps lived at Little Holland House, Kensington (on the site now occupied by Melbury Road). Their Sunday afternoon 'At homes' were a feature of London literary and artistic life. They assisted the young Edward Burne-Jones at the start of his career, and G. F. Watts made his home with them. Mrs. Julia Cameron the gifted photographer was a sister of Mrs. Prinsep.

[2] John Trivett Nettleship (1841–1902), animal painter who exhibited at the Royal Academy and the Grosvenor Gallery. An early admirer of Browning, he published essays on his poetry. His brothers were distinguished classical scholars—Henry, Corpus Professor of Latin at Oxford, and Richard Lewis, Fellow of Balliol. His early work was in black and white; he designed a Blake-like woodcut frontispiece for O'Shaughnessy's *Epic of Women* (1870).

[3] Edward Burne-Jones.

[4] The Ionides family, distinguished and wealthy members of the Greek colony in London. Other members of the colony were the Spartali family, and the Cassavettis. See *Ion—a Grandfather's Tale* by Alexander Constantine Ionides Junior (1927, privately printed).

[5] William Graham (1816–85), patron and friend of Rossetti from whom he commissioned the large *Dante's Dream* in 1868. Rossetti stayed in his houses in Scotland when recovering from his breakdown in 1872. Liberal M.P. for Glasgow and Trustee of the National Gallery. An intimate account of him is given by his daughter Frances Horner in *Time Remembered* (1933).

[6] Oil painting dated 1871 (S.224). Various studies for it were in hand during 1869. The full-length version does not seem to have been carried out. Bought by John Graham, uncle of Wm. Graham. Now in private collection.

[7] Penkill Castle, Ayrshire, the home of Rossetti's friend Alice Boyd. It was decorated with murals by Wm. Bell Scott illustrating the *Kingis Quair*.

[8] *Sibylla Palmifera*, 1866 (S.193). The sitter was Alexa Wilding. No duplicate for Leyland is recorded. The sonnet 'Soul's Beauty', no. 77 in *The House of Life*, was written for this picture which is now in the Lady Lever Art Gallery, Port Sunlight.

[9] Frederick R. Leyland (1831–92), wealthy Liverpool shipowner who lived at Speke Hall on the Mersey. Collector and patron of Rossetti, Whistler, and Burne-Jones. The famous Peacock Room decoration which Whistler executed for his London house and his portrait by Whistler called 'Arrangement in Black' are in the Freer Gallery, Washington. A portrait drawing by Rossetti is in the Bancroft Collection at Wilmington, U.S.A. For note on his Botticelli paintings see Letter 61. His tomb in Brompton Cemetery was designed by Burne-Jones.

[10] It is difficult to identify this picture. It may be the *Beatrice* (S.256) which is a replica of the head of the 1870 *Mariana* (S.213). Having such difficulty with the hands he may have cut down the canvas and kept the head and shoulders which he finished off in 1879. The picture remained unsold at his death, and is now in private possession. I owe this suggestion to Mrs. Surtees.

[11] Daughter of the Greek consul-general in London. She often sat for Rossetti and was herself an artist of talent. She married W. J. Stillman, American journalist, sometime consul in Crete, as his second wife in 1871. Her sister, also a noted beauty, is portrayed in Whistler's *La Princesse du Pays de la Porcelaine*.

[12] 'The M's at Ems', British Museum caricature (1939-5-13-1(1)) (S.605).

[13] Frederick Startridge Ellis (1830–1901), scholarly bookseller and publisher who published Rossetti's *Poems* in April 1870. He was a close friend of Wm. Morris and for a time co-tenant of Kelmscott Manor. He was associated with the Kelmscott Press and was one of Morris's executors. Purchased a version of *Proserpine*, and *La Donna della Finestra*.

[14] Elizabeth Burden and possibly Lucy Faulkner, sister of Charles Faulkner one of the original members of the Morris firm. She embroidered tapestries and painted tiles. Or he may refer to Lucy Madox Brown.

[15] Charles Eliot Norton (1827–1908), distinguished American man of letters, a friend of Emerson, Lowell, and Henry James. He contributed to the *Atlantic Monthly* and was co-editor of the *North American Review* with Lowell. He made a prose rendering of the *Divina Commedia* and was the first professor of Fine Art at Harvard. An early admirer of the Pre-Raphaelites, and on friendly terms with Ruskin and Carlyle.

16, Cheyne Walk, Chelsea
Tuesday 27 July [1869]

6 My dear Janey,

I got a nice letter of yours from Calais on Monday evening of last week, and on Wednesday wrote in answer to Poste Restante, Cologne, as you told me. I now find Ned has heard from Top at Cologne and as I have no letter from you I fear it is possible mine may have miscarried. I find on enquiring that the stupid people at the post office here never weighed it and only stuck on a fourpenny stamp. I am afraid this was under single postage, and I believe the letter must have been double as it contained a splendid cartoon. If you have not got it, you must indeed have thought me a beast for not answering your good kind letter written when you could hardly write.

It is no use making this a long letter, as I do not know if it will ever reach you, since by the time it gets to Ems you will be no doubt at some hotel. It enrages me beyond measure to think that, through a detestable blunder, days may yet pass leaving you under the impression that I did not answer your letter.

I have heard from others of your progress and health since Calais, and await most anxiously the next news of you. As soon as I know that what I write is sure to reach you, I shall write again; and if I hear from you meanwhile and learn that my letter did not miscarry, it will be the greatest relief to me.

        With love to Top

Ever your affectionate
Gabriel

Mrs Morris
Poste Restante
Ems
Germany

16 Cheyne Walk
30 July 1869

7 Dear kind Janey,

It is a great consolation to know that you have reached Ems at last, and that at any rate for the present the annoyance of travelling is at an end. All was well with my letter to Cologne which only mattered so far as you might have thought by not receiving it that I was capable of neglect in your regard. No doubt you have got also my fidgetty note to Ems. Pardon my troubling you with it.

I got yours from Ems last night but delayed writing because I was to receive the proofs[1] of my poems today and thought I might send them. However they are so huddled and blundered that I must wait to send a better copy. Besides they will not be of much interest to you as they are only those you know already.

Kate Howell[2] was sitting to me yesterday for a drawing I am giving her and I showed her your letter which induced her to write to you. The news of you must be considered hopeful on the whole so far as you seem by all accounts to have borne the journey pretty well after all. With what hope I await still better news and with what joy I shall receive it, pray believe better than I can say. All that concerns you is the all absorbing question with me, as dear Top will not mind my telling you at this anxious time. The more he loves you, the more he knows that you are too lovely and noble not to be loved: and, dear Janey, there are too few things that seem worth expressing as life goes on, for one friend to deny another the poor expression of what is most at his heart. But he is before me in granting this, and there is no need for me to say it. I can never tell you how much I am with you at all times. Absence from your sight is what I have long been used to; and no absence can ever make me so far from you again as your presence did for years. For this long inconceivable change, you know now what my thanks must be.

But I have no right to talk to you in a way that may make you sad on my account when in reality the balance of joy and sorrow is now so much more in my favour than it has been, or could have been hoped to become, for years past. The great question now, before which all else is as nothing, and for which God knows I would sacrifice all else, is that of your dear health. Never mind what I could not help writing, and of course do not say a word of any kind in answer to this foolish part of my letter.

I shall be going soon away for awhile I suppose—as you may be sure I am most anxious not to be away and miss seeing you improved on your return. I have been receiving all sorts of country invitations and several to Scotland but shall stick to quiet Penkill unless I am obliged to go to Graham's also for a few days. There seems some danger of a short stay at Speke with Leyland becoming inevitable and this will be a sad bore because of his family. He himself is a good friendly fellow.

I hope to give you some decided news of work soon. I have done the drapery of that drawing of you with the head resting on the hand,[3] and think it certainly the best I have done. I shall not let Norton have it of course but keep it and make him a copy. I must paint it for myself, if you will let me, as soon as you can sit again. Also I *must* do the full-length Pandora as soon as I have finished this one which will do well enough for Graham as he is delighted with it. Mary Spartali has given me one sitting to paint the hands of the Beatrice I did from you, and she is to give me another. I think they will come well enough, though it is provoking to have made a mull of them from you. However this will be one thing got rid of I hope before long.

Poor Nettleship I find is sold after all. It seems the Keeper of the Academy (that old fool Charles Landseer) takes on himself to kick out the drawings he doesn't like before they go up to the Council at all; and unfortunately God, when creating evil, appears to have created an evil opinion of Nettleship in the mind of Charles Land-seer.[4] This seems a great shame.

I was at Ned's the other evening and saw what he is doing. I was particularly struck with a most beautiful single female figure in profile with some smaller figures by a door in the background. This I thought one of the finest things he has done. I dont know what he calls it.[5] Ned, Webb,[6] Val[7] and Leyland dined in the tent with me one day lately. Howell[8] was to have come but didn't. Val supplied his place well so far as the impossibility of his narratives went, but he did not add the final charm of saying they had all happened to himself, so must be pronounced on the whole inferior.

I believe I may say I have really got my stables now, and that I shall really set to work on the studio in all probability before leaving town.

Val's studio filled me with envy as it always does one day that I called there, and the sight of it will I think expedite my movements. I cannot say that the same mean feeling was awakened by his pictures. He has begun one which he calls the *Lion's Mouth*,[9] and which represents a number of cheap supers acting in the way they do when the 'walking of the ghost'[10] on Saturday night is very uncertain. In the corner a female 'dresser' who has apparently taken the leading lady's part at a moment's notice, is doing something to your knocker in Queen Square, which as I told Val, he had better borrow to paint, as thus one character at least in his picture would be something like the real thing. Val has also done a sketch of Mary Spartali which seems like a faint reminiscence of Watts's feeblest portraits of

Beatrice by Burne-Jones

his mother. I said so to the lady, and found her an entire sympathiser as to the nature of Val's art. She said that he was about 4 hours doing it (it looks like 20 minutes' work) and that her maid said afterwards that she supposed that when that gentleman drew heads he liked to have one sitting 'for company's sake like'. I am glad you saw the Van Eyck at Ghent[11] which I have seen 2 or 3 times and always with the greatest delight. It is certainly the noblest picture of that school I know, though when first I went to Belgium I was I believe more attracted by the curious variety and interest of Memmling's pictures at Bruges. These I suppose you did not see, nor do I indeed know yet whether you stopped at Bruges at all. If so, I suppose it would be at the Hotel du Commerce (I think it is called) which is a splendid old mansion with a most curious stair-rail in which each upright consists of a duck with a bullrush in his mouth all painted in colours.

I have never myself been at Cologne, but no doubt you must have enjoyed the Cathedral as far as fatigue would let you.

I suppose you will have heard of the sad accident to poor P. P. Marshall,[12] involving I fear for certain the loss of the forefinger of his right hand. I hear he is progressing favourably, but only I fear as regards speed of recovery not the saving of the finger.

I must try after all and see Cousins[13] the engraver about your portrait. Robertson, who knows him, has made enquiries and finds that he really is at present very much out of sorts and not working but that he trusts to resume work. I saw the other day his engraving of Millais' *Minuet* which I had not seen before, and which certainly seems to be more satisfactory than other people's work.

Let me hear *something* from you, dearest Janey, but do not on any account weary yourself with writing, or rack your brain for any news except of your health. All love to Topsy from your loving

Gabriel

Mrs Morris
Poste Restante
Ems
Nassau
Allemagne

[1] The trial proofs for the *Poems* 1870. See *The Letters of D. G. Rossetti to his Publisher*, ed. Oswald Doughty, 1928.
[2] Cousin of Charles Augustus Howell whom she married in 1867. Rossetti made two portrait drawings of her (S.338, 339).
[3] Probably *Reverie* (S.206). Private collection.

[4] Charles, elder brother of Sir Edwin Landseer. Historical painter. Keeper of the Royal Academy 1831–73. It is perhaps worth noting that Nettleship first exhibited at the R.A. in 1874 and from then on showed almost without a break.

[5] *Beatrice*, watercolour dated 1870. His model was Maria Zambaco. Burne-Jones was indebted to Rossetti's *Early Italian Poets* for the Beatrice theme. Private collection.

[6] Philip Webb (1831–1915) architect, pupil of G. E. Street. Built Red House, Upton, for Morris, and with him was a founder of the Society for the Protection of Ancient Buildings.

[7] Valentine Cameron Prinsep (1838–1904), artist, son of Henry Thoby Prinsep of Little Holland House. Friend of Watts and Leighton. Painted many once popular Victorian subject pictures and was one of the artists who decorated the Oxford Union Debating Hall in 1857. Married the daughter of Leyland. He gives a lively account of Rossetti and his team at Oxford in 'The Oxford Circle: . . . A chapter from a Painter's Reminiscences', *Magazine of Art*, XXVII, 1904.

[8] Charles Augustus Howell (1840–90), an Anglo-Portuguese adventurer of handsome appearance and much personal charm who came to England as a youth. He became intimate with Rossetti, Whistler, and other artists, and was for a time Ruskin's secretary. He acted for Rossetti in the recovery of the poems from his wife's grave, and became his agent in negotiations for the sale of his pictures. He was associated with Rosa Corder, an artist of some talent, in forgeries of Rossetti drawings. Described by Madox Brown as 'one of the biggest liars in existence'. Howell and the model Ellen Smith are portrayed in *Washing Hands*, Rossetti's watercolour of 1865 (S.179) and there is a late portrait-drawing of him by Frederick Sandys in the Ashmolean Museum. An account of his picturesque career is given by Helen Rossetti Angeli in *Pre-Raphaelite Twilight* (1954).

[9] Unidentified. Prinsep was at this period interested in the theatre and in theatrical scenes. He sometimes changed the title of his pictures for exhibitions. This picture may never have been finished.

[10] Theatrical slang for salaries about to be paid at end of the week.

[11] *The Adoration of the Lamb* in the cathedral of St. Bavon. In a letter from Bruges in October 1849 Rossetti writes of 'the Miraculous works of Memling and Van Eyck' (D. and W. 50).

[12] Peter Paul Marshall, a founder member of the Morris firm. He contributed some cartoons for glass and designs for furniture.

[13] Samuel Cousins R.A. (1801–87), skilled and successful mezzotint engraver, made plates after Reynolds, Lawrence, and other artists. Beginning with *The Order of Release* in 1856 he made many popular engravings of pictures by Millais who praised his work. *The Minuet* was engraved in 1868. He presented a complete set of his engravings to the British Museum.

4 August 1869   **8**

My dear Janey,

You see your great idea has not been sown in barren soil but has immediately borne fruit. I fear that the legitimate helplessness of the pictorial and ideal Topsy has somewhat communicated itself to the German maid in the cartoon,[1] and even you have rather a Georgian air. But these are minor defects. The poetry and philosophy of the subject are I hope complete, while you will see that even Scriptural analogy has not been neglected.

What a joyful hearing it is that you have passed two days almost without pain. I must study donkeys[2] that I may be able to make a cartoon of your first expedition. What a good thing you went after all. I have no doubt now that you will return greatly benefited, and what could happen in the world so good as that?

I shall leave London as soon as ever I find possible, and shall not

The M's at Ems

The German Lesson

work much while I am away in order that I may profit by it much and be back soon. It would be too bad to miss the first sight of you in your improved condition. I had already been thinking of this, and may probably, if I find you are sure of being back by the time fixed, return then and if necessary go elsewhere afterwards. But I hate going anywhere if I can stay and work. As it is I see no prospect of getting away before the end of next week, but then I think I shall. Of course I shall be writing you again, and I hope hearing again from you before then.

I am thinking of making a drawing of Mary Spartali if she can sit to me one or two days next week. I began one in the fag end of the 2nd sitting for the hands (which I have got done) but it was not satisfactory and I shall begin another if she can sit. She is very difficult, but putting her against the light as you sat for the Pandora, I found the expression and character perhaps the finest and want to make the drawing in that way. I have been doing one or two other drawings to raise the wind,—drawings from models. Brown has begun a second drawing of Mary S. It is much prettier than the first, but somehow does not seem to have the amount of likeness which that had in spite of its want of beauty.

Kate Howell wrote that note here after sitting to me for a drawing I am going to give her. We talked a great deal of you, you may be sure. I saw Bessie and Lucy since their return. Bessie seemed to me to look very ill. You have no doubt full accounts of their vicissitudes, so I need not tell you.

I hope to have copies of my verses to send you before long. I think I shall have to get the sonnets printed only on one side of the paper, in order that as I write more I may be able to slip them into their proper places in the series—so far as it can be called a series. I find I have just 50 sonnets which I shall print after rejecting a good many I have by me. I shall reprint those in the Fortnightly.[3]

I see Topsy is proluded upon in Temple Bar[4] in the inevitable company of Matthew Arnold. I have not seen it but hear that the series is all bestial and written by a little ass named Austin who once wrote a stupid satire.[5] Some one has done Christina[6] in 'Tinsley'— the same series in which Top appeared and it seems William and I are to follow. It is weak beyond even the usual mark and may I suspect turn out cheeky too before it is over—The author I suppose may be one Forman who I believe did Topsy's article, only this seems worse written.

You see I have no news to speak of since last writing. May the news of you be better still!—is what is most in my mind. Good bye, dear Janey. Love to Top.

Your most affectionate

Gabriel

I hear Topsy wrote a lovely poem at Lille.[7]

Mrs Morris

Fortuna

Bad-Ems

Nassau

Allemagne

[1] 'The German Lesson', British Museum caricature (1939–5–13–1(2)) (S.603).

[2] 'when . . . she gets better there are splendid mokes and mules here, whereupon she may climb the hills.' Morris to Philip Webb, 31 July 1869. *Letters of William Morris*, edited by Philip Henderson, 1950, p. 26.

[3] Sixteen Sonnets which had appeared in the Fortnightly Review of March, 1869 with the title 'Of Life, Love, and Death' were included in *The House of Life*.

[4] *Temple Bar*, August 1869, 'The Poetry of the Period—Mr. Matthew Arnold and Mr. Morris'. Alfred Austin blamed Morris for giving his age the go-by, ignoring the present, and reverting to vanished days. The article did not worry Morris. See letter to F. S. Ellis—*Letters of Wm. Morris*, p. 28.

[5] Alfred Austin, *The Seasons: a Satire*, 1861.

[6] *Tinsley's Magazine*, August 1869. First of three articles on the Rossettis in a 'Criticism on Contemporaries' series. Articles on D.G.R. and W.M.R. followed in September and October. The writer was Henry Buxton Forman.

[7] Unidentified, but evidently one of the *Earthly Paradise* tales on which he was working.

Monday night [9 August 1869]

9 My dear Top,

I confess to a feeling of great discouragement on not seeing Janey's handwriting when I opened your letter this morning. I hope it does not really mean that she is worse than you say. I would not of course for the world have her write when she is too ill to do so easily but her previous letter had led me to hope more perhaps than was reasonable in so short a time. It would reassure me greatly to hear something like better news from her as soon as possible.

I have been feeling extremely used up myself, and shall leave for Scotland I believe, either Saturday or Monday next. It would be a relief if I could hear before then. In any case, all letters will be immediately sent on, so I will hope to continue hearing as usual and shall write regularly myself.

You do not say when you expect to return, and I suppose you hardly know as yet. I would make up my mind to one thing if I were you; and that is, to take care now you have made the journey, that the baths have a fair chance, even were the delay a little longer than you intended. The journey back too, might undo the good done were not full time for rest allowed.

With love to Janey,

Yours affectionately,

D. G. Rossetti

W. Morris Esq
Fortuna
Bad-Ems
Nassau
Allemagne

Saturday 14 Aug. 1869   10

Dearest Janey,

You may be sure that my joy on receipt of your letter last night was proportionate to the extreme discouragement I had felt at the last news of you through Top. Perhaps after all the attack of illness has been beneficial as clearing the way for improvement now you are using the baths again. I wonder impatiently as to every hour's result upon your health. But it is a glorious thing that you can say so decidedly that you are getting free from pain. The weakness must be expected for the present. If you come back, as I now really hope, set up (to the extent of reasonable hope in so short a campaign) I shall bless the name of Ems which does not take up much room in one's thanksgivings. It seems quite a shame to call it Bad Ems on the envelope and I should write Good instead if I thought the postman had an intuitive soul.

Now that I know you are on the mend, I shall really get off to Scotland on Monday morning. Even if I do not stay long, it is the readiest and best thing to do at once, as I am most sorely in want of a change, having been for some time more thoroughly seedy than I can tell you. As for my head and eyes, they have been far from well, but I do not now experience the absolute inconvenience in work that I did at one time. So I may (I hope) look on the question without great anxiety at present. However I mean to take no work with me to Scotland, as I am sure perfect rest is what I need. Were I to be staying I could send for some. I am afraid what I tell you of my used-up condition may induce you to look for much work done, but such is far from being the case. I hoped on getting the hands put into your picture from Miss S.[1] that I might be able to take it up and get it out of hand; but other things have come in the way and it sticks as it was since then; so after all perhaps I might have done the hands again from you, which is a provoking idea. Since she sat for the hands Miss Spartali has given me two more sittings and I have made 3 chalk heads of her. The last I think is not unsuccessful, though the 2 first were completely so. I find her head about the most difficult I ever drew. It depends not nearly so much on real form as on a subtle charm of life which one cannot recreate. I think it would be hardly possible to make a completely successful picture of her, and feel a great deal humbler now when I look at other peoples' attempts. During her sittings she was very much amused with the Polly, who became very expansive towards an old Miss Young who accompanied her. This old body seemed to consider Polly her elective affinity, and many love-passages passed between them, though for some time, on the Polly imploring a kiss, Miss Y. said that it should be earned when they were alone, which she really seemed to look on as a question of propriety. Now and then Polly would launch an expression at her admirer which used to cause me to bury my nose deeper in the drawing with terror till the air was clear again. It was not till the second sitting that Miss S. relieved my mind very much by saying—'Why Miss Young, she calls you an old *wretch*!'

I have received from America the water colour by poor Lizzy[2] for which I am to give Norton a drawing of you. It looks very fine though certainly quite quaint enough. I wish I had any amusing news. The stable business[3] has still been hanging on, but this very day seems perhaps about to conclude. However it is no use my thinking of building till my return from Scotland at any rate. Nettleship and Brown dined here yesterday. N. showed me his Academy drawings which are remarkably good, so their rejection was disgraceful. He is painting beasts and the gardens and has done a crouching one for which I have commissioned him (!)—also a roaring one in progress, which is splendid as is mine also. He seems to be getting over his difficulties in painting. I asked him if he had got Top's books, which I know were meant to be sent, but he had not, so I suppose it was deferred in the hurry of leaving.

I believe I have got in type all the verses[4] I can scrape together at present. They will be finally struck off in a few days and I will cause a copy to be sent you unless time gets too late for it to reach you at Ems. However there is nothing to interest you much as they are all old things you know, but I have improved some. The chaotic copies of other things I have not yet tackled, but may possibly do so before long though with uncertain results. Now writing seems to have departed from me, as I have done nothing for ever so long. Perhaps Scotch air and the neighbourhood of Burns may set me piping. I suppose Topsy is roaring and screaming through the Parnassian tunnels and junctions in his usual style now,[5] not without an occasional explosion. Did he remember the couple of blouses he promised me from Lille, or will he remember them on his way back? The one you gave me gets dirty and not having another to wear while it is washed, I become oblivious and discontinue its use.

You have heard I suppose that poor Marshall's forefinger has had to be amputated. He is going on well now, but was only just in time, as a stupid country doctor had dozed over the question, and it was only through Marshall's calling on John M.[6] that he was roused to the necessity of having it off at once.

Ned is gone to Crom's Tower[7] for some days, as you probably know. When you are able to answer this, you can do so either straight to

Penkill Castle
Girvan
Ayrshire

or else to Chelsea, as I take care to leave envelopes duly directed which will ensure all letters being sent on at once. But perhaps the best will be to write straight there. You know without my saying it that I am far from wishing you to write when you do not feel in sorts but you know also how glad I am whenever I can hear from you.

What you tell me seems to infer a fortnight longer at Ems from the date of your letter, Thursday last. Thus with a week on the way home which I suppose will be fully required, I judge you may be expected in London in all probability about a fortnight from Thursday next. Will you be sure to keep me exactly informed? I suppose the Doctor has not raised the question of you being sent on to the place in Switzerland which you told me was sometimes made a second stage after Ems.

Conceive if your cure were now to proceed so rapidly that there remained a glut of surplus baths, and Topsy were induced to express

Resolution; or, *The Infant Hercules*

a thanksgiving frame of mind by that act which is next to godliness! Give him my love, and if he wishes to be revenged for the apposite diaphragm—i.e. diagram,[8] let him know that I have bought the works of the poet Banting,[9] that 'idle singer of a too full day'.[10] God bless you, dear Janey. Let me hear from you, and I will answer from Penkill.

Most affectionately yours
D. Gabriel R

Mrs Morris
Fortuna
Bad-Ems
Nassau
Allemagne

[1] Two chalk portraits of Marie Spartali are recorded (S.519, 520).

[2] The drawing which Norton returned at Rossetti's request was *Clerk Saunders*: now in the Fitzwilliam Museum, Cambridge. He offered to do a drawing of Mrs. Norton or send one of Mrs. Morris instead. Letter 23 April 1869 (D. and W. 817). Norton owned Rossetti's watercolour *Before the Battle*, now in Museum of Fine Arts, Boston. He also had a version of *Beatrice meeting Dante at a marriage feast denies him her Salutation* which is in the Ashmolean Museum, Oxford (S.50, R.1).

[3] He is referring to the conversion of the stables at 16 Cheyne Walk into a studio.

[4] One of the Trial Books privately printed in preparation for the 1870 *Poems*.

[5] Morris while at Ems was working on the second volume of *The Earthly Paradise*.

[6] John Marshall (1818–91), Rossetti's doctor and friend. Professor of Clinical Surgery, University College, London, Professor of Anatomy to the Royal Academy, and Fellow of the Royal Society. He attended Rossetti through his breakdown in 1872 and was present at his death in 1882. Marshall sat for the jester in Madox Brown's *Chaucer at the Court of Edward III*, painted in 1851.

[7] Cormell Price (1835–1910), friend of Morris and Burne-Jones. Educated at King Edward's School, Birmingham, and Brasenose College, Oxford. Housemaster at Haileybury, and the Headmaster of United Services College, Westward Ho, N. Devon, 1874–94. Dedicatee of Kipling's *Stalky & Co.* He lived at Broadway Tower, Worcs, and in later life at Minster Lovell, Oxon. His Diary, now lost, was used by Mackail as a valuable source of information about the Pre-Raphaelites in Oxford in 1857.

[8] 'Resolution or The Infant Hercules', British Museum caricatures (1939–5–13–1(8)) (S.604).

[9] William Banting, London undertaker, who dieted for overweight and in a few weeks lost 46 lb. Published *A Letter on Corpulence*, 1863, which went into many editions, the fourth in 1869. Hence the phrase 'to bant'.

[10] Cf. *The Earthly Paradise*, 'The idle singer of an empty day'.

Penkill Castle Girvan   **II**
Ayrshire
Monday 23 August [1869]

My dear Janey,

I have got your letter to-day and certainly it is rather tantalizing after the great hopes your former one had raised. But after all we know that there are all kinds of delays and disappointments in the cure of a long standing evil, and we must remember that certainly there does not seem to be any traceable deterioration in your constitution from the first so that it is reasonable to feel convinced that the local affection is in all probability open to remedy even though time should prove the principal agent in bringing it about. I cannot but think that possibly a return to London at present is not the surest road to health. Brown and I were talking about the matter often before I left London, and he was decidedly of opinion that the invigorating air of Switzerland should be tried after the Ems system. Some of your friends could come out if you were making any stay, and so save Top and you from suffering too much from blue devils. Perhaps the suggestion is impracticable, though of course could its advisability be known as *certain*, nothing should prevent its being carried out. The best of all would be that such an improvement should take place before you leave Ems as to render further probation unnecessary: but you must bear in mind that, if this does not after all prove the case entirely, the trial will still have been such a short one that to complete efficacy within the time would have appeared from the outset to be something like a miracle. And indeed your telling me that you cannot consider yourself worse than at your former writing shows that something has certainly been already effected.

By the bye, let me most humbly apologise, after your grave rebuke, for the too naked truth of my last historical portrait. You see a feeling of denunciatory duty is involved for Taylor and myself in our letters and cartoons; and Ezekiel and other prophets, if you remember, are not too particular as to the mere outward form of the truths which they are bound to convey.

I have been here since last Thursday, having spent a day on the road at old Miss Losh's[1] house near Carlisle. The neighbourhood there is a beautiful one, and there are some really extraordinary architectural works—a church of a byzantine style and other things —erected from her own designs by a lady of Miss Losh's family who has been dead some years and who must certainly have been a true genius. The works are very original and beautiful, very much more so than the things done by the young architects now, and they were done as far back as 1830 without any professional assistance or directed study, though the practical part of them is quite as remark-able as the invention. I was very much interested and should like Webb to see them. The place is called Wreay.[2]

Since I have been here, I occupy myself chiefly in walking, and am I think benefiting much by the change. It is very fine weather, though the last 2 days were so hot that a walk became very like a warm bath. Scott[3] is making some designs from Burns for etching, and produces one daily with the most sublime calm and satisfaction. Some of them are really the best things he has done in that way. He has been getting through the proofs of his book on Albert Durer, and a most amusing correspondence has gone on between him and William who has been consulted throughout. Pig-head or even pig-lead conveys but a faint symbol of the immoveable conviction of either party on every vexed point. Scott's absolute certainty that he has hit upon a splendid idea in proposing to call Durer's Melancholia *Il* Penseros*a* as the best means of conveying the artist's thought, and the raging scorn with which William visits both the grammar and the proposition; together with many other similar conflicts—are really so delightful that they should by right be printed in an appendix. The book however will be a very interesting one—especially as regards a diary by A.D. of his journey to the Low Countries, and some private letters of a curiously joky order much reminding one of Holman Hunt's style in letter-writing.

While I write Scott is busy on a Burns Illustration, produced as it seems in watching him, by dint of aimless groans and fragmentary sleep. One rises and looks over his shoulder and finds the mystic subject which has thus rapt his being to be Tam-O'Shanter in a state of roaring intoxication.

Yesterday I got a note sent on from Mrs Coronio to apprize me that Luke[4] is going to be married next Saturday,—also one from Miss Bird asking me to a party at her house on Friday evening! So she means to die game.

My proofs[5] have hung on hand very much with tattooings that I have gone on giving them. I fear I shall hardly have a set in trim before you return, which shows that Scott might not find it hard to retort on me as to the use of sleep as a productive agent. However I hope to get some new work done perhaps, though here Topsy's mountain must indeed view my mouse with scorn even if he finds his way into the world at all.

I wonder whether we shall be able to realize some sittings on your return. They shall be *such* careful judicious and considerate ones! I have been conceiving a great desire to paint you as Fortune and have the design clearly in my head now, having been long knocking it about there. Fortune will be seated full-faced dealing cards on which will be visible the symbols of life, death, etc. Behind her will be her wheel. The spokes wound with festive and fatal growths, and on either side of it will be seated a dove (or a white peacock) and a raven. I also want awfully bad to get about the full-length Pandora and to do the Beatrice[6] in the big picture. The last will be a nice easy sitting.

But a thousand times more than any work do I desire your renewed health, dear Janey, and you know how anxiously I await all tidings on the subject. Pray take my love and give the same to Top, and believe me

Ever affectionately yours

D. Gabriel R

P.S. Miss Boyd and Scott desire me to send kindest remembrances.

Mrs Morris
Fortuna
Bad–Ems
Nassau
Allemagne

[1] An elderly cousin of Miss Boyd; she made Rossetti a loan of £500, unrepaid at her death in 1872. For Rossetti's correspondence with her see J. C. Troxell, *Three Rossettis*, 1937, Chap. VI.
[2] In a letter to his mother (D. and W. 855) Rossetti describes the remarkable architecture at Wreay on the Losh estate at Woodside near Carlisle. The church of St. Mary was designed by Sara Losh, a kinswoman who had travelled in Italy and was a scholar. For a description and illustration see article by M. A. Wood, 'A Memorial to Two Sisters' in *Country Life*, Vol. CL, No. 3882, 4 Nov. 1971.
[3] William Bell Scott, 1811–90, Scottish artist and writer working in Government School of Design, Newcastle upon Tyne. His paintings are mainly of historical subjects, his most important work being the decoration of the hall at Wallington with subjects from Border history and legend, done for Sir Walter Trevelyan. There are also murals illustrating the *Kingis Quair* at Penkill Castle, the home of Alice Boyd, with whom he had a lifelong relationship. A vivid portrait of the young Swinburne is at Balliol College. Scott was also skilful in his etchings for book illustration. Rossetti admired his poem 'Rosabell', and became a friend. Scott wrote a memoir of his brother David Scott (1850), and *Albert Dürer: His Life and Works* (1869). The illustrated edition of Burns, though commissioned and paid for, was never published. His *Autobiographical Notes*, published posthumously, caused some controversy. See W. E. Fredeman, 'Prelude to the Last Decade of Dante Gabriel Rossetti', *Bulletin of the John Rylands Library*, 1971.
[4] Second son of Alexander Ionides and brother of Aglaia Coronio. Married Elfrida Bird in 1869. Author of *Memories* (privately printed, Paris, 1925).
[5] i.e. the Trial Book for the 1870 *Poems*.
[6] Wm. Graham commissioned the big picture, i.e. *Dante's Dream*, in April 1869 (S.81).

Penkill Castle Girvan
Ayrshire
Monday 30 Aug: 1869

12 My dear Janey,

Your letter must on the whole be pronounced satisfactory. Miracles are not to be expected unless perhaps from bread puddings; and one day with another improvement seems the rule. Moreover the malady itself is of such a capricious nature that it may be expected to benefit quite as much by rest after the baths as by the baths themselves I should think. It is also satisfactory to know that, with apparent good reason, you do not think it necessary to procede to Switzerland; although I thought it my duty to suggest the possible wisdom of such a course. However I believe you to be quite right in abstaining, after what you say.

I am getting good I think by my stay here, though till yesterday the heat was so excessive, and the swarm of flies so annoying, as to render my daily walks a martyrdom. Now a good wind has sprung up, and I walk in comfort. During the two last of the hot days I only crawled about the sheltered glen. There are many enchanting spots in it, and particularly a little cave[1] in a concealed position on a slope overhanging the bed of the stream—the very place for Topsy to spin endless poetry in, and for you to sit in and listen to the curious urgent whisper of the stream—though perhaps a better approach than the present one would have to be made before you could reach it conveniently; but this is going to be done, so much have I praised the cave and its capabilities. All this you know is perfectly private, and I cannot go about without thinking that this above all places would be the very one in fine weather for you to get about in to some salutary purpose. How nice it would be to see you here, at ease and liberty, and with an air likely to do you good!

I cannot say by the bye that I have yet made much of the poetic properties of the cave in the way of absolute verse. Some scraps have come into my head but not to much purpose as yet. You may be sure I shall send you anything worthy to be sent. I have been working on what may be called the flea-bite principle, however, at my poetry going through the press, and I find that correction, when one suffers from the vain longings of perfectibility, is an endless task,—and Topsy will I fear look with utter scorn on this fidgetty fretting over old ground. He is in the right for himself, I know; but I have nothing of his abundance in production; and to attain confidence first in the plan of any work, however small, and afterwards to aim at rendering it faultless by repeated condensation and revision, is the only system that gives me a chance. I have done a very great deal lately to bring these little things into a state which may lead me to hope they deserve all the extension of such life as is in them. Thus their getting finally printed off is prolonged from week to week.

A Tinsley's Mag. for Septr. was sent me by Dunn[2] containing a good-natured though shadily written article[3] on me. I sent it on to old Miss Losh, but afterwards it struck me you might like to see it, and I wrote to Dunn asking him to get another copy, tear out the article and enclose it to you; so you will probably get it before this. I do not know whether you can see the English Mags. where you are—There was a former article on Christina, and I judge that one on Wm is forthcoming. It is very loud about a thing I once wrote called *My Sister's Sleep*,[4] of a fearfully pious and sentimental kind. I had left it out of my present reprint, but may now perhaps be obliged to include it; as any attention gradually attracted to it might otherwise lead to its ultimately getting into print again without the necessary corrections.

My reprint consists (to avoid raising undue expectation in so friendly a reader as yourself) much of the following:—Firstly; some poems, all shortish: viz: The Blessed Damozel; Nocturn; the Burden of Nineveh; the Card-Dealer; the Staff and Scrip; Ave;

Sister Helen; Stratton Water; Dennis Shand. The most important of them I fancy you already know, but I have worked at all I think to great advantage up to the present moment as they have been going through the press. Secondly:—a section called 'Songs and Sonnets towards a work to be called *The House of Life*'. Nearly all these you know. Thirdly: Sonnets on Pictures and other Sonnets. Lastly: a prose piece called *Hand and Soul*,[5] which is much more of the nature of a poem than anything else, and which I have thought well to include and revise, as I should not wish it to be lost. I have got very imperfect copies of some other longer poems in M.S. but I cannot remember many important alterations which I had once made in other copies now lost;[6] and this has deterred me as yet from tackling them. But it is very possible that I may before long set about doing so and re-writing what is necessary. In this case I fancy I should have a vol: of quite 300 or probably 350 pages without reckoning new things which might probably get written meanwhile. In such case I should rush into publication. Ellis has advised me with that view to have the type of these sheets kept up and pay a rent for it. I find from the printer that this would not be very expensive, and shall probably do so.

I forgot I think to tell you that, the day before leaving London, I actually got at last full possession of my stables and broke open the communication with the garden. On soberly considering them, they afford a mass of space of extraordinary capabilities and as soon as I return to town I must see about building projects with Webb. Before building, I ought to try for an extension of lease; but I have already nine years still to run; so if the people would only extend the lease with the considerable immediate increase of rent, I think I should be induced to build at once and postpone the question of extending the term till its expiration, if indeed I myself am not the first to expire. In building my studio, I should have an ante-room for people to wait in, and I think also a bed-room for myself, as I feel sure in some weather it might be a great advantage to avoid the necessity of running about between house and studio. Moreover if I did not sleep there myself, it might probably be advisable not to leave the place uninhabited at nights. I should also have a communication by bells between the studio and house. This would make the place completely convenient.

Well, dear Janey, I am going out on my daily tramp now, and only wish you too were capable of such daily constitutionals. I believe

that in this retired region you might soon make some way towards
them. I assure you my great anxiety about my own health as I
walked these roads last year was a less troublesome companion than
the impotent longing for your rapid restoration and constant hope
of better news which possess me at present. However there is no
cause up to this to view the matter in any but a hopeful way. You
do not tell me how much work Topsy has accomplished. I suppose
doubtless a great deal, and that the first section of his 2nd vol.[7] will
really appear in October. Give my love to the dear old thing and
bear in mind how much you are loved by

Your affectionate
D. Gabriel R.

Mrs Morris
Fortuna
Bad–Ems
Nassau
Allemagne

---

[1] Not only for Topsy to spin endless poetry in, but also suggestives of the setting for Rossetti's poem
'The Stream's Secret'.
[2] Henry Treffry Dunn (1838–99), from Truro, succeeded W. J. K. Knewstub as Rossetti's studio
assistant *c.* 1867; he remained with him (with a break), till Rossetti's death. Wrote *Recollections of Dante
Gabriel Rossetti and his Circle*, 1904. See also Gale Pedrick, *Life with Rossetti*, 1964.
[3] Written by H. Buxton Forman.
[4] Written *c.* 1847 when Rossetti was aged 19.
[5] Had appeared in the first number of *The Germ*, 1850.
[6] Rossetti had instructed Howell to make arrangements for the exhumation of the MS. from Lizzie's
grave in Highgate Cemetery; this took place in October, 1869.
[7] *Earthly Paradise*, Part iii, published December 1869.

Penkill   **13**
Tuesday [7 September 1869]

My dear Janey,
  Your former letter had discouraged me more than I cared to say:—
so provokingly small did the improvement seem to be after all your
efforts. So you may suppose how proportionately happy your
present letter makes me: to think of you restored to daily comfort
and activity by so simple a means, and to think of it as a resource
always in case of fresh attacks, is indeed reassuring. No doubt you
will take the precaution on your return to London of having proper
arrangements made to enable you to take the baths at home. I quite
agree with you in thinking it desirable to return as soon as the
improvement has shown itself to be in any degree permanent. I hope

this will have been the case by the time of your starting. I suppose by what you say it will be the safest plan for me to write to Ghent. I judge you will reach London about Tuesday or Wednesday of next week if you travel as leisurely as before. Glad indeed shall I be to see you there in safety.

I have been so feverish and unwell here, and have had such bad sleep, that I do not feel confident in a longer stay being the best course to improve me. However I may perhaps think it well to complete the month, which will not be up till Thursday of next week, as I lost one or two days on the road here. Thus it is possible I may not add one to the number of your congratulatory visitors till you are fairly settled at home again. But perhaps I may leave earlier.

I have begun one or two new poems, and one of them will I hope be the best thing I have done. It is called *The Orchard-Pit*,[1] but I have made little way as yet. I have sonneted a little too and added importantly to some of the old things which wanted working up at the joints.

Tinsley is as you say laughably shady, but I only look at these things so far as they are likely to do good or harm, and this cannot at any rate do harm.

I am rejoiced to hear of Topsy's mighty doings and shall expect much enjoyment from them on my return. By the bye I have long seen him eyeing that poor young man's ewe-lamb, 'The Death of Paris',[2] and am delighted to find him so far after God's own heart as to be no better than the royal bard of Israel; only I hope you learned where Bathsheba bathed and kept an eye on her at Ems. I really think the ewe-lamb business suggests a cartoon which should be carried out with myself as Nathan, but to-day I have no time as I must be gadding about.

News is sadly scarce, and then I hope to be really seeing you so soon now. One sad thing perhaps you have heard—poor Burnett Payne's[3] death after a few days' illness.

A farmer who is a tenant of Miss Boyd's here resembles Topsy in visage, waistcoat-gusset (as I noticed the other day while he was working his corn-cutting machine) and manner no less. He enters his landlady's boudoir suddenly, stands still and glares with his hat held in front of him and his legs apart, and ejaculates 'Ah! about those rabbits!'

Work has been going on in the regular pot-boiling line while I have been away under Dunn's auspices, & Agnew has been buying the drawings I did just before I left. So you see the coast will be clear for your sittings when they become possible.

And now good bye for the present, dear Janey. Don't forget to let me have the further news of your health which you promise, or I shall think all is not well.

With love to Top,

Your affectionate Gabriel

Mrs Morris
Hôtel Royale
Ghent
Belgique

---

[1] This poem remained unfinished and was not included in the 1870 *Poems*. The fragment was printed by W. M. Rossetti in the *Collected Works* 1890, along with the full prose plan which Rossetti had prepared.
[2] The September tale in *The Earthly Paradise* written during the stay at Ems.
[3] A clergyman who became art critic and died young. Rossetti paid tribute to him in a letter to Madox Brown written from Penkill (D. and W. 865).

Penkill **14**
Saturday [11 September 1869]

My dear Janey,

I got Top's note from Ghent this morning. I hope you found there my letter posted on Tuesday to Hôtel Royal as you told me. It is a comfort to think that this letter will reach you in friendly London and that your wanderings are over.

What Top tells me is most reassuring. Then, thank Heaven! all the labour has not been lost. I rejoice to hear that you are getting the baths ready at home. Do let me have a word from you when you get this,—just a word to say how you are after the journey. I long to see for myself how much better you are, but think it will hardly be wise to leave here before the month, so expect most probably to be in town by this day week. So you will have one visitor less to beset you before you are quite rested. I hope and hope that you may be able to come to me soon and preside at a dinner in honour of your restoration. Not of course that I am expecting miracles, but it is evident much has really been done.

What do you think? I have got a Wombat[1] at Chelsea, come the other day, whose portraits (by Dunn) I enclose.

Your affectionate
D. Gabriel R.

Wombat drawings by Dunn

Death of a Wombat

I never reared a young Wombat
To glad me with his pin-hole eye,
But when he most was sweet & fat
And tail-less, he was sure to die!

P.S.   Oh! how the family affections combat
Within this heart; and each hour flings a bomb at
My burning soul; neither from owl nor from bat
Can peace be gained, until I clasp my Wombat!

[1] Madox Brown suggested that Rossetti's wombat was the original of the dormouse in *Alice in Wonderland* published in 1865. As it does not appear among his pets till 1869 this is unlikely. On his return from Penkill he wrote enthusiastic accounts of the animal to Miss Boyd and Miss Losh. It survived till 6 November and was then stuffed. It is commemorated in a memorial drawing showing Rossetti grieving for his pet (S.606), British Museum (1939–5–13–1–(3)).

    G. P. Boyce records in his Diary 14 Feb. 1871, 'Just as we were sitting down to supper Rossetti sent for his marmot which trotted about the floor for the rest of the evening.' In his Diary W. M. Rossetti mentions a racoon, a Virginian owl, a raven, and a kangaroo among the pets, and there were others. Some disappeared, some died from lack of attention.

Dearest Janey,   Sunday [30 January 1870]   **15**

    You were so sweet as to ask me to let you know how I got on, so I write to say I am all right again this morning after the mustard last night. The sight of you going down the dark steps to the cab all alone has plagued me ever since,—you looked so lonely. I hope you got home safe and well. Now everything will be dark for me till I can see you again. It puts me in a rage to think that I should have been so knocked up all yesterday as to be such dreadfully dull company. Why should it happen just when you were here? I shall look you up on Wednesday evening. Will you see if those spectacles of mine have got into Top's room, as I am quite sure I must have left them at your house. As soon as you are able to sit to me again I will send you that chalk drawing to hang up, and indeed may probably do so before if I find I am not needing it. How nice it would be if I could feel sure I had painted you once for all so as to let the world know what you were; but every new thing I do from you is a disappointment, and it is only at some odd moment when I cannot set about it that I see by a flash the way it ought to be done. Such are all my efforts. If I had had you always with me through life, it would somehow have got accomplished. For the last 2 years I have felt distinctly the clearing away of the chilling numbness that surrounds me in the utter want of you; but since then other obstacles have kept steadily on the increase, and it comes too late.

Your most affectionate
Gabriel

Mrs Morris
26 Queen Square W.C.

16 Cheyne Walk, Chelsea
Friday [4 February 1870]

16 Funny sweet Janey,

A bloke is coming here tomorrow with a frame, so I think I had better take the opportunity of sending you that chalk drawing as said bloke can hang it up. If he should happen not to come tomorrow, then I suppose he will on Monday, and I will send it then.

Dear Janey, I suppose this has come into my head because I feel so badly the want of speaking to you. No one else seems alive at all to me now, and places that are empty of you are empty of all life. And it is so seldom that the dead hours breathe a little and yield your dear voice to me again. I seem to hear it while I write, and to see your eyes speaking as clearly as your voice; and so I would write to you for ever if it were not too bad to keep reminding you of my troubles, who have so many of your own. It is dreadful to me to think constantly of a sudden while my mind longs for you, that perhaps at that moment you are suffering so much as to shut out even the possibility of pleasure if life had it ready for you in every shape. I always reproach myself with the comfort I feel despite all in the thought of you, when that thought never fails to present me also with the recollection of your pain and suffering. But more than all for me, dear Janey, is the fact that you exist, that I can yet look forward to seeing you and speaking to you again, and know for certain that at that moment I shall forget all my own troubles nor even be able to remember yours. You are the noblest and dearest thing that the world has had to show me; and if no lesser loss than the loss of you could have brought me so much bitterness, I would still rather have had this to endure than have missed the fulness of wonder and worship which nothing else could have made known to me.

When I began this I meant to try and be cheerful, and just see what vague and dismal follies I have been inflicting on you—I hope to look in tomorrow evening and see how you are, even if I only stay half an hour.

Your most affectionate
Gabriel

Mrs Morris
26 Queen Square
W.C.

[18 (?) February 1870]   **17**

Dearest kindest Janey,

How good of you to write to me so nicely when you are suffering torments in your dear throat. I really feel, seeing you so little, as if I must seem neglectful and careless of all you have to endure. But I hope you believe that it is never absent from my thoughts for a moment and that I never cease to long to be near you and doing whatever might be to distract and amuse you. To be with you and wait on you and read to you is absolutely the only happiness I can find or conceive in this world, dearest Janey; and when this cannot be, I can hardly now exert myself to move hand or foot for anything. If I ever do wish still to do any work, it is that I may not sink into utter unworthiness of you and deserve nothing but your contempt.

I shall come up on Saturday evening and see how you are. But if I *should* be prevented then (or rather to speak plainly if I should resolve that it would be much pleasanter to come when no visitors were at your house) I will then come on Monday.

As for the Academy question,[1] I do not see that I can suggest anything; I suppose all Top has to do is to signify that he wants my book as soon as it appears. If it is necessary it should be advertised to enable him to do so, then Ellis had better advertise at once—I think on the whole I had better write at once to Ellis and tell him he had better do so.

Most affectionately yours
Gabriel

Mrs Morris
26 Queen Square
W.C.

---

[1] Rossetti's *Poems* were published at the end of April 1870. Wm. Morris's review appeared in the *Academy* on 14 May. 'I have done my review, just this moment—ugh!', he had written to Aglaia Coronio.

Friday night [4 March 1870]

18   Dearest Janey,

I hear from the Greeks[1] that you are going to make one at a party to Evans's[2] on Monday night. I hope it is safe for you to do so, and in that case should stay and go too. I shall see you on Sunday or perhaps tomorrow (Saturday) evening. I am sending a copy of the proof[3] for Top, and shall bring one for you when I come.

I have received an invitation again from Mme Bodichon[4] to go down to her cottage near Hastings, and really incline to think it will be the best thing to do. Only now unluckily it has been lent to Stillman and he has been asked to try and still get me to accompany him. I wish I had taken it when first offered and had it to myself. There is one rather uncomfortable point. Chariclea Ionides told me today that when she was lately at Hastings she found the sea air aggravated the bother in her eyes very much, and who knows but I might find the same? To be sure this cottage is a goodish way from the seaside.

I think I have made a good portrait of Mary Zambaco,[5] and Ned is greatly delighted with it. Indeed I enclose a note from that poor old dear which I have just got, as it shows how nice he is. I like her very much and am sure that her love is all in all to her. I never had an opportunity of understanding her before. Today I have been doing Aleco's[6] flame who is a cousin of Mary's and no great matter to look at, but seems niceish. The party at Evans's will it seems be a large one including her, Mary, Ned, etc. I like Mary because she said the sweet one was far more beautiful than any one else in the world. And she is really extremely beautiful herself when one gets to study her face. I think she has got much more so within the last year with all her love and trouble. But rainy walks and constant lowness are I fear beginning to break up her health.

Your most affectionate
Gabriel

Mrs Morris
26 Queen Square
W.C.

[1] The Ionides family.
[2] W. H. Evans, friend of Wm. Morris who accompanied him with Faulkner and Magnusson on his first visit to Iceland in 1874.
[3] Rossetti's forthcoming volume of poems.
[4] Scalands, Robertsbridge, near Hastings, the home of Barbara Leigh-Smith who married Dr. Eugene Bodichon in 1857. Before her marriage Rossetti had visited her with Lizzie Siddal in 1854. Now in 1870, with W. J. Stillman as fellow guest, he stayed there during March, April, and part of May. Mrs. Morris was there for part of the time and he made a drawing of her reclining on a sofa (S.376). Barbara

Bodichon was an advocate of women's rights and one of the founders of Girton College. See H. Burton, *Barbara Bodichon*, 1949.

'Ah if you were only like Miss Barbara Smith . . . blessed with large rations of tin, fat, enthusiasm, and golden hair, who thinks nothing of climbing up a mountain in breeches, or wading through a stream in none, in the sacred name of pigment.' D.G.R. to Christina (D. and W. 131).

[5] Maria Cassavetti a young relation of the Ionides family who married Dr. Demetrius Zambaco. Rossetti's account of Burne-Jones's involvement with the 'Greek damsel' is given in a letter to Madox Brown (D. and W. 809). Burne-Jones blamed Howell for spreading scandal about the episode. Rossetti made four drawings of her (S.540–3).

[6] Third son of Alexander Ionides whose other children were Constantine, Luke, Aglaia (Mrs. Coronio) and Anthea Chariclea (Mrs. Dannreuther). The Morris firm decorated Aleco's house in Holland Park.

16 Cheyne Walk, Chelsea **19**
Monday [7 March 1870]

My dear Janey,
I have bethought me that you wore the blue dress at your party and may possibly want it for tomorrow evening.

Your affec: Gabriel

Mrs Morris
26 Queen Square
(by hand)

[Fragment]   [10 March 1875[1]] **20**

tactics of that kind. However I was glad to see him, and we spent 2 or 3 hours pleasantly together. He seemed to me better than when I last saw him.

I have been finishing the Sphinx design[2] I spoke of, and shall enjoy showing it to you. The idea is that of Man questioning the Unknown, and I shall call it either 'The Question' or 'The Sphinx and her Questioner', but I think on the whole the shorter title is the better. In the design, a youth, a mature man, and an old man, have made their way up a rocky ascent to a platform embowered in laurels which is the shrine of the Sphinx. The youth has fallen in death before he can question the oracle,—the man peers into her eyes with his question, but they have no answer, staring at the unseen sky beyond the horizon of the picture—a creek of sea hemmed in with sharp rocks and having only the image of the moon reflected in its centre. Meanwhile the old man still toils up towards the Sphinx, eager to the last for her secret. I have made the design nude, but propose to drape it in some degree when I paint it, which I fancy must be on rather a small scale, for 2 reasons; one being that to sell a big picture

The Sphinx or *The Question*

without women in it wd be a double difficulty, and the other that a moonlight subject on a large scale is always monotonous. The subject is in fact the same as that of my little poem 'The Cloud'.[3]

> 'And eyes fixed ever in vain
> On the pitiless eyes of Fate.'

I have told you about the design and hope it will not therefore dis- . . .

Mrs William Morris
Horrington House
Turnham Green
Chiswick

[1] Defective letter—beginning and end missing. Postmark Turnham Green, 10 March 1875. The Morrises moved to Horrington House, Turnham Green Road, Chiswick, towards the end of 1872. There is a gap of five years between this letter and the previous ones written when they were still at 26 Queen Square, Bloomsbury; and a gap of two years between it and the next letter dated November 1877.
[2] Pencil drawing known also as *The Question* (S.241). Design for a picture which was never painted and may have reference to the untimely death of Oliver Madox Brown. In his *Autobiographical Notes* Bell Scott accused Rossetti of stealing his subject from an early poem of his. Rossetti returned to the subject during his last illness in 1882. He wrote two sonnets for the drawing which was to be an illustration in a joint volume of poems by Watts and himself. These sonnets, dictated to Hall Caine, were privately printed by T. J. Wise and are reprinted by Doughty and Wahl in note to Letter 2615, and by Surtees in catalogue No. 241.
[3] *The Cloud Confines*, a poem which ponders the question of survival after death, was written at Kelmscott in 1871.

Monday [19 November 1877] **21**

My dear Janey,
    Pardon a line at last moment when you must be so busy: but it is to impress on you not to fail to write as soon as possible after your arrival,[1] as I shall be most anxious to know how you have stood the journey. Thanks for the things sent. I never meant Dunn to come in boring you, but told him the things wd be left out for him.
    God bless you.

                                        Your affec.
                                        Gabriel

You never left your Italian address, so I cannot write till you do so.

Mrs William Morris
Horrington House
Turnham Green Road

[1] Mrs. Morris with her two daughters spent the winter at Oneglia on the Italian Riviera. They were joined by Wm. Morris in late April 1878 for a visit to Venice and the cities of north Italy.

16 Cheyne Walk, Chelsea. London.
2 Dec. 1877

22 My dearest Janey,

What a relief it was to me to know that you had not quite broken down during such a journey in so weak a state! You give me a clear idea of your surroundings, and as to yourself I could have no clearer vision than is at all times present to me. How I wish I could look with you on everything you are seeing. I fear from what you say that the weather is not perfection with you, but surely it cannot equal the shivering shadowland which surrounds us here. Nevertheless I have my misgivings as to Italy in the winter, and wish you wd have been more explicit on this point. Please be so in your next. I highly approve of the pattern of your sofa—the most appropriate imaginable—and should almost suggest such a quaint piece of furniture being purchased, were it not for the distance it wd have to travel. I am surprised indeed that you can understand your Genoese landlord: better-educated men of his province even have sometimes well-nigh baffled me. I trust you will return a thorough Italian. What progress do the girls make in the language? or did they already know it? I suppose however that they think Icelandic ought to be the social language of Europe.

I have been very busy beginning a picture from Mrs. Stillman, as she is on the point of leaving England for the winter. Her husband is to meet her and the children at Turin, and they are to proceed to Corfu for the winter. I have misgivings that they will settle there. I am becoming most unfortunate in my models. She is the only person who wd in any degree have suited me for ideal subjects now that you can hardly be hoped for as a sitter; and now she must needs take herself off, with the best will in the world to sit if she were only staying. I have finished the head of the picture—'Fiammetta',[1] from Boccaccio's sonnet on his last sight of her,—and it is far better than I ever painted from anyone but yourself. She has given me the sittings most kindly under great difficulties,—her own little girl having had an accident and broken her collar-bone: however it is going on quite well.

I think I told you of Macdonald's house[2] in Hammersmith Mall: favorable reports of it continue, and I am going myself to see it in a day or two. I have written to Mrs. Cowper Temple[3] to let me know whatever she knows about it. I have some idea that Ned is on the

look out for a house, so don't mention this one to any soul lest he pounce on it.

Thanks about the Kelmscott matter—I was just making my mind up to get Dunn to go down there and fetch the drawings etc. which I want. I still think this will be best plan, and will write to Top and ask him whether it will be convenient for Dunn to go while he is there or whether it wd be better after he is gone. I must also get Top either to send key or leave it with Philip for Dunn, suppose D. goes there after Top's return. By the bye, Dunn told me there was a girl like May in the room when he called on you. Does this happen to be the daughter of your costermongering relative? If so, I could give her some sittings, which wd be as profitable as the smoky chimney business.

What a wretch you were to *remind* me that you had honored that furniture by your acceptance. That shows that *you* wd strip *my* house if I'd let you! But I don't want any of the furniture away, except perhaps an old cabinet in the tapestry room which is useful in studio.

How I hope you won't be such a bemuffled banshee as last time when I see you again. And when and where will that be, I wonder? Write again immediately, for I want to get every word I can from you.

By the bye, Mrs. Stillman told me of her calling in Paris on poor Mary Z. who it seems must be dying of consumption. She was very pale, very ill dressed, and (added Mrs. S.) 'she *must* be very ill, for her hair was quite black'.

I've got no foreign paper and hope they won't charge you more postage than I pay: but I wouldn't put off writing over today (Sunday) because then I could not find time to write till Monday evening.

Write soon to

Your most affectionate
Gabriel

By the bye the wretch Howell's house[4] *is* coming down for a railway!! The devil takes care of his own.

Mrs Morris
Villa della Cava
Oneglia
Italia

[1] *A Vision of Fiammetta* (S.252), completed in 1878, was purchased by W. A. Turner of Manchester. Mrs. Stillman sat for the figure. Not to be confused with the earlier *Fiammetta* of 1866 (S.192). Fiammetta was Boccaccio's name for his beloved Maria d'Aquino. Rossetti's sonnet on the picture was published in *Ballads and Sonnets*, 1881.

> Behold Fiammetta, shown in Vision here
> Bloom-girt 'mid Spring-flushed apple-growth she stands . . . .

On the difficulty of finding good apple-blossom see letter to Shields (D. and W. 1909).

[2] Horrington House, Turnham Green, being now too small, Morris arranged in April 1878 to take the Retreat, Upper Mall, Hammersmith, which had been occupied by George Macdonald the novelist. They moved there in October, and changed the name to Kelmscott House. Rossetti gave Janey the furniture he had left at Kelmscott Manor.

[3] Georgiana Tollemache m. the Hon. William Cowper (1811–85) in 1848. Stepson of Lord Palmerston he became Cowper-Temple in 1869 and Lord Mount-Temple in 1880. Statesman and one of Rossetti's early patrons, he purchased the original version of *Beata Beatrix*. This was left to the nation by his widow as a memorial to him and is in the Tate Gallery. Rossetti visited the Cowper-Temples at Broadlands in 1876.

[4] There was a current rumour that Howell had a habit of extracting compensation from railway companies which threatened his houses. The matter is explained by Mrs. Angeli in *Pre-Raphaelite Twilight*, p. 223.

19 Dec. 1877   **23**

My dear Janey,

I had laid in a stock of thin paper before your warning arrived so may as well proceed to use it. I cannot say your accounts are very brilliant: as for the climate I dont believe a bit in it on your showing and am certain that I for one should be chilled to the marrow. I fear you are still incapable of exercise, though indeed a decided improvement might hardly be hoped for as yet: do tell me how far you are able to walk. Also let me know how near you are to the Howards,[1] and what amount of society of any kind you get. Also whether Jenny[2] is better in the important respect, and how May is. I wot not of Signor Ravizza, but if he can speak English I dare say he wd prove a more helpful Italian teacher than another. Nevertheless I shd think you might get on pretty well without him, and indeed the girls too, unless they are bent on talking Icelandic in Italy.

I saw the last of Mrs Stillman on Monday. She came here with the 3 girls[3] and was to start next day for Turin where Stillman meets them. He must have had a narrow escape when the Prince of Montenegro's house was blown up: he is almost always there, and wd probably have lost his life had he not already started on his way to meet his family. I was most charmed with little Effie, who will be extremely like her mother. Lisa is a charming dreamy looking girl, almost as tall as Marie S. now: and Bella is very engaging through her extreme intelligence, and comely though the only one of the three who is not beautiful. They all draw and design no end, and

Lisa has quite settled to be an artist: she is a lovely and loveable creature. I accomplished the complete head and neck from Mrs S. for the Fiammetta subject, and it is certainly as good as anything I ever did: I am better contented with the design now, as I have developed its meaning better, and feel confidence now in the carrying out; I forget whether I showed you some lovely flame-coloured oriental drapery I have for it. I could not get time to do the hands from her, which is very bothering, but in the last sitting I made an additional study of her hand in another action. She is extremely pressing that I should join them abroad; but I suppose there is little chance of this, though her sittings wd be precious, and I also might compensate her somewhat by being of use to her work. She showed me 2 of her latest watercolour pictures,—life-sized half figures with a good deal of elaborate and sometimes excellent imitative painting in the floral accessories but I am sorry to say I found them disappointing: they are not nearly as good in the higher sense as some things she did before her marriage.

You will be glad in one way and sorry in another to hear that I have sold both the Proserpine and the little picture of you painted at Kelmscott: together with them I have sold the as yet only commenced Fiammetta, all to one purchaser, a Mr Turner[4] of Manchester, a new buyer to me. He is a real lover of my work and told me that very early in life he got wildly enamoured of my illustrations in Tennyson,[5] and swore that if he could ever buy pictures he wd buy mine. He is still not more than about 35 I shd think, and is only able now to begin launching out at all as a buyer. In these horrid bad times, to sell pictures to a good amount is, I can assure you, rare indeed; and I may congratulate myself that, after my long illness and with the worry of moving close at hand, I have been able to lay in a lump of money to meet exigencies. I was really mortally sorry to part with the Kelmscott picture, but after one or two disappointments in business matters lately, felt that there was no alternative. It is a great thing to get works into Manchester where the principal buyers are, and these works will do me credit. Hitherto, except a few water colours, I had nothing there. The few who yet know of the sale are surprised and congratulatory, for both artists and buyers are crying out about the bad times. I have hung the drawings of you in the studio now and finished the one of Pandora which before look[ed] undraped. I want to start an important picture of this, full-length to the feet, as soon as possible. It has certainly occurred to me

45

Water Willow

sometimes to try and work out some of these drawings as pictures, using any nature at hand for the mere surface and light and shade of the flesh and adhering in all respects to the drawing as a guide. All my models of any value—to wit 2 only, yourself and Marie S.—are leaving me in the lurch, and I may be forced on this alternative. Pictures from common models folk will not buy from me, witness the Gretchen[6] which I began, which I offer cheaper than others, but which sticks to me yet.

I think it probable that the large profile head of you which was autotyped[7] and of which I retouched a copy for a fresh negative may be immediately reprinted and published. The *Silence* you know is out. They have tried the drawing I did at Scalands in several forms but they never get the tone to please me nor will they, I am sure, without retouching and a fresh negative.

I dont think the house in Hammersmith Mall will answer for several reasons: one very important one being that I am assured the garden is generally being overflowed by the Thames. I suppose this is the case all along there. I went to see it, as I think I told you, and it has many advantages. I also saw another house at Percy Cross, Fulham, which has attractions and objections. Heaven knows where I can find rest for the sole of my foot.

I will occupy the last page with an amusing anecdote of Howell. He has lately taken to pressing his society on Whistler as a last resource, though that worthy had not spoken to him for years. His plan is to go there early, set to work printing W's etchings for him, and stick on all day long till people come to dinner (W. now knows some swells) and thus force an invitation and try to make a fresh circle. One day he was printing etchings as usual, when the servant came up with a long face and said there was someone downstairs who wanted to see Mr Whistler. W says at once: 'Oh I see,—a writ, of course. Well, how much is it?' The servant goes down and asks: 'Fifteen pounds, Sir.' W. says: 'Well, perhaps I'd better try and pay: I've got eleven pounds.' 'Well' says H. 'I've got something in my pocket.' and together they made up the sum. Then H. says: 'I'll tell you what, you'd better let *me* go down and settle this. I understand these fellows and shall get something taken off the costs.' Accordingly down goes H. and in due time returns looking quite another H.—most awfully crestfallen. W. notices this at once, but to his enquiries H. only says, 'O yes, it's alright, he's gone.' W. insists that H. looks very queer, but H. only exclaims 'O d—n it, I want to get

47

to my work,' and bolts to the etching-press. However W. is so persistent in his urgencies for an explanation, that at last H. says:— 'Well if you *will* have it, it's this. That d—d fellow has been hunting me down for a year with a writ for £100; he knows me perfectly well, had the writ in his pocket and served it on the spot. If your servant had only said his name, I should have known and not gone down to him.'

Of course W. was vastly amused and told the story to Watts[8] who told me: but *I* should not wonder if H. had gone down with the full intention of pocketing W.'s 11£ and saying he was out and the man must call again, in which case he is extremely likely to have paid that sum (with the above information) to stave off his own writ, & W's writ will come home to him yet again. So fares it between Portugal and Portugal Street.[9] The origin of H's intimacy with W. was that one day Watts ran against W. in the street, and just as they met Howell rushed past in a cab: they were both congratulating themselves that he had gone by, when down he comes upon them, with a slap on the back to Watts, and a 'How's Gabriel?'. He then turns to Whistler, fraternizes, and departs. A few days afterwards Watts meets Whistler again in the street, and asks (for fun) 'Have you seen any more of Howell?' But W. replies 'I should rather think I have indeed. He came the first thing in the morning after we met him, and has been every day since, printing my etchings off and sticking on till dinner-time.' The last reported result is the anecdote given above; but report also says that those who meet H. at W's table dont seem to see it at all.

I hope to hear again from you very soon dear Janey.

Your affectionate Gabriel

Mrs Morris
Villa del Cavo
Oneglia
Italia

---

[1] George James Howard (1843–1911), Liberal M.P. for East Cumberland, succeeded as 9th Earl of Carlisle in 1899. Married Rosalind, daughter of Lord Stanley of Alderley in 1864. Friends of the Morrises they joined Janey at Oneglia, and later Janey and the children stayed with them at Naworth. Lord Carlisle was a gifted amateur artist and had studied with Legros and Costa. Both the Howards were ardent temperance reformers.

[2] Jane Alice, the Morris elder daughter born 1861. At the age of 15 she became subject to recurrent epileptic fits, but lived on to the age of 74, dying in 1935.

[3] Little Effie is Euphrosyne, the Stillmans' daughter born in 1872. Lisa and Bella were the daughters of his first marriage. His son Russie died in 1875 aged 13.

[4] Rossetti sold three pictures to W. A. Turner, a Manchester manufacturer, in December 1877 for

1500 guineas—*A Vision of Fiammetta*, *Proserpine*, and 'the Kelmscott picture'. For the complicated history of the various versions of *Proserpine* see M. pp. 170–4 and S. 233. The Kelmscott picture is *Water Willow*, a portrait head of Mrs. Morris with the house in the background painted in 1871. The original is in the Bancroft Collection; a copy by Fairfax Murray is at Kelmscott (S.226).

[5] Rossetti contributed five designs to the Moxon illustrated Tennyson, 1857: *The Lady of Shalott*, *Mariana in the South*, *Saint Cecilia*, *King Arthur and the Weeping Queens*, *Sir Galahad*. They were engraved by the Dalziel brothers.

[6] *Risen at Dawn*, or 'Gretchen discovering the Jewels', an incident from *Faust*. The whereabouts of the picture is unknown but two studies for it exist (S.253).

[7] A process of permanent photographic printing which reproduces photographs or works of art. An Autotype Company was formed in 1878. Rossetti, Shields, and Charles Rowley of Manchester were interested in the process and several of Rossetti's works were reproduced by it. The autotype *Silence* was made from a favourite drawing. For details see S.214.

See letters to Shields (D. and W. 1851, 1861, and 1888), and Ernestine Mills, *Life and Letters of Frederic Shields*, 1912, pp. 204–6.

[8] Walter Theodore Watts (1832–1914), solicitor and writer. Introduced to Rossetti by Dr. Hake he became his friend and legal adviser. He was a regular contributor to the *Athenaeum* after 1876, and author of *The Coming of Love* (1897), a narrative poem, and *Aylwin* (1898), a novel describing some of his contemporaries. He rescued Swinburne from his life of dissipation and looked after him at No. 2 The Pines, Putney, till the poet's death. Watts added Dunton to his name in 1896, giving Whistler the occasion for his well-known witticism.

[9] The joke is that Portugal Street is where the Bankruptcy Court used to be before it moved to Carey Street.

16 Cheyne Walk **24**
24 Jany 1878

My dear Janey,

I have not heard from you since your letter dated 30th Dec: last, by which you seemed then to be far from well. I answered it within a few days, and am of course anxious at having received no news of you since. I suppose it is hardly possible that my letter miscarried.

In my last I mentioned my purpose of renewing the lease of this house. I am now doing so, and shall therefore have less difficulty in awaiting the convenient moment for a change of abode. At least I suppose as yet that I shall take this course, but matters are not yet concluded. Every one tells me that as soon as I wish to leave, there are plenty of excellent tenants who will be too happy to take the house at an advance on what I shall be paying now—i.e. 200£ a year.

I merely tell you this in order to fill up a little space, and in *case* by any possibility you did not get my last. But my real object in writing is to get some news of your health, which I hope will not now be long delayed, since the time which has already elapsed is quite sufficient to give anxiety. Should you, by evil chance, be very unwell, perhaps Jenny or May would write me a line.

Affectionately yours
Gabriel

16 Cheyne Walk
10 Feb: 1878

25 My dear Janey,

I was much relieved by receiving your letter, though the news was not very encouraging up to your writing. I hope however that by this time the anticipated Spring change has set in for good, and that there is no more tramontana to rake your system. I should have written before this only was anxious to be able to tell you something positive about this house matter,[1] which of course, like all such matters, hangs on for ever. However I believe I may say for certain now that no building is likely to take place hereabouts at present,— indeed they say probably not for several years. I am taking a renewed lease, at £200 a year, but cannot obtain a longer term than 7 years, as they are unwilling to be hampered in the matter. This lease does not include the garden, but I am to have it till needed for building and with due warning of such need. Unfortunately the shortness of the lease makes it a far less profitable investment, as any tenant to whom I let it would have to rely on getting his lease renewed at end of my term, or on my being able to do so. However it was Hobson's choice with me, as no other house whatever of a suitable kind had turned up.

However these are small matters to report to your part of the world, where a Pope has just followed a King[2] out of their joint supremacies. I suppose there is no great stir in your quiet quarter, and that no inconvenience is anticipated: neither probably are you so much bedevilled with rumours of wars as is the case in London. Morris, I hear, is dealing about him on all sides,[3] and you will see my prophecy as to his parliamentary career will come true yet. However I suppose the picture market will soon be nowhere. My reason for not telling you about any work is that really I have done nothing to speak of. I made a small water colour Proserpine,[4] and am getting to a finish with the predella of Graham's eternal Bd. Damozel picture;[5] the predella representing the lover lying in an autumn landscape and looking upwards. I shall soon no doubt make way with more important things, but these had to be got done and the figure in the predella gave me just as much trouble as if it had been four times the size. Before sending away the Proserpine (with which the owner is delighted) I tried to get it photographed, but the result was a lamentable failure. However perhaps I may retouch a proof and

The Blessed Damozel

take a second negative. The profile head of you is being issued in autotype as well as the *Silence*: I have called the profile *Twilight*, which title seems to be viewed as very appropriate to the shadowed eyes and penetrating sweetness of the expression. Ah! when shall I draw from it again? Nevertheless these autotypes never seem really to come out, as they seem waiting for an overwhelming list (to include Ned and others) before they are issued. You know I retouched a copy of the profile, and the second negative is now taken but I have not seen the result.

I hear nothing from Mrs. Stillman who promised to write forthwith: I hope nothing is amiss. Brown and Shields[6] have really got the job of painting the new Town Hall at Manchester with historical subjects which *must* bring poor Brown out at last I should think. I think you must have met Smetham,[7] but do not know if you have seen any work of his. You will be sorry to hear that he is—as one may say—out of his mind; having succumbed to a fearful attack of Melancholia which has now kept him lying in bed without speaking (except in monosyllables to his wife) for three whole months! What the result can be, it is impossible to surmise: the doctor gives some hopes of a tardy recovery; and one thing to be said is that I understand he had an equally bad attack of the same kind some 20 years ago. I have got some pictures of his here—quite admirable in the *highest* sense but unfortunately not faultless—and am doing my utmost to try and effect some sales. I suppose the Howards wd not buy one— the prices are from £100 to £25. If you thought there was any chance, I would send you a copy of a letter of Mrs. Smetham's respecting his case. He is the most loveable and one of the most gifted of men.

I hope the girls continue as much better as when you wrote, and am above all glad to infer that Jenny is freed from the special evil. But all is nothing if *you* do not mend: I do hope for a better account next time.

P. P. Marshall was here the other evening in his usual condition, and turned into bed with his clothes on. His leading opinion, as I gathered it, is that he ought to shoot down every man he ever knew if he would not be hanged for doing so.

Hoping to hear before long

I am your affectionate
Gabriel

PS Watts has asked me more than once to remember him kindly to you.

Mrs Morris
Villa del Cavo
Oneglia
Italia

[1] The lease of 16 Cheyne Walk was due to expire on 24 June. With the prospect of increased rent and the possibility of building development Rossetti was looking for a new residence. With the help of Watts he was able to renew the lease on satisfactory terms.

[2] Pius IX died 7 February, and Victor Emmanuel 9 January 1878.

[3] Morris was deeply concerned with the 'Eastern Question', organizing and speaking at meetings of the Socialist anti-war party.

[4] Watercolour replica sold to F. S. Ellis, present whereabouts unknown (S.233).

[5] Wm. Graham commissioned the picture in 1871 and the predella in 1877. This depicts the lover lying in a wooded landscape gazing up to the heaven where his lost lady is. Now in the Fogg Museum, Harvard (S.244).

[6] Madox Brown and Frederic Shields were commissioned to decorate the new Town Hall designed by Alfred Waterhouse. There were to be twelve pictures illustrating episodes in the history of Manchester from Roman times till the nineteenth century, each artist responsible for six; Shields resigned his share in the work and Brown carried out the whole series in eight years from 1878 to 1886.

[7] James Smetham (1821–89), Methodist artist who taught drawing at the Normal Wesleyan College. A friend of Rossetti and the Pre-Raphaelites. He suffered a mental breakdown and was in an asylum for the last ten years of his life. Author of essays on Reynolds and Blake; his literary works were edited by Wm. Davies in 1893. Rossetti helped his family by promoting the sale of his pictures to friends.

27 Feb: 1878

26   My dear Janey,

Your letter is far from consolatory indeed. The very writing does not look like your firm hand, but reminds me of poor Lizzy's in days gone by. But you do not despair and I will not do so. It is too provoking that you should have made all this effort in the very winter which might have been passed at home without possibility of bad results—so mild has it been. Mrs. Sumner[1] (who suffers greatly in winter) writes me that this time she has got on perfectly well so far. However it has been so unwinterly as yet that the worst may in fact be to come—probably enough about April and May.

I also am anxious about Mary Stillman. She has never written to me, but did answer a letter of Lucy's. She was then at Corfu after spending some time in Venice and elsewhere. Her husband is reported very well. I cannot help fearing that there is every risk of her being integrated in a harem along with the 2 girls and the baby who wd be brought up as a first-class odalisque. Of course this is only joking or one would not view it as funny: nevertheless it must be a risky sort of sojourn just now.

I had a visit from the secretary of the Grosvenor[2] the other day, kindly informing me that they had reserved space for my benefit; but I told him I should not exhibit. Yet I do wish to come out somewhere and somehow, but am never finally pleased with what I have to show. The Blessed Damozel is enormously improved by its predella and looks very brilliant now both are finished. I wish you could see it. I have finished an old watercolour of the head of your portrait, and it comes well: it is for Valpy. I did not want it to be talked about among strangers by your name, so have christened it Bruna Brunelleschi,[3] of course bearing on the dark complexion—I did think of calling it Vittoria Colonna, who I find was *certainly* the original of those heads by M.A. which are portraits of you; but I thought it would not do to tackle Mike. Soon I hope to have some news of work to tell you, but lately the finishing of trifles has cut into my time.

It seems Ned will not have an equal show at the Grosvenor this year, but is to come out next year with a big series from the story of Perseus which he is painting for a man named Balfour.[4]

I will enquire of Watts as soon as I see him about the dividend; but of course I will not hear of your being mulcted for poor Smetham's sake, though it is very kind of you to suggest it. You will be glad to hear that I am beginning to have some luck with his work. Cowper Temple has bought one picture for £100 and Vernon Lushington[5] another for 65 guineas. Other friends promise help, and I dare say I shall get at least a couple more sold. I must buy one myself if necessary, but not if I can do well without, as I really can't afford it. The matter is costing me both trouble and time, but I shall think both well bestowed if Smetham is helped to real purpose, as I always had a high regard and great affection for him. I think I told you that he has lain for months without noticing person or thing, only answering his wife in monosyllables, though not apparently unable to understand what goes on about him. It is what doctors call Melancholia. I have got the 2 cheques made *to order*, in the hope of his being roused to sign his name at the back of them; but perhaps it will only result in my being obliged to trouble the drawers of them to draw fresh ones *to bearer*.

It seems they have been smashing Gladstone's windows: if you were in town, perhaps the air would come in without your throwing the windows open, considering Top's political bias. He is the Odger of the Future,[6] my dear Janey, depend on it, and will be in parliament next change.

It quite pains me, much as I covet your letters, to think of you having to undergo undue exertion in writing them. You must only write just as much as you can; but a *word only* is better than letting too long interval elapse.

Your affectionate Gabriel

Mrs Morris
Villa del Cavo
Oneglia
Italia

[1] Mrs. Holme Sumner, friend of the Cowper-Temples whom Rossetti met at Broadlands. He made a portrait of her, and she was the model for *Domizia Scaligera* (S.246, 521).

[2] The Grosvenor Gallery founded by Sir Coutts Lindsay in 1877 as an independent gallery where artists of original talent were invited to exhibit their own selection of their work. The pictures were well spaced and each artist's work was grouped together. Madox Brown and Rossetti (who was always reluctant to exhibit his work) refused invitations to contribute to the opening exhibition in May 1877. Rossetti objected to the inclusion of work by members of the Royal Academy, giving his reasons in a letter to the secretary in January 1877 (D. and W. 1745). Burne-Jones and Whistler became mainstays of the Grosvenor which was given 'greenery-yallery' fame by W. S. Gilbert in *Patience*. Ruskin's criticism of a *Nocturne* by Whistler in *Fors Clavigera*, 2 July 1877, led to the famous law-case which awarded a farthing damage to the artist. See The Palace of Art by Barrie Bullen, *Apollo*, November 1975, pp. 352–7.

[3] Probably a study begun in 1868 for the portrait of Mrs. Morris now at Kelmscott Manor. The water-colour is in the Fitzwilliam Museum (S.251, 372).

Rossetti was probably thinking of the Michelangelo drawing 'Ideal Head of a Woman' now in the British Museum (B M 1895-9-15-493). In the past this was fancifully identified as a portrait of Vittoria Colonna, and was reproduced under the title 'The Marchioness of Pescara' (i.e. Vittoria Colonna) in *The Lawrence Gallery* published in 1853. So it could well have been known to Rossetti. Swinburne may have infected Rossetti with his own enthusiasm for Michelangelo's studies of Female Heads which he had seen in Florence in 1864. He wrote about them in his 'Notes on Designs of the Old Masters in Florence', published in *Essays and Studies*, 1875.

[4] Arthur Balfour was introduced to Burne-Jones by Lady Airlie. He commissioned a series of eight pictures illustrating the story of Perseus for the decoration of the drawing-room at 4 Carlton Gardens. During the last fifteen years of his life the artist was at work on the series which was still incomplete at his death in 1898. The pictures, acquired from the Huntington Hartford Gallery in New York in 1971 are now in the Staatsgalerie, Stuttgart.

[5] 1832–1912. Fourth son of the Rt. Hon. Stephen Lushington, M.P. Educated Trinity College, Cambridge, Barrister Inner Temple, Secretary to the Admiralty, and finally County Court Judge. He and his brother Godfrey contributed to the *Oxford and Cambridge Magazine* and helped at the Working Men's College. He introduced Burne-Jones to Rossetti. Lushington retained his friendship with Rossetti and was present at his funeral.

[6] George Odger (1820–77), shoemaker, London trade-unionist, President of the International Association of Working Men, who made five unsuccessful attempts to enter parliament. A well-known speaker in the Socialist cause. Matthew Arnold said of him in *Culture and Anarchy* 'he may very well stand for the beautiful and virtuous of our present working-class'.

5 March 1878

27 My dear Janey,

What a pleasure to see your handwriting again so soon while I am feeling so anxious about you at this great distance! I assure you I have thought very seriously as to exhibiting this year at the Grosvenor: and your urging me is of course the strongest incentive. But a lifelong abstinence from exhibition makes me perhaps over-anxious; and it is certainly a fact that an unfavorable result would have the effect of damping the few who remain to help me to a livelihood. Graham is as dead as ditch-water: he was here the other day to see the predella to the Bd. Daml. and not a living word wd come out of his Scotch throat, though I know the picture does look well now altogether. I have vastly improved it by adding roses in the hedges, aureoles round the heads, etc. and enlivening the whole colour which is now most deep and brilliant at same time; and the predella vastly enhances it, being too a fine picture in itself—one of my very best.

Another dead 'un is Leyland who I feel sure won't buy again at all: and the only man really that I have to look to now is this Turner (of Manchester) who after all may draw back in spite of his good start, or may not really be rich enough to go on buying.

Thus I am quite between 2 stools as to coming forward with work; and above all (while you say how much my exhibition wd encourage you) I am haunted with the idea of the *dis*couragement which must result for you from a public failure at my age. Had not I lost 5 months this year through illness, I should have had the replica of the large picture finished, which I mean to make superior to the large one; and I could then have judged better how I stood for exhibition.

I suppose you have heard that Ruskin[1] is dangerously ill with brain fever. However I view his constitution as very strong.

I am getting on about Smetham. Graceless Graham did buy one (reluctantly enough) for 75£. I think I told you of the Cowper Temples buying one for £100: this (with Lushington's) comes in all to 243£. I have now sent 6 of the pictures to Manchester to Turner's care, who expresses himself willing to help. Ned Jones said Constantine Ionides *might* buy one: but hearing the other day from Aglaia (who wrote offering spontaneously to look over that house in Hammersmith Mall for me!) I asked her if her brother wd buy, and find she thinks not. Smetham may perhaps be considered as slightly improving: he now rises for an hour—sometimes two daily, but takes no notice of anything nor shows any other advance. Still I fancy he may get over it.

I have got 3 drawings of May and 3 of Mary Stillman framed in two triple frames and they look very well.

Today I received the most grotesque begging letter I ever *did* get; and as I know you love a laugh, I copy it verbatim et literatim. If you can read it seriatim (in the Brunonian sense)[2] you must be far gone indeed.

Young Street Kensington

To Daniel Gabriel Rosetti Esqre.
   Hon. Sir,
There was a time when Evening's Twilight came so gently stealing upon man that he went forth to fulfil his duties—so gratifying to humanity and to himself—with joy. Alas! what expectations, what results! Driven almost on the verge of destitution through stubborn misfortunes, he begs—so utterly desolate!—for a small charity in the way of old clothing or boots or a change of linen. Your noble resolutions ever thankfully appreciates, Sir,
   Your most humble servant,

Jean D. Schneider.
Choir-Singer

from the Herzdeutsche opera at Rotterdam.

The qualifications of Mr. Schneider I have copied as best I could. I judge he must have *dictated* the letter to some begging scribe. He came while some one was here, and being very busy I simply said there was no answer: but on examining the racy epistle, I enquired what the applicant was like; and was told he could not speak a word of English but was very well dressed! On hearing that there was no answer, he seemed much depressed but uttered to the servant the only English words he seemed to know which were 'Good Afternoon'. I am really sorry I did not see and even help him, though if I had I dare say his tribe wd have been upon me.

It has been a great happiness to me to hear from you this evening, and I hope you may be able soon to write again if only a few words. May's superscription alarmed me somewhat at first for your health, but you are quite right to get her to write addresses, as no doubt the letter itself is fully enough for your forces: but I do hope the weather will help you soon. Why not make your way to Rome? That is where every one is going at this time of year. I happen to know 2 people who are there now: viz: Valpy[3] and Davies[4] (a friend of Smetham's): and their reports of climate are most inviting, though Valpy was groaning about it when at Genoa. If you by chance *did* think of going to Rome, Davies is the nicest cleverest and comfortablest of men (a friend of Ned's and no Methodist though intimate with Smetham) and wd be most helpful, knowing Rome thoroughly—find you quarters, look you up in them, take you out, and everything. Still of course I suppose you wd find it impracticable to get to Rome; but I fancy it wd really be desirable, and do not see, if so, why it shd not be done.

Your affectionate
Gabriel

Mrs Morris
Villa del Cavo
Oneglia
Italia

[1] Ruskin's mental breakdown which had been threatening for some years finally overwhelmed him in February 1878. He made a slow recovery, but resigned his Oxford professorship in November.
[2] Evidently an allusion to Madox Brown, possibly to his solemn manner and malapropisms.
[3] L. R. Valpy, London solicitor, a steady patron of Rossetti from 1867 onwards. He acquired the original large version of *Dante's Dream* when Wm. Graham relinquished it. For Rossetti's complicated financial arrangements with 'Valpy the vampire' over this picture and others see his letter 10 Sept. 1878 (D. and W. 1958) and M. p. 184. Valpy was a desperately religious man with a particular objection to nudity in art.
[4] William Davies of Liverpool (1830–96), writer and artist, friend of Rossetti and Smetham. Wrote various volumes of poetry including *Songs of a Wayfarer* (1869). Rossetti admired his poetry and Hall Caine included him in *Sonnets of Three Centuries*. Davies wrote an article on British painting in the *Quarterly Review* (1873), contributed a memoir to the letters of James Smetham (1891), and edited Smetham's literary works (1893).

16 Cheyne Walk
18 March 1878

28 My dear Janey,

It is sad to see you writing in pencil, but still a thousand times better than no writing, and I am most thankful to you for making the exertion. Your state of weakness would seem rather unaccountable but I suppose it is in great measure due to your inability to take exercise: it cannot be greater than mine was in the middle of last year: indeed of course it does not approach what that was at its worst: so I will still hope for improvement in you. I really am sure I derived benefit—very considerable benefit—from taking a prescription of iron medicine. Have you been in the habit of trying this?

An aunt of mine who had fallen into *great* weakness just lately has rapidly revived by the same remedy.

Simultaneously with your letter, I got one from Davies at Rome. He speaks with rapture of the advanced state of Spring beauty there, and I suppose it must be much more forward and advantageous to health than with you. I do not quite understand your reasons for feeling sure you wd not be inclined to go on to Rome,—particularly as you have a helpful maid with you. I feel certain it wd be much more beneficial than Venice, which certainly has not a promising sound for one in your state. To tell you the truth, by the way, I do really believe in Iceland. Meanwhile Rome is nearer you at present. Have *funds*[1] anything to do with the question? That wd be easily remedied. I could get you some of that capital forthwith. The dividend (which I mentioned to Watts) has been due some time and I will take care it leaves me for you *without fail* in a day or two. I will send it in notes registered.

I wish I had much news of work. I am getting on at last with the *Fiammetta*, have painted the arms in, and shall now have to get the drapery done before the latter end of next month when apple-blossom will be forthcoming, after which I trust the picture will find itself finished before it can say Jack Robinson or Giovanni Boccaccio. I have taken up the Pandora drawing again[2] with a fresh system of bogies round the head, and have now made it very complete indeed. My studio abounds in the old drawings of you all round now,—the Scalands one—the Pandora, Proserpine and no less than 6 others, including the profile, now called Twilight in the autotype which they succeeded in getting right by a second negative taken from the copy I retouched. I have ordered a copy to send out to you (which could easily be done unmounted) but they have not yet sent it me.

The number of illnesses in our circle is terrible at present. Ruskin, as you doubtless know, is in the most precarious state with brain fever. Stephens[3] fell ill nearly a month ago, with quinsy and other things resulting in pyæmia, and would not be alive now had not Marshall operated on his throat last Wednesday. Since then he is much improving and it is hoped will recover. A report comes through a private source that Holman Hunt is well-nigh given over at Jerusalem, his complaint being a long and most painful attack of carbuncles, now followed by dysentery.

Poor Smetham shows some symptoms of improvement at last,—to the extent of sitting up for a good many hours daily in another

room and noticing external matters somewhat but without much improvement as to speaking. I have made some further steps as to his
work—sold one to Graham for £75 and have a prospect of other sales.

I should *certainly* think that in your case some strengthening
medicine should be adopted, particularly if you have not been trying
such lately: in that case I cannot doubt of its proving efficacious to
some real extent.

I have just bethought me where to find a copy of Marshall's
prescription for the iron, which I enclose accordingly. Do try it if
you are doing nothing of that sort now. I used to take (by Marshall's
prescription) *2* teaspoonfuls twice a day at one time; but perhaps it
might be better to begin with doses of one. I shall hope to hear again
soon if only a few words.

Your affectionate
Gabriel

I want to know how you are looking.

PS I ought to mention (what perhaps you know) that the weather
in London has become much more severe just lately, and that every
one is looking forward to a probable winter during April and May.

2.7.76

Tinct Fer Sesquie 3ij
Syr Limonis aq 3iij

Take a teaspoonful twice
a day, in water.

J. Marshall.

D. G. Rossetti Esq
Copy

Mrs Morris
Villa del Cavo
Oneglia
Italia

[1] When the original partnership of the Morris firm was dissolved in 1875 Rossetti received a compensation of £1,000. This he settled on Mrs. Morris, but later took it back paying her interest on it.
[2] Later crayon version of the 1871 painting. Now in Winthrop Bequest, Fogg Museum, Harvard (S.224D–Ri).
[3] Frederic James Stephens (1828–1907), original member of the P.R.B. He contributed to *The Germ* and later became art critic to the *Athenaeum*. Published a monograph on Rossetti in 1894.

16 Cheyne Walk **29**
1 April 1878

My dear Janey,

I was encouraged at once by the sight of your writing which is decidedly firmer: but it is very hard that, after my bread-puddings and other remedies have all been systematically rejected, you should now begin to take a remedy of mine just as my letter and prescription are on their way to you! However I am glad to hear it is doing you good already, since it generally takes a little while to act. Mine was at first very unpalatable, but afterwards I got it flavoured with lemon by Marshall's leave, (I suppose it is so in the copy I sent you,) and thus it is quite an agreeable and refreshing drink. However I must warn you of one thing,—that is, a tendency it has to destroy the enamel of the teeth and so loosen them. I took it for a long while, and I must say some of my teeth *do* show signs of loosening since decidedly. The way of guarding against this is to drink it through a glass tube or straw (I believe the chemists sell glasses for the purpose), and were I to be taking it again, I should use such means.

As to the house at Hammersmith, it is a nice one, a good deal like this in arrangement and accommodation,—the garden good but now a good deal overlooked by a new road which forms an approach from the main Hammersmith road; before which it could only be reached through a labyrinth of slums. There is one objection to the garden however: a cottage flanks it, the windows of which are *in* the garden and on a level with your face. However this cottage is near the further end, so that, were you to wall or fence that bit off, you wd not be losing much. The most serious blemish to the house is a frightful kitchen floor, perfectly dark and very incommodious,—the kitchen stairs being a sort of ladder with no light at all, in which smashes would I should think assail the ear whenever a meal was going on. You would hardly get good servants to stay there (it is all stone moreover) unless some alterations were made, which would be difficult. Besides these objections, the place is very damp: masses of dead leaves forming a complete swamp in the garden when I was there: I fear really it is *not* the place to suit the health of any of you,— though I am sorry to say so, knowing the difficulty of such a search. There are two stations within reach, but neither at hand; one being in the Broadway as you know, and the other to be reached in some quarter of an hour or so through a very squalid slum. The Mall I suppose you know: it is almost exactly like what Cheyne Walk was before they spoilt it,—with a low parapet and fine old trees. There is hardly any traffic, and I think I am right in saying there is even no paved footpath in front of the houses.

I know of another house which I fancy is still to let,—Arundel House,[1] Percy Cross, Fulham. It must certainly stand much higher than the Mall. The rent is £100—there is a premium but not a high one I think, the present lease having only some 7 years to run if so much. It is a very old and even historical house (being named in the local histories) built of red brick, thoroughly genial in aspect and comfort, but the rooms not so large or so high as those at Hammersmith. The garden is specially fine, but has an Irish colony in a lane flanking it; still I do not suppose most people wd mind this much. When I was there, it was in the possession of some people named May, who wanted to let the remainder of their lease. If you wished to learn about it, a letter to Mrs. May at the address I give wd no doubt be answered, if it is still to let. Of course it is much nearer town than the Mall, but what the nearest station is I am not quite certain. It is not very much past the main Cremorne entrance, but quite sufficiently to be out of the way of it entirely; but I dare say you know where Percy Cross is. Old Hallam used to live in the house, and Tennyson wrote some of his poetry in the garden; so those sylvan shades would recognize Top's thunderings of composition. As I say, the house is best at the Mall (the Fulham bedrooms being none of them really large or lofty) but the kitchen and garden are incomparably better at Arundel House, and it cannot be nearly so damp. It is quite walled in, and has roomy stables which wd be convertible to other uses. The Stables at the *Mall* are the finest I ever saw, wall to wall with the house, and easily convertible into a fine range of studios.

You see I have nearly filled 2 sheets with house news: I think Dunn made sketches of both houses before I saw them. These I will try and look up for you.

PS I was forgetting about Ruskin. I hear it *reported* that there is a fear, since brain fever has not yet killed him yet he does not recover, that softening of the brain is setting in. But this I only hear said, and don't want to be an alarmist, as I was regarding Hunt who I now hear is said to be better and on his way home. Stephens is slowly getting round again I understand. Smetham shows more activity but hardly improved state of mind. He sits up now all day and will listen to reading but cannot be got to talk more than before, or hardly at all more! Nor can he be got to endorse the cheques I have sent, amounting now to over £340.

I should have told you that the vast Macdonald family mended the kitchen difficulty at the Mall by living on that floor entirely, by gas light! This with the exception of the long drawing room (as long as mine but without the bow) which Mac used as his study, and has made fearful to the eye with a blood red flock paper and a ceiling of blue with gold stars! The dining room (a fine room) was I understand in constant use by fits and starts, a perpetual table being laid for everyone to cut and come again but hardly any other meals I think. Certainly the plan was not badly suited to the nature of the house. They kept I believe only one undergrown slavey. I fancy Macdonald's term is not yet quite up. When I heard, he proposed repapering and other repairs to a small extent for any tenant who wd take the place off his hands: but I fancy it must now be nearly falling in to the real landlord.

I should say that if you wrote to Mrs. May about Arundel House, she would not know my name; but is conversant I think with Dunn's who was there several times, and also probably with Watts's. The latter has often asked me to send you regards. By the bye, are you so forlorn then that nobody will go to post for you?

As for news of myself, the main piece is that Turner (who bought the Proserpine) has so urged me (though expressing himself prepared for either decision on my part) to exhibit the picture at Manchester (in an exhibition of some 200 picked works only from Lancashire collections for the Building Fund of Art Schools there,) that what between the object being urged on me, and the desirability of pleasing Turner who remains alone as a buyer of mine just now, I have consented to its being sent, but absolutely with no other of mine. I have weighed the matter well, and taken the advice of Shields who knows Manchester thoroughly, and oddity as he is, is very practical and sensible; and he thinks the advantages *in posse* more than balance the objections *in esse*. I have told Turner that he must make up his mind to lots of abuse or else not send it. As for me, I shall look at no papers. Turner was very helpful with the Smetham pictures and really exerted himself I know, though the result was only that he himself bought to the amount of £90, but this was good of him, as I know he did it mainly to please me; and I feel really under obligation to him for buying of me bravely in these sad bad times. I am getting on with his Fiammetta now. Next year I do really purpose exhibiting in all probability at the Grosvenor, if they are not yet sick of me; and shd then show the Proserpine in London with others. You never say how the business is flourishing in London. Or has Top perhaps thrown trade after poetry, and now executes none but wholesale orders in philanthropy,—the retail trade being beneath a true humanitarian? But no, without a shop he could not be the Odger of the future!

Pardon this nonsense and believe me ever

Your affectionate
Gabriel

I hope to hear again soon that iron is entering not into your soul but system to some purpose.

Don't forget the tube—a straw or reed will do.

Mrs Morris
Villa del Cavo
Oneglia
Italia

---

[1] The house was in the Fulham Road, a little way SW. of the present Walham Green. C. J. J. Fèret, *Fulham Old and New*, 1900, Vol. II, pp. 202 ff., gives two photographs and a description of the house.

16 Cheyne Walk
19 April '78.

30 My dear Janey,

It is good news indeed that the iron medicine has done you so much good. I thought it must, but view the taking it on lumps of sugar as a very nasty way. I hope now you will really be fit to enjoy Venice,[1] and that the damps of that sojourn may prepare you somewhat for the Hammersmith house, which I really do not think a wise choice, if *you* are a person to be at all considered in the matter.

I wish I had any news worth telling of myself and work. I am still waiting for apple-blossom to put in the picture of Fiammetta, but hope to get it daily, though indeed these blasts of rain make me tremble for it every time I hear them. Meanwhile I took up that eternal incubus,[2] the replica of the large picture, and found myself less satisfied than ever with the figure of Love which I never thought quite right throughout. Thus I found the shortest and most thorough

Dante's Dream

plan was to alter it first in the large picture itself, which I have now done, and can proceed to transfer the figure as altered to the replica.

The Proserpine is only exhibiting at Manchester (as I think I told you) in some exhibition got up for the building of art schools there; and it was the urging of this object on me which made it so difficult for me to decline, as Turner (the purchaser of the picture) was anxious, and would probably have thought me deaf to public appeals if I had refused. I am haunted with an idea that the horrid Fry will have sent my Astarte[3] (which I know he wants sorely to exhibit) to the R.A. where they wd of course sky it and ruin me. Last year he tried hard to get it into the Grosvenor against my will, and is capable of anything.

I think you are quite mistaken about Hammersmith Mall being more within reach than Percy Cross: at any rate it is much further from the centre, and has no contiguous railway station such as you had at Turnham Green.

I am only writing this that you may not fail to hear from me before you leave Oneglia. By-the-bye little Murray[4] looked in on me the other day, as modestly oracular as ever. When he went away I remembered that I had failed to ask him, as I had long wished to do, respecting the particulars of his Italian home and facilities for settling agreeably in the neighbourhood.

I hear Ned has a good many works in the Grosvenor,[5] but whether as many as *ten* I know not. He and Crom Price have taken Phil to Paris and Normandy, but I believe will be back next week.

Your affecte:
DGR

Mrs Morris
Villa del Cavo
Oneglia
Italia

[1] Wm. Morris joined the family at Oneglia in April for a visit to Venice and the north Italian cities. The trip was not a success as Janey fell ill in Venice and Morris was crippled with an attack of gout. After a break at Verona they returned to Horrington House by the beginning of June. Morris was out of sympathy with the Italian architecture despite its 'magnificent power', and longed for 'the heap of grey stone with a grey roof that we call a house northway'.
[2] The reduced replica of *Dante's Dream* painted for William Graham was finished in 1880. The original picture, finished in 1871, was bought by Graham who found it too large for his house and returned it. With Howell as negotiator it was then acquired by Valpy in 1873; five years later he too returned it for resale on moving to a smaller house at Bath. Through the efforts of Hall Caine it was finally purchased by the Liverpool Corporation in 1881 and hangs in the Walker Art Gallery. The young Johnston Forbes-Robertson was the model for the figure of Love. See also note to Letter 136.
[3] Commissioned by C. E. Fry partner of Elliot and Fry, photographers, and purchased for £2,100 with Howell acting as agent. This was the highest price Rossetti ever got for a picture. Later sold by Fry to the Manchester City Art Gallery (S.249).
[4] Charles Fairfax Murray (1849–1915). Subject painter and imitator of Rossetti from whom he may have had instruction. Paintings by him are in the Birmingham City Art Gallery and Walker Art Gallery, Liverpool. He became a collector and dealer in works of art. His unrivalled collection of Pre-Raphaelite drawings was acquired by the Birmingham Gallery.
[5] Burne-Jones had sent eleven works to the Grosvenor Gallery Exhibition. His son Philip became a competent minor portrait painter. Morris spent Easter Sunday with the party in Paris on his way to Oneglia.

Friday [? 31 May 1878] **31**

My dear Gabriel
I had better put off coming to see you. I am so much thinner than when I saw you last you will scarcely thank me to pay the visit. I had thought little about my looks till I got your letter yesterday

starte Syriaca

reminding of our last meeting in London, and when I came to think of what I was then and what I am now, I feel more and more that I must stay away for a time. I am several inches smaller in the waist, and proportionately thinner everywhere else, a good deal of my hair came off after I got the slight fever at Oneglia, but still there is a good deal left. I care nothing at all about my altered looks for my own sake, only I hate to appear before you as a Guy after this long absence.

We went to see the new house one day, of course much will have to be done before we go in, but really it does not seem damp after 6 or 7 months without fires; Webb says the overflow of Thames water can be prevented if proper means are taken and you know how difficult it is to get any house than is not quite new, for my part, I should not mind a bran-new one of a good size, but the price would be far beyond our means.

Your affectionate
Scarecrow

D. G. Rossetti Esq
16 Cheyne Walk
Chelsea S.W.

An unpublished letter from Janey to which Rossetti No. 32 is a reply. It is found in British Library Ashley MS. 5755, fol. 107.

Friday [31 May 1878]

32 My dear Janey,

I cannot help saying your letter is no less than a shock to me. Is it possible that mine can have contained anything by which you could really suppose that the question as to your looks influenced in the least my great desire to see you again? The supposition would be an outrage to my deep regard for you;—a feeling far deeper (though I know you never believed me) than I have entertained towards any other living creature at any time of my life. Would that circumstances had given me the power to prove this: for proved it *wd.* have been. And *now* you do not believe it.

Your telling me that Mrs. Howard and that queer old dowager said how well you looked induced me to mention the point and well —better in the highest sense than anyone—I doubt not you *do* look: though what you tell me as to your increasing thinness is very serious. Have you tried cod liver oil lately? I should do so if I were you.

You surely cannot seriously mean that you project deferring a visit here beyond your original intention. Today the weather has made a step towards improvement; but I do not forget that next Wednesday is the Derby Day, and that your road becomes all but impassable in the racing season. Do banish all even the faintest impression that you must now unhappily have derived somehow from my last, and come the very first day you can. Pure desperation would result to me if I were to come to your house and find it impossible to be alone with you. There is much I want to hear from you, and much to say.

The Blessed Daml.[1] picture is still here, and you wd like the little predella; and the Fiammetta wd of course be shown—though, far as it is to completion, it is still scattered as to effect and not yet framed. My buyers have hit on the happy idea of buying from each other instead of from me. Leyland is very anxious to buy the Damozel from Graham, and Turner wants to buy a picture of mine from Rae.[2]

Now never sign anything again but your own dear name: it is no joke to substitute nonsense for that. As for me I might fairly enough sign Paint-rag or Dishclout or worse, but will not.

Your affectionate
Gabriel

Mrs Wm Morris
Horrington House
Turnham Green Road

[1] The picture was finished in 1877. Graham then asked for a predella which was finished early in 1878.
[2] George Rae of Birkenhead, a banker and discriminating collector who was one of Rossetti's early patrons. He acquired many of the best oils and watercolours of the 1850s and 1860s. The Tate Gallery purchased many of these when his collection was sold by his descendants in 1916.

Sunday [June 1878]   **33**

My dearest Janey,

When shall I have a chance of another visit from you? I quite forgot after all to come to any conclusion about the overdress, nor did I quite understand your explanation. The underdress also (which is in good condition) was never finished. You remember—it is a green silk.[1] I am rather wanting to get on with the picture now, as it is necessary Dunn shd be again turned on to parts of Graham's replica before I can proceed further with it myself.

When you are able to come again (no impediment on my part) try and come earlier as you proposed, so that I may do *something*—even

Perlascura

if only a very little—towards the hands in the drawing I spoke of. I am sorry you did not leave me May's ballad[2] which was funny.

Watts would like to call one day on you, and I said I thought you wd let him in. At last I believe the lease will really be concluded this week.

I shall send the 2 autotypes and your faverite ugly drawing to be framed as small as practicable so as to occupy the least wall-space.

Your affectionate
Gabriel

PS. I think of calling the profile autotype of you Perlascura.[3]

[1] Difficult to assign this to a picture.
[2] Unidentified.
[3] The name is a reference to the first Canzone of the *Vita Nuova*, lines 47/8.

My dear Janey, Thursday [July 1878] **34**

I am sending you the 2 autotypes. At some moment you can let me have them again for framing. I hope you will be able to send me just one line to say how you are.

Your affectionate
Gabriel

I copy overpage a label which is to be printed and put on the Silence—[1]

Silence holds in one hand a branch of peach, the symbol used by the ancients; its fruit being held to resemble the human heart and its leaf the human tongue. With the other hand she draws together the veil enclosing the shrine in which she sits.

[1] Crayon drawing, 1870, a favourite of Rossetti. Sold without his knowledge during his illness and absence in Scotland in 1872 to Aldam Heaton. Bought back and sold to Charles Rowley of Manchester in 1876 (S.214). Now in Brooklyn Museum, N.Y.

My dear Janey, Friday [August 1878] **35**

I had better enclose a list of things I have remembered from time to time and noted down, as being desirable to get from Kelmscott when convenient. Do not be appalled by its length: all I propose to trouble you about at present (besides all drawings and pictures of mine whatsoever—some even in attics I think)—are the few items I have marked with a cross. The case for drawings you might open and put the best drawings inside locking it again and sending me the key.

Silence

The 2 paper screens wd be useful if you can send them, but wd require careful packing—do: the musical instruments of which there are at least 2. Of the French blue ware—whether yours or mine—I should like one or two of those pretty *small* pieces sent to paint from. The Lay Figure could come if convenient but I hope is safe. One item not marked—the Lac Screen—is very valuable and I hope safe—it used to stand I think in the store room.

Reverie

I know there should be a lot of cases of mine there—but however this may be, the drawings and pictures must of course be carefully packed. You know if 4 slices of cork are cut and fixed to the 4 front corners of a drawing, another of same size can be packed face to face with it: but battens may be needed to steady them in the cases.

I enclose my debt to you. I dare say you will write a line at once, just to say you have got the letter, otherwise I shall fancy it has been prigged, packing directions and all. How I long to see you again when possible! Mrs. Howard must be a fool to prefer the Silence of those 2,—the profile is much the most like you.

My reason for not exhibiting with the Fine Arts Compy. in Bond

Street is that I hear the Gallery is inferior and Agnew's the only right place. Of course there is also the question—what should I get in real money gain? Without this it is not improbable that my best course is to stick to my old plan for the present. However I now hear that they *did* pay Ruskin £1000 lately or some time since—perhaps more by this time. But I think I told you a vile portrait of Whistler has been stuck into the place, which seems to show they are a dirty lot— considering that W. is actioning R. at present.

I sent Ellis his little Proserpine[1] yesterday and he is delighted with it. I hear he has given his man a note addressed to Howell in case that worthy shd call at the shop, in which note he declines further acquaintance.

Your affectionate
Gabriel

P.S. Please write labels for packages yourself to ensure correctness.

    Black Cabinet in Studio
XPaper screens
    Lac Screen in several leaves—I think 4 or 5
    2 Marble Urns
    black stand for same
XMusical instruments
    Old Pictures—specially portrait of man in drawing room
    Pair of brass candlesticks
    Little table with drawers bought at Lechlade
    Chippendale washstand
    2 sets of Bookshelves bought at Lechlade
    Chest of drawers (I think in servants' room)
    Picture rods (I think in small side room)
XCase for drawings with grooves inside
XFrench blue ware
    Cabinet for photos etc. made at Lechlade
XLay Figure probably case for this exists
X3 Dante drawings framed in hall
    Marble frieze
XInkstand given by you
    2 Corner Cupboards with Stands (in small side room)
    Topsaic Tapestry (small side room)
    2 Ram's head arm chairs

PPS. Did I tell you I thought of bringing out some dozen autotypes of you in a book—done on a moderate scale so as to make a large folio shape. I might call them

Perlascura:
Twelve Coins of one Queen.

and quote a motto from Dante's first canzone in the Vita Nuova:—

'Color di perla quasi informa, quale
Convieni a donna aver non fuor misura:
Ella è quanto di ben puo far natura:
Per esempio di lei beltà si prova':

with my translation:—

She hath the paleness of the pearl that's fit
In a fair woman, so much and no more:
She is as high as Nature's skill can soar:
Beauty is tried by her comparison.

The expression 'quasi informa' means that the pearl-colour clothes her as it were with a garment. This is rather obsolete in language and I generalized it.

I should put a sonnet to each autotype.

PS. I judge the musical instrument you diagram is one that is sent—a broken model of a lyre made by Stennett.[2]

I suppose there is nothing of consequence in the drawers of that black cabinet in the tapestry room. This cabinet and a case I had made by Mitchell for photos, etc.—together with 2 corner cupboards and stands from the side room—and those only if not wanted—are the only things I should propose to remove some time when convenient if *you* care to have the rest.

I think it possible that the 2 missing musical instruments may have got lying *perdus* at the back of the shelves put up in the closet in tapestry room.

I dare say I shall get the key of the grooved case immediately.

Your affectionate
Gabriel

The copy of Dunn's from a drawing of you with head on hand[3] has got much damaged—I believe it was lying about in attics. It is really better than I thought.

---

[1] Small replica in watercolour sold to F. S. Ellis for £262 (S.233).
[2] Probably a craftsman in the Morris firm.
[3] This is probably *Reverie* (S.206).

Friday [August 1878]

36 My dear Janey,

Thanks for your affectionate zeal and care. I see your list does not quite tally with the marks X on mine. I did not specially suggest the sending of the Urns at present because I am conscious of their requiring very careful packing to prevent damage. Indeed one of them got severely grazed on its sides (after 1000 yrs.) in sending it down to Kelmscott. They ought I judge to be packed in boxes larger than themselves and well stuffed round with hay or tow. One of them has a separate lid.

The Moscow cast I did not send for because I got another since in London. I am greatly obliged to you for remembering the green marble which I had not mentioned. There are 2 pieces, a large and a small one, the small being the most beautiful, and I think there is also a grey piece. All might come advantageously if packed to prevent breakage. If the 2 Urns come, the little black stand made to fit one of them shd come also. I mentioned in my list a 'Marble Frize',[1] meaning a long strip like a mantelpiece with Cupids etc. on it. Have you met with this?

In haste for post

Your affectionate
Gabriel

PS Dunn went yesterday to Turnham Green for the dress but getting there rather late could not make any one hear his knock.

Mrs Wm Morris
Manor House
Kelmscott
Lechlade

[1] No doubt the marble in the *Roman Widow* (S.236) which he painted at Kelmscott.

Wednesday [21 August 1878]

37 My dear Janey,

Thanks for *key* which came yesterday after I wrote. By the bye, the hammer of Thor, the head of Topsy, or some other Icelandic weapon must have been employed to jam the drawings into that grooved case. Something like steam-power had to be brought to bear in getting them out, regardless of consequences.

Strange to say, the only drawing I reckoned for certain on finding therein—(a paltry black chalk sketch of a head and perhaps a hand, quite worthless but for which I am being endlessly pestered by its owner Valpy)—was not in the case. Was it perhaps taken out as worthless and forgotten to be sent at all? This may not be so, however, as my (or rather Valpy's) only authority for its being in said case was an assertion of Howell's, who, if it is not at Kelmscott at all, probably stole it.

Among books sent up by you before, I don't find 'Love is Enough'[1] of which I know I had a copy at Kelmscott,—also I think one of my own book. These might be brought by your kind care when you return, with any other portable one that seems worth bringing—not poetic waifs etc.

Your affectionate
Gabriel

PS I have some notion that there is a copy without cover of a book with the tremendous title

Studies of Sensation and Event
by Ebenezer Jones[2]

If there, it might come by post, as being asked for now, but I am quite uncertain about it.

Mrs Wm Morris
Kelmscott Manor
Lechlade

[1] Published 1872.
[2] Poet with Chartist interests (1820–60). Author of *Studies in Sensation and Event*, 1843. Rossetti found his poems 'full of vivid disorderly power' and showed his interest in Jones in a letter to the Editor of *Notes and Queries*, 5 February 1870 (D. and W. 920). A presentation copy from the poet's brother Sumner Jones was among Rossetti's books.

Monday [2 September 1878] **38**

My dear Janey,

It is a great anxiety to me to hear so poor an account of your strength as winter approaches. Have you any plans of going abroad again? You know there is that money at hand to help, and if done, it ought to be done in time,—much as I should sorrow at losing all prospect of seeing you for so many months. I fancy it might really be a great gain if, instead of having so specially damp a country resort as Kelmscott is, Top were to consider well what place wd be the dryest and best, and try to find country quarters there. This is still more urgent now that he is making so mistaken a move towards a house in town even damper than the old one.

I have got into rather a hobble with Valpy—who is a vampire in his requirements—as to the Dante exchange business, but may write you about it ere long, unless indeed I should have the happiness to see you.

I never read *Erewhon*, but recollect meeting the author whose name I think is Butler.[1] At that time (abt 6 years ago) he seemed a man perhaps approaching 30, and was a great friend of Nolly Brown.[2] What I chiefly remember of him is that he had eyebrows which were exactly like two leeches stuck on his face. He afterwards brought out another book which I saw. It was I think in the form of a clergyman's biography, and was intended of course as a skit on religion, but was so deceptive that it seemed like nothing but a very devout work, and I think fell flat.

Weather is very bright generally but very stormy and changeable here of late.

Your affectionate
Gabriel.

Mrs Wm Morris
Manor House
Kelmscott
Lechlade

[1] Samuel Butler, 1835–1902. Published *Erewhon*, 1872, and in 1873 followed it with *The Fair Haven*, *a work in defence of the miraculous element in our Lord's ministry upon earth . . . by the late John Richard Owen.* A second edition in the same year revealed Butler's authorship. Rossetti was right, it fell flat.

[2] Oliver Madox Brown, 1855–74, gifted son of Ford Madox Brown. Author of two novels, *Gabriel Denver*, 1873, and *The Dwate Bluth*, published posthumously, 1876. He was also an artist of talent in watercolour. Rossetti's memorial sonnet 'Untimely Lost' appeared in the *Athenaeum*, 21 Nov. 1874. See W. E. Fredeman, 'Pre-Raphaelite Novelist Manqué: Oliver Madox Brown', *Bulletin of the John Rylands Library*, 1968.

39 My dear Janey,   Friday [6 September 1878]

I enclose a too apposite work of art.[1]

I have a very nice Vita Nuova (Italian Edition 1829) with nothing else attached, which I will get bound for you if you like. What is the nature of the edition you have?

In speaking of furniture, one other thing I might like to retain if useless to you is an old gilt chandelier which I had put up on the staircase,—this simply as of possible use to paint from. There *may* be a small round table with a tripod leg given me by Lizzie—this I shd like to keep. Also perhaps a funny old square washstand with *utilities* which used to stand in the closet of the dining room. This wd be all, and only these if not needed by you. I don't know if any of these embroidered cushions remain at Kelmscott, if so, wd like to have them when all comes up.

I am afraid the stay cannot have greatly benefited your health, if so little able to get out. I trust the press of inmates may have done more good than harm, as giving you some occupation.

I will write more anent the big picture anon.

Your affectionate
Gabriel

[1] An engraving from the *London Journal* was enclosed. See Letters 41 and 42.

Wednesday [September 1878]   40

My dear Janey

How dear it always is to see your sweet handwriting again!—and it is not bad as you say, but very different to your bad times.

I have had several strange miscarriages with letters lately. Did you get one in which I begged YOUR acceptance of all furniture belonging to me at Kelmscott except an old black cabinet in tapestry room, an oak cabinet made at Lechlade (and all started at the joints) for holding photos: etc.; and (if not needed) 2 corner cabinets and stands in side room? Did you get this letter? Your references to the furniture seem rather to argue that you did not. I should be obliged for the urn-stand when easy to forward. The musical instrument could I dare say be needed so had better come—also oil colours. The Dutch picture of course is yours with the furniture. All will come in in the new big house.

I valued that inkstand as your gift, but have one for use here and a Flemish one you gave me, so need not trouble you about another.

Have you an *Italian* Vita Nuova, or only mine? The lines occur in the first canzone commencing

Donne che avete intalletto d'amore

and form part of the description of Beatrice. There is a similar reference to pearl colour

Con quel color angelico di perla

in a canzone by Fazio degli Uberti which I have translated[1]: the canzone is commonly attributed to Dante but on quite insufficient grounds.

Christina has been making some admirable Italian versions from her Sing Song[2]—most ingenious adaptations of the originals—of course very free. I send you a few I received the other day, which please return.

Your affectionate
Gabriel

I will write you details as to the Dante transfer when I am quite sure about it.

Is the lay-figure's head discoverable? If so it might come some time, but doesn't matter.

[1] In *The Early Italian Poets*, 1861, p. 162.

[2] Christina made Italian versions of thirty-three of the *Sing Song* poems. They were printed with the title 'Ninna Nanna' by W. M. Rossetti in his edition of her *Collected Poems*, 1904. She wrote to Dante Gabriel in Sept. 1878: 'It would need a better Italian than I to translate the whole series. . . . The Pig, I avow, causes me much inward triumph' (*Family Letters of Christina Rossetti*, ed. W. M. Rossetti, 1908, p. 77). She is referring to No. 19, 'If a pig wore a wig'—'Porco, la zucca fitta in parrucca.'

Tuesday

41 My dear Gabriel,

I return the verses of Cristina's, they seem very funny as far as I can understand them, I still find difficulties with poetry, as you can imagine—I should be delighted with the 'Vita Nuova' you speak of, I have not one of my own, the one I use here is a little Florentine copy printed 1863. very small type, and trying to the eyes—I have had some trouble with my particular eyes lately, which has kept me from using them in any way, but they are suddenly better today.

I will see to anything more of yours you wish before I leave, the gilt chandelier is still where you left it on the staircase, and also that comic clock belonging to George Hake,[1] the embroideries were all sent before, if you remember, the washstand is safe, but I see not the little table you mention.

What is the paper you cut the engraving from? I see there is a story of an intensely sensational character at its back, for I still keep up my old habit of reading every scrap that comes in my way, the hero seems to be one Boddlebak, which name would be enough to excite one's curiosity without the picture.

I am going to walk out a little way, the day is fine, and sunshine is rare.

Your affectionate Janey.

[1] Son of Dr. Hake; Rossetti's companion at Kelmscott.

Wednesday [September 1878] **42**

My dear Janey,

It always rejoices me to see your loved writing, and know that your living loving hand has rested again on lines addressed to me.

I am so glad you care to have the Vita Nuova which I send with this to Ellis to be bound. It is a very nice copy, with marginal notes giving the various readings. I never saw another Vita Nuova apart from Dante's other prose works some of which are for a different class of readers.

I dare say the Italian Sing Songs puzzled you:—

Porco, la zucca
Fitta in parrucca,—

Zucca (literally pumpkin) is used colloquially to mean a stupid head.

Buon legale
Gli farebbe un codicillo

is an ingenious parallel play on words to the English

Send him to the tailoress
To get one new.

The codicil bears the same relation to the *coda* as the tailoress does to the tail.

How sad to hear about difficulties with your eyes when you have so little means of occupation apart from them! I am glad you did not tell me till they were showing signs of improvement.

I did not mean that anything else of mine was worth sending up now, but that the few things I named might be viewed as still claimable by me. If quite feasible the black cabinet in tapestry room (too shabby for furniture but very useful for chalks etc.) *might* perhaps be sent up—of course its stand with it. The urn-stand really ought to come. The table or little cabinet I named is one Mitchell made with shelves that slide out for photos: etc. The woodcut came I suppose from the London Journal. It was one of many (all cut out) which Shields brought here one evening to show me as good things of Gilbert's[1] and examples of his manner. I saw in it a more awful example and begged it to send to you. I also read the story at the back and could only view its Icelandic character as symbolic.

Your affectionate
Gabriel

P.S. Urn-stand is a tallish black thing with a square top and I think a sort of second space underneath.

There used to be some Topsaic tapestry: it hung in the side room. This I shd rather like to keep, but fear you had no hand in it. I bought it of Taylor[2] I think.

---

[1] Sir John Gilbert (1817–97), a pioneer of pictorial journalism and a master of woodcut illustration. He was a mainstay of the *Illustrated London News* and provided the *London Journal* with illustrations to its melodramatic and sensational serials. Another instance of cutting-out and of preserving Gilbert's illustrations is found in G. P. Boyce's Diaries, 22 March 1851: 'Gave Miss Cook 7 numbers of the London Journal, having cut out Gilbert's frontispieces.' Search in the *Journal* has failed to find Boddlebak.
[2] Warrington Taylor, business manager of the Morris firm.

Friday [20 September 1878]

43 My dear Janey,

There is truly one good piece of news in your letter,—i.e. your speedy return, when I will hope for your spending a day with me ere long. It is a shame to think that I after all have no work to show since you left—all has gone on the replica, and in minor muddle. What a painful matter this is of your eyes! Ought you not to see an oculist? I wouldn't go to Critchett again, but try Bowman[1] or Power. Would it not be desirable perhaps to try Devonshire for the winter? The absence of great labour in travelling might of itself be a sanitary advantage, and the air is mild. No doubt you will let me know when you reach town without delay. I am writing this in haste to save country post as you talk of coming up in a few days, and I don't want my letters to reach when you are gone.

A great deal of bother has been caused me by the professed exchange for the big picture; and lawyer Valpy proves so exorbitant in his demands that I have just now come to a dead lock with him: but I dare say we shall arrange it somehow.

Your affectionate
Gabriel

Mrs Wm Morris
Kelmscott Manor
Lechlade

---

[1] Sir William Bowman (1816–92), distinguished ophthalmic surgeon at the Royal Hospital, Moorfields, whom Rossetti had consulted.

Friday[1] **44**

My dear Gabriel,

After many delays, we got into the new house only last night, workmen will not have done for another week, and then there will be carpets to fit and various things to finish. Still I thought it would be better to get in as soon as possible, as every week it gets colder and colder.

I am doing nothing myself except feeling tired and lying awake at night.

Your affectionate

The Retreat   Janey
Hammersmith Mall

[1] This and the following four letters relate to the move from Horrington House to The Retreat, Hammersmith Mall, where the Morrises took up residence in October, 1878. There is a gap of some months in the Rossetti letters which resume in the spring.

Tuesday **45**

My dear Gabriel,

Will you give me the address again of Mr. Walkins the man at whose house servants congregate? I can't lay my hands on my address-book, and to wade through a drawer-full of your letters would be the work of a day for me. I have not yet applied to him, but wish to do so at once, having suddenly discovered a most promising place for the Italian maid, who left yesterday. I am grieved indeed to hear of your bad nights, mine are improving I expect I am over-tired and anxious to get things straight, and moreover I have got used to the noise of the river-steamers which seemed at first to go on all night.

Your affectionate

Janey

Tuesday **46**

My dear Gabriel,

I must give up trying to get to you this week. I think I have succeeded in finding a third servant, then I shall be more free to go out as I like; and as you seem a little tied this week, we shall both meet more comfortably after a little time.

I am suffering somewhat from the horrible cold, though the house is by no means a cold one I find.

Your affectionate

Janey

Kelmscott House, Upper Mall, Hammersmith.
Thursday

47 My dear Gabriel,

I am but writing a line to show that I am still thinking of you, and to say how glad I shall be to get news of you some time when possible, but of course you are not to think of wearying yourself to write.

I shall not be going away at all this year for Xmas, I want to get the house as much in order as possible. I will settle about the china, the crate should be returned or a sum will be charged for it.

Dear Gabriel it would be but a mockery if I were to wish you a happy Xmas, I can only say that I hope and trust you may not be suffering more then than your last letter led me to expect.

Always yours affectionately
Janey

Kelmscott House, Upper Mall, Hammersmith.
Wednesday

48 My dear Gabriel,

I am writing a line of congratulation on the return of Spring, or more correctly on the disappearance of the horrible darkness of winter, it is quite true that everything these last two days has presented an entirely different aspect. I can breathe without gasping, you will paint without bad language or have you quite given up the habit?

Don't think I am yet in the 7th heaven of delight, but I get out again, and that, you know, makes an immense difference to my health and spirits, I only hope you are benefiting too by the change. My dear old pussy Jack succumbed to the cold a few days ago, we buried him in the garden—alas poor Pussy! We never shall look upon his like again.

I never saw so many birds in a town garden, they come in scores to be fed, and reward me by singing sweetly in every tree or bush. Did you get Murray's address?

Your affectionate Janey

Kelmscott House, Upper Mall, Hammersmith **49**
Sunday

My dear Gabriel,

It is true that I began to chirp much too soon as to weather, we have had dreary days since, and no doubt shall have many more, but you know what a babyishly hopeful creature I always am. The Grosvenor meeting seems to have given general dissatisfaction, I hear that some literary men considered that the artists had taken a narrow view in not combining with them before getting up a petition, then I saw a letter from Samuel Fry in the Daily News claiming equal rights as a photographer; Sir Coutts it seems began his speech with an account of his personal ailments. Top was persuaded to go by Richmond,[1] who is much excited about the matter. What a pity it is something can't be proposed and carried out by able men! Or soon painters will become the mere slaves of these dealers.

I am most sorry to hear about poor Murray, I heard that the 2nd baby was doing well some time ago, his wife appears incapable of taking care either of herself or her children, soon after the last baby was born, Murray wrote to some lady friends of Ned's in Florence (he had not then left Siena) to beg them to come to him, for his baby was dying, and his wife could do nothing for it, when they got there, they found the poor little creature apparently dying of cold, they rubbed it well, and wrapped it in flannel, and in a very short time it began to crow and take its food vigorously. I suppose it succumbed again when left to the sole care of the mother—but after all, I think it is a great charm in Murray's eyes, this entire ignorance and total incapacity on the part of his wife, she loves him, and that is all he cares about, and they can make more babies.

Your affectionate
Janey

I shall see no more of Marzials I suppose, he came out as a public singer at Liverpool a few weeks back.

---

[1] William Blake Richmond. See note to Letter 114.

Wednesday[1]

50 My dear Janey,

I must write another line, merely for the sake of some communication with you, for there is nought of news.

On looking at yours again, I see a mention of one *Samuel* Fry. If you give the Christian name correctly, it is not my man, who is no less than Clarence E. Fry. But indeed some botherment is sure to occur in this copyright matter. Ned, luckily for him, finds it impossible to take the slightest interest in it or know anything of it—so dear are Affghans and Caffres.[2] His family may rue it later. What fearful news though about this war! I should not be surprised to hear of some general massacre if troops there are not sufficient.

You give a very sad account of poor Murray[3]—paternity and chances of ever maintaining the character in the teeth of so shiftless a partner. Surely the woman must be an idiot. Top ought to send him that thick stick he used to walk with, for surely sense wd require beating into such a mother. But I thought the mother-in-law was there too. *She* ought to know something of babies. I heard of the 2nd death from Dunn who heard it from Ted Hughes: I suppose it must be true.

Ned says he has given up all thoughts of Art for Phil. It seems a great pity. He spoke in a rather wild way, as if dismal dumps afflicted him. After all I was obliged to let old Mme Cassavetti buy that drawing of Mary[4] about which I think I spoke to you.

There is really nothing worth saying about work. I jog at jobs, and that is all. As for buyers, they seem to have disappeared altogether. Some cartoons of old Brown's[5] (made as I find for Top's firm) are being published in an architectural paper. Really I must say they are inconceivable. Every figure (it is a long series) is passing one hand through the stone mullion of the window into the next panel of glass!!—each panel containing one figure. It is called the Story of St. Edith. I must say if this series was what reduced Top to desperation, I think every one wd have sympathised with him if he had only shown the cartoons. However, if too public, the incident might have ended in a strait waistcoat for old B.

Your affectionate
Gabriel

I cannot condole with you on losing the society of the gentleman

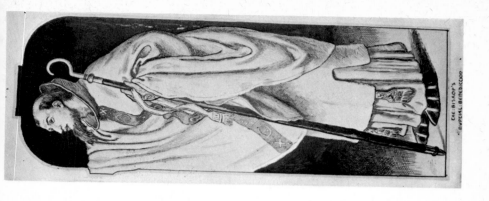

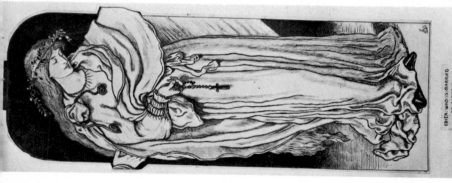

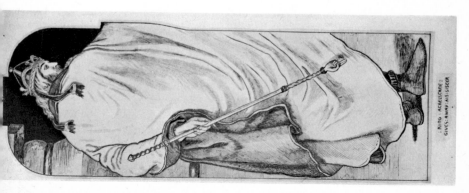

St. Edith cartoons by F. Madox Brown

who has turned singer,[6] as you know my opinion of him. Please oblige me by not mentioning him again.

Mrs Wm Morris
Horrington House
Turnham Green Road

---

[1] The address of this letter implies that it was written before the move to Hammersmith Mall, but the envelope may be misplaced. As it is a reply to the preceding letter from Janey it follows here.

[2] England was engaged both with fighting in Afghanistan and with the Zulu War. At the same time Morris and his friends were taking an active part in the 'Eastern Question' campaign, in protest against Turkish atrocities in Bulgaria and concerned lest England be drawn into the Russo–Turkish war in support of Turkey.

[3] Fairfax Murray.

[4] Mary Zambaco. Rossetti did four drawings of her. This is probably S.531 or 542. Mme Cassavetti was her mother.

[5] *The Story of St. Edith*, a set of twelve panels made for St. Editha's, Tamworth, 1873. Madox Brown sold the cartoons in 1877/8, probably to Charles Rowley of Manchester. A set of four is in the Whitworth Art Gallery. Reproduced in A. C. Sewter, *The Stained Glass of William Morris and his Circle*, 1974, Plate 455.

[6] Théophile Marzials, b. 1850, poet and musician who composed the words and music of many popular Victorian songs. Having a fine baritone voice he popularized his own songs. He was joint author of the libretto of Goring Thomas's opera *Esmeralda*. He sent Rossetti two volumes of his poetry in 1873. See D. and W. 1332.

Kelmscott House, Upper Mall, Hammersmith.
Tuesday

51 My dear Gabriel,

I have been so far from well of late that I would not write, I am better now but still not free from pain. I got out yesterday as far as Kensington, and now the weather seems improving, I shall improve and get out oftener.

The christian name of *Samuel* Fry was correct, I took particular notice wondering if it was your buyer.

I wish I could send something more of a letter.

Always your affectionate
Janey

19 Feb. [1879]

52 My dear Janey,

Your dear handwriting does not look quite so firm this time, and I can see that you have not been well. Still, if you are getting out again I trust you may mend, but everyone has been shaken by this terrible daily change of climate. Watts has been very seedy, and Davies (whom you have heard me speak of) has had a sharp touch of pleurisy. He is kindly acting as mentor and protector to a young artist—if he can yet be called so—of great and curious talent.[1] He is a youth of 18, a nephew of Smetham's. His father (now dead) was a Wesleyan parson and would not let him draw, so he hit on the plan of cutting out his designs in paper silhouettes. Of these he has some myriads. Any subject given him he will cut out in a few minutes with the celerity of lightning and hand it to you. The first I saw were a long series from Milton's Allegro and Pensieroso,—inconceivably various and really wonderful—everything (groups, animals, foliage etc.) perfectly varied in character and in a very high style. The only things one can liken them to are the designs on Greek vases or the finest Flaxman work, but they abound in reality. I ordered a set from Hamlet which has reached me today, and is excellent, but not affording so much scope for variety as the Milton series, fails to interest so strongly. Still you will be much struck when you see them. Davies told me that the young genius lays two sheets of paper together and so cuts duplicates of each design at the same time: so I told him if there is a duplicate set of the Milton I will take it. My Hamlet,—25 designs in a very pleasant grey tint of paper mounted in a handsome cardboard album,—only cost me 25/——so they are not ruinous. If I don't see you before long, I must send them by Parcels Compy to amuse you a little.

You remember my beginning a picture from the old head of you done at Scalands. I began it a second time (not liking the first thoroughly) and it is now well advanced. The head is as like you I think as if done from nature, and is satisfactory in execution. I have lately done in replica the drawings of Pandora[2] and Proserpine for the market as I wouldn't part with the originals; but haven't spotted a buyer yet. Of course indeed no one has yet seen them. The Proserpine is fully carried out as in the picture and the Pandora somewhat extended in length, and both look very well, so I suppose even in these bad times something will come of it.

Your affectionate

Gabriel

Mrs Wm Morris
Kelmscott House
Upper Mall
Hammersmith

---

[1] George Allen. Rossetti was enthusiastic about his skill and enlisted patrons. He later advised him to enter a regular course in art training at the Slade School.
[2] See Letter 28.

Monday [3 March 1879]

53 My dearest Janey,

Who the housemaid's bridegroom may be I have not the least idea. She is not communicative, and even the cook knoweth not. I am glad to say that I have seen an applicant today who seems exceptionally respectable and likely to suit, and whom I suppose I shall engage. I have been advertising, which I find the shortest plan perhaps on the whole. But I should think it might be worth while for you to try a line to the brush shop again.

How dear of you to stick to your old belief in me and my doings and to frame and hang up the autotypes. I have another autotype (not published) from the Scalands drawing, but I never thought it thoroughly good. Of course it shall be yours if you care to have it.

I really couldn't read anything by Auerbach[1] or any German whatever. I must say the Greville Memoirs[2] are a dastardly business: this old wretch waiting till he is safe and dead, and then backbiting every one from his tomb. As for the poor old King he was nearly 70 when all this happened, and could not be expected to be very much up to the mark. There is no ability to speak of in the book, though every one who hates his neighbour as himself will enjoy the reading of it.

Your most affectionate
Gabriel

Some relics he sees at Rome are amusing—viz: the column on which the cock crew at Peter's third denial; etc. There is a very funny story of the Duke of Gloucester[3] who went by the name of Silly Billy. He was being shown over Bedlam one day, when a madman called after him 'Silly Billy!' The Duke started and exclaimed, 'Why surely that man has not lost his reason'.

Another good story. Some Irish had settled in some part of Jamaica, and the niggers soon learnt their brogue. Some more Irish came, and while they were landing they were saluted by the natives from the coast with 'Och Paddy my boy, and how are ye?' They were stupefied and exclaimed: 'Arrah now! and sure are ye turned black already?'

Another fine bit. A barrister in court was asked by a stranger: 'I beg your pardon, Sir, but is that Baron Wood?'[4] The answer returned was, 'Yes, Sir, but his *name* is Richards.'

Mrs Wm Morris
Kelmscott House
Upper Mall
Hammersmith

[1] Berthold Auerbach (1812–82), translated Spinoza, and wrote popular novels of German peasant life.
[2] Charles Cavendish Fulke Greville (1794–1865), Clerk to the Council and intimate with the statesmen of his day. His *Memoirs* edited by Harry Reeves were published in 1874. In a letter to Wm. Davies (D. and W. 2024) Rossetti describes them as 'a dastardly business—the very grave-worm still snarling and back-biting'.
[3] William Frederick (1776–1834), only son of William Henry, 1st Duke of Gloucester of the new creation. Nephew of George III.
[4] Sir George Wood (1743–1824), Baron of the Exchequer—'his apprehension being rather accurate than quick' (*D.N.B.*).

Wednesday [12 March 1879] **54**

My dear Janey,
    Of course I never used any mounts except oak, gold, or white. Murcott has ruined his morals by working for Howell and Corder.[1] You should make him alter the mounts. Surely you do not mean *black*! There is a lightish French grey now much in use, but I never use it. They must look dreadful. The frame-makers charge all alike, but if you don't wish to go to the notoriously dear Foord and Dickinson (90 Wardour Street) who are the best, there is the firm of Steward and Brown (56 Eagle Street, Red Lion Square). They have made cheaply and well for Brown and Mary Stillman, but I gave them (on the strength thereof) an order for a lot of frames for drawings a year ago, without getting an estimate, and the result is a bill just such as I shd have got from F. and D. I mean to contest it amicably. If you went to them for anything, you shd get an estimate beforehand, or indeed from any one.
    I am at present getting some frames made in Manchester where I find they can be made much cheaper.

Your affectionate
Gabriel

Mrs Wm Morris
Kelmscott House
Upper Mall
Hammersmith

[1] Rosa Corder (1853–1904), daughter of a London merchant, trained as a portrait painter and exhibited at the Royal Academy. A portrait of Dr. Pusey by her is at Pusey House, Oxford. Her brother Frederic Corder was Curator and Fellow of the Royal Academy of Music. Well known in Bohemian circles, she was Howell's mistress, and was probably associated with him in the faking of Rossetti drawings—'nervously perpetuating the touch of a vanished hand' (Max Beerbohm). A portrait of Rosa by Whistler—*Arrangement in Black and Brown*—is in the Frick Collection, New York. It was purchased from the artist by Howell for £100—'the only thing he ever paid me for in his life'. A sympathetic account of her is given by Helen Rossetti Angeli in *Pre-Raphaelite Twilight* (1954).

Tuesday [15 April 1879]

55 My dearest Janey,

Long absence and many disappointments have inured me to missing the sight of you, and today at least it was best I should miss it, as the weather is not fit for your being out to any distance. I shall be very glad when I hear from you, but am kept in such uncertainty as to the noise and bother of building[1]—i.e. when it may commence here—that nothing seems to be reckoned on. Still I will trust to a chance of seeing you yet.

I have got a bottle of the medicine I spoke of for neuralgia, and if your cold is of that nature, will forward it to you at once.

Your ever affectionate
Gabriel

Your letter dated Sunday only reached me by last post on Monday. By the bye I don't know whether you have heard that Graham is getting rapidly well. So Ned wrote me.

It is better not to talk about the building here. I found that old babbler Scott had it from you. Of course it doesn't matter.

Mrs Wm Morris
Kelmscott House
Upper Mall
Hammersmith

[1] Rossetti had renewed his lease of Tudor House in 1878; building work was threatened in the stables at the back of the house adjacent to his studio. As he grew older he became increasingly sensitive to noise.

Thursday [22 May 1879]

56 My dearest Janey,

Really you ought not to be paying my debts—no one can afford that luxury to a friend nowadays. I must see about a settlement.

I have heard nought of Constantine Ionides.[1] I think I told you old Graham was better. I had a long letter from him (dated Cannes) in which he enquired about his commissions but when I answered I judged from a letter his daughter wrote me that letters were not sent on to him. He is likely to be in town now I believe in a month or less. Both from him and Leyland I have dues in reversion, and must see about getting them in now that the buying world is at a standstill.

Next week is the Derby week,—after that perhaps we might in better weather think it possible to take some sort of look at each other.

Your affectionate
Gabriel

Mrs Wm Morris
Kelmscott House
Upper Mall
Hammersmith

[1] Eldest son of Alexander Ionides, member of the prominent and wealthy Greek family with financial interests in London. One of Rossetti's important patrons. He commissioned *The Day Dream*, Rossetti's favourite portrait of Janey, in 1880. He left his art collection to the Victoria and Albert Museum.

My dearest Janey, Sunday [1 June 1879] **57**

You would be a joyful sight to me, were I not so sorry an one for you. But I hope we may meet yet this summer—as yet weather still looks uncertain. I have felt a good deal out of sorts lately and my work has not much prospered. A little later there *may* be rather more to show.

I am afraid, my dear Janey, you have found me more than once an afflictive phenomenon, and I feel I truly am so.

I hear Marie Stillman is in London, but have not felt the right to trouble her for sittings, nor the certainty that I could fully avail myself of them.

Old Graham is close on his return I think, and I am getting to work on the 2 predellas[1] for the replica of the big picture—which predellas he wished to be added to it. Now all such fag-ends of commissions have to be looked up and done to bring a little grist in.

Your affectionate
Gabriel

Mrs Wm Morris
Kelmscott House
Upper Mall
Hammersmith

[1] The double predella for the smaller version of *Dante's Dream*. The subjects are described in the next letter.

Predellas for *Dante's Dream*

Monday 2 June [1879]

58 My dearest Janey,

I fear I wrote last night in a stupid disconsolate way calculated to make you uncomfortable. But I think it will be best to defer meeting for a little, particularly as this is the blessed Whit week, and most because of the daily drenches. I am making drawings for the 2 Predellas for Graham's picture. When done I shall give the drawings to you. They will be very pretty and full of full length figures—each drawing nearly as big as the drawing of the Damozel groups you have, and done in the same way. The first (which I have nearly done) represents the lady at the head of Dante's couch watching his troubled sleep while the Dream hovers over his head,—on the other side of the composition is a sort of loggia with 4 ladies, one of whom

94

is perceiving the grief of her friend and beckoning to the others to go to her.

In the 2nd Predella Dante will be sitting up on his couch and relating the dream to the group of ladies. In the loggia (which is parted by a curtain from the rest) I shall here show the figure of Love standing by himself while a sort of tabernacle cloud full of wing-points hovers in the midst. I know you will think them nice compositions—they embody as it were the first and last lines of the Canzone[1]

'Donna pietosa e di novella estade,
and
'Voi mi chiamaste allor, vostra mercede.'

Your affectionate
Gabriel

Mrs Wm Morris
Kelmscott House
Upper Mall
Hammersmith

[1] *Vita Nuova* XXIII, Canzone ii.

My dearest Janey,   Thursday [5 June 1879]   **59**

The moment I got your letter I bethought me of Shield's bottle[1] for neuralgia, and am now sending it by post. Do try it, as I am told it is very efficacious.

I am so glad you care to have the Dante sketches. I hope to write again immediately and try for an appointment. Today there seems a truce to the daily drenches, but how long it will last one does not know.

Your Vasari[2] is quite safe here, but I have got on to Crowe and Cavalcaselle[3] (the worst of writers and most valuable of authorities) and to Grimm's Life of M. Angelo,[4] which you should read if you do not know it. But then I suppose a collection of Gladstone's speeches wd be far more attractive. Perhaps some day you may be able to peruse the Parliamentary works of so great a legislator as George Howard, to say nothing of the coming Parliamentary Man,[5] whose career is now a certainty in the Future.

Your affectionate
Gabriel

Mrs Wm Morris
Kelmscott House
Upper Mall Hammersmith

[1] Frederic James Shields (1833–1911) met Rossetti in 1864 and became an intimate friend of his later years. He was present at Rossetti's death and designed the memorial window at Birchington. His most important work was the decoration of the Chapel of the Ascension in Bayswater. This was bombed during World War II, and is now demolished. See Ernestine Mills, *Life and Letters of Frederic Shields*, 1912.

[2] Giorgio Vasari (1511–74), *Lives of the most eminent painters, sculptors, and architects*, translated from the Italian by Mrs. J. Foster in 5 vols., 1855–64.

[3] *A History of painting in Italy from the second to the fourteenth century*, by J. A. Crowe and G. B. Cavalcaselle, 3 vols., 1846–66.

[4] Hermann Grimm (1828–1901), Professor of the History of Art in the University of Berlin. *Life of Michael Angelo*, 1860.

[5] Wm. Morris and his involvement in politics as Treasurer of the National Liberal League.

Monday [16 June 1879]

60   My dearest Janey,

The weather is so wet still that no appointment could have been made with certainty; but truth to say, depression of spirits (not monstrous however) has been one cause for my not trying to see you. I hope it may happen soon. You don't tell me whether you tried the bottle I sent. I suppose you sniffed and scorned it.

Mrs. Stillman came in yesterday with the divinely lovely Effie. The mamma says she is thinner herself every day and that her bones are coming through. Certainly she and her husband must weigh the least of any such tall couple in the world.

I am painting the first predella, but have not made a thorough start with the design for the second one yet. Today I laid in a figure wonderfully like you I think and one of my best.

Your affectionate
Gabriel

Mrs Wm Morris
Kelmscott House
Upper Mall
Hammersmith

Wednesday [2 July 1879]

61   My dearest Janey,

If tomorrow (Thursday) is such a deluge as today was, of course I could not think of your coming, but otherwise will hope to see you. Afternoon no doubt and to stay as late as possible. Better ring the gate bell as well as that by the street door.

Your affectionate
G.

Mrs Wm Morris
Kelmscott House
Upper Mall
Hammersmith

My dearest Janey,

My mind has been dwelling ever since we met on your gentle
kindliness and my dullard state. As I told you, I have become so
subject to depression that this has been the main reason of my not
laying hold of my appointment lately till last week. I am so sorry too
that I failed to get out at your gate and lend you a hand, as I fear you
found it awkward, but I thought to bother you by pushing by you
to get out. The step was steeper than I judged.

I wish there were any thing to tell you. I hope we may meet again
ere long if I don't feel too serious a nuisance to inflict myself on you
again. Just now I hardly go to my mother's, so do low spirits beset
me and the idea of producing a sad impression on her mind.

I keep altering the last predella design, but ere long the two must
get painted, and then the sketches will reach you, such as they are.
Your sweet faithfulness in the value you set on what I do is most
touching to me. Those who made apes of themselves and kissed my
hands with insane obeisance in early days now ignore me or make
me a figure of fun; but you are always faithful, and always will be,
I know.

This is not a letter worth sending, but I have been thinking so much
in the direction since the other day that it may as well go.

Leyland has bought the 4 Botticellis[1] mentioned by Vasari from
Boccaccio—Giorn: 5: Nov: 8. He has had them cleaned with
perfect success, all restoration being quite recent and easily removed.
This restoration consisted in draping the naked lady and painting out
the horrors. They belonged to Barker's collection which was sold
some few years ago: these Botticellis had a high reserved price and
were then bought in. They were now sent unreserved to Christie's
and Leyland bought them for 1100£—dirt cheap as they are large
and leading works. Till Barker bought them, they had remained in
the Casa Pucci for which they were painted.

Your affectionate
Gabriel

There were not 6 vols of your Vasari, were there? I only see 5 now
in the parcel.

[1] Four pictures illustrating the story of Anastasio degli Onesti, the eighth novella of the fifth day of the
Decameron, were painted by Botticelli in 1486 for the Casa Pucci in Florence, on the occasion of a
marriage between the Pucci and Bini families. These were acquired by Alexander Barker in 1868, and

The Story of Nastasio degli Onesti by Botticelli

after his death were bought by F. R. Leyland in 1879. After the sale of the Leyland collection in 1892 the pictures passed through various hands. One picture, *The Marriage Feast*, became detached from the series and was bought by Vernon Watney in 1894. It remained at Cornbury Park, Oxfordshire, till the Watney collection was sold in 1967, when it was bought by a descendant of the Pucci family and returned to its original home in Florence. The three other pictures finally reached the Prado, Madrid, by gift in 1941. Some modern scholars attribute the pictures to one of Botticelli's pupils. Rossetti also writes about these pictures in a letter to Shields, 16 July 1869 (D. and W. 2064).

The story is that Anastasio degli Onesti, a nobleman of Ravenna, was in love with a young lady who refused to marry him. Retiring in grief to the pineta near the city he sees there a beautiful naked woman pursued by a horseman with hounds who captures and tortures her. He is told that this is her punishment for the cruel and scornful way she treated her lover in life. The vision is repeated, and Anastasio then brings the lady who has scorned him with her family to see it. Whereupon she relents and marries him.

G. F. Watts chose the same incident for his huge early picture, *A Story from Boccaccio*, painted in 1844.

Wednesday [July 1879] **63**

My dearest Janey,

As I have not got a line from you, I will not believe you are worse in health, but only that you did not know what to say to my Jeremiad. Pardon—I'll never do it again. But I had been thinking troublesomely and did not duly reflect that it is one thing unbosoming oneself in words and another putting it in ridiculous black-on-white.

I write now chiefly to tell you that I have had in these bad days what must be called the rare luck to sell the picture of you—La Donna della Finestra.[1] Ellis has bought it. Last year when he bought the water colour Proserpine, he admired the cartoon, and when I told him I proposed painting it, he wished to see the picture. I had felt backward about writing him, but the other day I did so and he is greatly delighted to have the picture. I asked him such a price as one needs must in these days, but still enough to be useful—400 guineas, but of course this is *quite* in confidence, as one must hope to raise prices again eventually. Still it was better to sell, as thus I shall briskly get another in hand, which I should have felt tardy about as long as this was unsold—indeed it does not do to have many unsold pictures. While Ellis was here by appointment, the Cowper Temples came, but Dunn had orders that nothing was to interrupt the interview with E.—so they went. As I suspected and as it turns out, they also came to buy the picture! Mrs Cowper Temple was here with a Lady C. Gaskell[2] a week or so ago, and both were enraptured with the work. In fact, I fancy Lady Catherine will want another instead, —she was immensely struck with the one seated in the tree[3] over the mantelpiece. So the old studies of you may go on being useful yet.

Best of all if I could manage to paint one again from life in an easy position and by short stages.

Let me hear from you when you can.

Your affectionate
Gabriel

Mrs Wm Morris
Kelmscott House
Upper Mall
Hammersmith

¹ The Lady of Pity compassionate for Dante's grief at the death of Beatrice. The sitter is Mrs. Morris. Finished in 1879 (S.255). Now Fogg Museum, Harvard University (Winthrop Bequest). An unfinished replica dated 1881 is in the Birmingham City Art Gallery. For purchase by F. S. Ellis see D. and W. 2059.
² Lady Catherine Wallop, daughter of the 5th Earl of Portsmouth; married Charles Milne Gaskell in 1876.
³ The drawing from which Constantine Ionides later commissioned *The Day Dream*. Now in the Ashmolean Museum, given by May Morris (S.259).

Kelmscott House, Upper Mall, Hammersmith
Thursday

64 My dear Gabriel,

You are right, I really did not know what to say to such a very sad letter, and am only glad to receive another with the good news of the sale of the picture, and the prospect of doing others on commission—as to sitting again, I should be but too happy to feel myself of use again to any human being, but it is scarcely likely, that my back will improve with age. Still I will not despair yet, and you may be quite sure that if at all possible, I shall let you know. I must see a doctor again one day next week, before any long space of time afterwards I shall hope to see you. Meantime and always I am

Yours affectionately
Janey

P.S. No more Jeremiads I beg—or you will not get let off so easily another time.

Sunday [20 July 1879]

65 My dearest Janey,

I write that our correspondence may not drop and hoping that you may soon fix for another visit. On Tuesday I have new servants coming in here—a housekeeper (middle-aged, wages £20, and 10 years excellent character from her last place) and a little rummy housemaid of 16 whom she recommended and whom I am taking

La Donna della Finestra

on trial. I suppose they wd have just to get used to the place for a day or two before we thought of making any appointment. The house-keeper seems quiet and pleasant enough.

Mary Stillman writes me word of a Miss Florence Moore[1] "a friend of hers" who wishes to do a little sitting on the usual model terms, in order to get some money for the expenses of a picture she is painting!!! She is described as of a refined order of beauty. Do you know anything of her? Dont tell other artists, lest she shd prove a treasure for one's pictures. What will the art-world come to next—Every artist his own model—except perhaps little Murray for legs![2] That wonderful little man passed yesterday evening with me, and astounded me by poking no end of fun at the legs of a costume figure of a Turk in a book he looked through. He wouldnt leave off and I didn't know what to say. They were much better legs than his own. I have done a portrait head of Leyland[3] as a wedding present to his daughter who poor thing is so plain that with all her money she has had to marry a man twice her own age and with 3 kids ready made. They were so tired of their honeymoon in Paris that they came back in 10 days.

Your affectionate
Gabriel

Mrs Wm Morris
Kelmscott House
Upper Mall
Hammersmith

[1] According to a letter from Rossetti to Shields (D. and W. 2064), she was recommended as 'refined and suggestive for Dante subjects'. See also Letter 107.
[2] 'His legs had a great outward curvature—the word bandy-legged only faintly expressed the pronounced nature of this strange deformity—which had, however, nothing either disconcerting or repellent about it, except for the wonder as to how he supported himself at all.' A. C. Benson, *Memories and Friends*, 1924, p. 208. It is said to have come from his sitting cross-legged on the floor when in his youth he was a tailor's apprentice in the East End of London.
[3] Possibly the crayon drawing (S.346) in the Bancroft Collection, Wilmington, U.S.A., bought from Fanny Cornforth in 1898.

Friday [25 July 1879]

66 My dearest Janey,

I am writing again in hopes you will give me another word as to your health, even though it is in pencil. I heard a great deal of the virtues of those Sneeze powders (or whatever they are called) and I really think you should give them a trial. I think I told you I feared my servants might not be staying. They—at least the housekeeper on behalf of both—has already complained of dullness etc. She seems a worthy woman and very suitable—a fair cook too. The house maid is a nice natural little thing—one of 6, 4 of whom are out in the world, and the 2 youngest still at school. She says 'Minnie is a house-maid, Emmy is a housemaid, Steeve is at sea and has made two voyages to Australia before he is 15.' She herself went to service at 11, but used to sleep at home till she was 13, since which she has earned her living entirely. She is quite clever, and capable, and forgets nothing. She will be 17 in September. It is difficult to think of such a kid as being only a year younger than your stately self when I first met you. However she is tall to look at, being very well pro-portioned, and wears a train!

I did not mean to fill this note with house-maids stuff, but havent much news. I am now putting the figleaves for foreground to your picture of La Donna della Finestra before sending it home to Ellis. I wish you could see it when finished as it will be greatly improved.

Would I had any more stories of little Murray's legs, or could invent any! The other evening he declared his wife was the most like a Botticelli that he ever saw in womankind, and produced from near his heart several photos of her, but I must say she seemed to me but an ordinary little wench. She however is another of Mary Stillman's beauties, who told me she was quite lovely! Murray is painting a picture for which he expects to get £1000, and 2000 for a Palma which he has picked up. I am sure he has the gift of getting on, if only from his unutterable Scorn of every one else who makes the mistake of being alive and not dead,—a sure sign of a successful destiny. There is a sort of superficial good nature about him, but depths of cynicism perhaps grown with the growth of his legs. Crowe and Cavalcaselle he already waives aside as infants, and is the only man who knows the arcana of art-history. I fancy he really does know a great deal, but seems to have not the slightest faculty of writing it down.

The two drawings[1] will soon be ready for you, and I shall have them framed like the one of the lovers,[2] to occupy little space. I am glad to think what a splendid view you have in the front of your house in summer. The night I went back with you it struck me as even finer than this used to be—the boles of the trees so grand and massive.

I heard the other day that Ruskin has only 9000£ left and lives on his capital, out of which he pays 2000 a year to helpless incapables whom he has on his back, having never all his life aided any man who was worth his salt but idiots only. One honest man alone he has—a certain Allen[3] who publishes his Fors, and this bloke manages to get him in 800£ a year, which he really lets him have, so it is to be feared he will not starve.

Let me hear from you.

Your affectionate
Gabriel

[1] Drawings for the predellas of Graham's replica of *Dante's Dream*.
[2] Study for the lovers in the background of the *Blessed Damozel* (S.244G).
[3] George Allen was Ruskin's pupil and assistant. *Fors Clavigera, Letters to the Workmen and Labourers of Great Britain* was issued at regular monthly intervals from January 1871 till Ruskin's illness in March 1878. Started again in 1880 and issued irregularly till 1884.

Kelmscott House, Upper Mall, Hammersmith.
Saturday morning

67 My dearest Gabriel,

I am writing you a line as you ask though but in lead-pencil.

I am still confined to the sofa, I just manage to sit up to eat my dinner, the violent pain in the back is gone but I have no use in it, I can't straiten myself. I was ordered a Sea Voyage for it—and curiously enough, yesterday we got a letter from a Scotch lady who has been to Iceland several times, who is going again and offered to take me with her—but the fact is I am too ill to think of moving yet.

I would like to see the pictures finished, but am afraid there is little chance of it.

Pray write to me whenever you can, letters are a great resource just now. I have been reading some manuscript poems of Dickson's,[1] they are most odd, not unlike Blake, with some very good things here and there.

Your affectionate Janey

[1] Mrs. Troxell suggests probably Thomas Dixon, the Sunderland cork-cutter, the 'Working-man' addressed by Ruskin in *Time and Tide, by Weare and Tyne*. See *Ruskin: Rossetti: Pre-Raphaelitism*, ed. W. M. Rossetti, 1899, p. 220, and Rossetti's letter to Christina (D. and W. 2295).

Monday [28 July 1879]

68 My dearest Janey,

I only wish my life were more eventfull, in order that I might have something to write to you daily. As it is, I enclose in another letter an article (or lecture in print)[1] just received from some enthusiast of whom I had already heard as lecturing in my honour. I only hope

Caine may manage to spell Able as regards enforcing my poetic claims. The object of the lecture is very good—being evidently to insist on the high tone of feeling in the poems, and I am much obliged to the writer, who has also written me a manly and excellent letter, and whom I shall try to know. I enclose a big envelope that you may return me the pages when read, as I want to send it to my mummy who is at the seaside at a place called Seaford which is I believe the very dreariest spot in this kingdom. Ergo, you may perhaps have to address me there some day.

I have put the figleaf foreground[2] to your portrait and it looks very well. I am in doubt whether or not to introduce a branch of laurel towards the upper part of the picture, but if I do not do this it is now well-nigh finished.

It is some relief at any rate to hear that the violent pain you suffered has left you, and I try to think—indeed I really know—that I recollect previous occasions on which there was an interval of inability to move yourself properly when lying down. It was distressing enough then, but a comfort to think now that this instance may not be absolutely exceptional. You will doubtless write me a line whenever you can. I am always divided between the unwillingness to press you and the knowledge that if I do not hear I shall get sorely troubled about you.

I suppose now, as to the servants, that I may probably be able to keep the housekeeper but that the girl will certainly go. She is very young and naturally enough finds it horribly dull here.

By the bye, I forgot to show you those silhouette designs when you were here. Wd it help to amuse you if I sent you a book or two of them by Parcels? I saw the young artist who is rather older than I had been told, being 22. He must be a very great genius—it is so absolutely impossible to believe when you talk to him that he could ever have done the things. He initiated me the other evening into the envious side of little Murray's nature. I showed him some of them, and he evidently refrained with difficulty from absolutely snorting with wrath and scorn. Nevertheless they have more power in original design than he will possess as long as he lives, or indeed I might say any one else either. You wd think them really phenomenal.

Dunn went down the other day to Epsom at Ellis's request to take my picture of La Bella Mano[3] out of the frame, clean the glass and paste it up, which had never been done at all, so that in fact Ellis has never really had a sight of the picture since he got it. I suppose you

La Bella Mano

know Ellis's place which Dunn says is most pastoral in spite of the Derby Day. However, that is not the only gaudy day there, for the whole time Dunn was there, the house was completely hemmed in with shows bands and merry-go-rounds. It was one of 3 fair-days and the noise was deafening. Ellis appeared perfectly happy and unconscious.

I have tried to eke out news but fear this is the last item at present from

Your affectionate
Gabriel

PS I see I have actually omitted mention of the Icelandic idea. Of course I think if you felt fit for it, it *might* be very beneficial, but even this does not seem a certainty, and only yourself can know if you are at all equal to the attempt. I fear indeed the reply must be negative, yet one feels a wish you could try.

Mrs Wm Morris
Kelmscott House
Upper Mall
Hammersmith

[1] Thomas Henry Hall Caine (1853–1931), then a clerk in a Liverpool architect's office, sent Rossetti a copy of his lecture delivered at the local Free Library defending the poems against the charge of immorality. Rossetti was pleased, and his acknowledgement is quoted by Caine in his *Recollections of Rossetti*. The lecture was printed in the *New Monthly Magazine*, 4th Series, Vol. I, July 1879. He met Rossetti in 1880.
[2] To *La Donna della Finestra*.
[3] Commissioned in 1875 by Murray Marks and bought by F. S. Ellis (S.240). The central figure is Alexa Wilding. Now in Bancroft Collection, Wilmington, U.S.A.

Thursday [August 1879] **69**

My dear Janey,

I am sending you the 2 Dante drawings,[1] and your books, Clarissa and Vasari. I am deeply grieved to say that I fear the 6th vol. of Vasari (for 6 there were, were there not?) is entirely missing. It is not the only book lost here for some time past, and I fear it will certainly not prove recoverable. The only consolatory point is that vol. 6 merely contains the *Opere Minori*—i.e. the long bumptious dialogues between Vasari and the Duke of Florence etc. and has no real value and contains no portraits. I ascertain its full contents from another

Vasari's Works here. I am very sorry about it, and that I shd have borrowed your book only to get it spoilt.

I have put labels on the backs of the drawings specifying the subjects. Dunn is no longer amenable to inscribing things and I am not a good hand at writing on oak which runs.

Your affectionate
Gabriel

Mrs Wm Morris
Kelmscott House
Upper Mall
Hammersmith

¹ The studies for the two predellas of Graham's reduced replica of *Dante's Dream*. The drawings are part of the Winthrop Bequest, Fogg Museum, Harvard. (S.81B.—R2 a and b.)

Kelmscott House, Upper Mall, Hammersmith.
Thursday night

70 My dear Gabriel,

I wrote you but a mere line saying that the drawings had come safely, the man who brought them asked if he should hang them for me, but I could not make up my mind just where to put them at the moment—I unpacked them myself and carried them carefully to my own room, where I have finally decided to arrange them over my bed, so that I may always have the pleasure of feeling them near me in bed, and seeing them when dressing and undressing, I think them more lovely than ever, you have finished them so delightfully, they are really more beautiful than I expected to see, even Top got enraptured with them, especially No. 2. Thank you so much for thinking me still worthy of making so lovely a present to, it is a great pleasure once more in this life. Do not worry about the Vasari, Vol. 6 never came to you at all, it is safe here. I returned by your man the 3 Vols. Coleridge (2 Cottle, 1 Gillman) I think I have no more of yours. Have I? As to embroidery, I do nothing except when I am lying down flat on my back, I find it hurts my eyes less than reading constantly. Good night dear Gabriel.

Always your affectionate Janey

My dearest Janey,

It was a very serious relief to me to get a letter from you this afternoon. I opened it with the greatest anxiety to see whether you had been able to write yourself, and was much cheered when I read that you had 'roared with laughing'. Since getting the Lecture back with May's address and no word from you, I had been feeling very anxious indeed. In your letter, you treat my poor admirer (the lecturer I mean, not myself—we are but two perhaps, he and I) with silent scorn. I grow more and more into the weakness of being thankful to anyone who will give me a little praise. Alackaday! it is much better, no doubt, to view all admirers merely as Slaves of the Ring, which is the current fashion. The above passage you will consider cynical, so don't allude to it.

I will send off the Silhouettes as soon as I possibly can. I wd like to do so tomorrow, but there is always a delay in getting the Parcels Delivery carts to call. I have 3 books—Hamlet, L'Allegro, and Isabella. The 3rd you mustn't look at much, being a horrid sort of subject if you think there is any danger that it may 'waken Snakes'. But I think you told me the Serpent family have deserted your slumber lately. L'Allegro is perhaps the most surprising—his command of every kind of animal seems miraculous. In other books I have seen lions elephants bears and everything else, all equally perfect.

After being praised for long cheerful letters, it is sad to find an utter dearth of news. I know it is vain to try and interest you in such a subject as the sale of Smetham's pictures, or anything one is able to do for any poor unit like oneself and not for wholesale mankind. I suppose Top never gave one farthing to Keats's sister,[1] but then he writes long epistles on every public event. Now there I'm at it again —as Shields says to himself (as he confessed to me on my chaffing his peculiarities) when he feels the hyena laugh surging up within his guts.

The name of Shields reminds me of an incredible narrative which is nevertheless true. S. had been in the habit of relieving some poor wandering street character and his son who accordingly were very attentive in calling as you may suppose. For some time suddenly they disappeared, and when the son came again he told S. that his father had fallen down in a fit in the street, and that some one passing had directed that he shd be taken to his (the passer's) house where he had lain ill ever since. When the man himself eventually appeared, he told the most astounding stories of the benevolence and eccentricity of his preserver who it appears entertained a whole shoal of cadgers at his table, and on Shields asking his name, he was told it was Savage Bear! This roused his wrath, the whole story having seemed to him very improbable, and he turned the man out of the house as a liar. He however reappeared in a few days with a gentleman's card as a witness, on which was printed *Savage Bear*. There are many more astonishing particulars which I have forgotten as the tale was told me some time ago, but I will try and hear them again and retail them if they seem worth it.

I forget whether I told you that I had got through Murray some wonderful photos from Italy—especially 2 of Botticelli's the original frescoes of which were lately recovered from whitewash in an old villa. The subjects are of a romantic kind full of lovely figures. Also a large one of his Spring. Isn't Ned Jones's Phyllis and Demophoon[2] just about as plain as a pikestaff in one corner—isn't it just! The principal head in the Spring and several in other pictures—are obviously the woman represented in that portrait I have got, and quite different from the types of his wife and family which I judge are those of his Holy Families and other subjects. By the bye there is a portrait of Botticelli in a fresco by Lippino which makes him the rummest looking bloke ever seen, something between a Newman Street artist of the smoke-and-beer type, and a thirdrate actor. I have the photo and must show it you one day. Vasari improved mightily on it in his version reproduced in your edition. Are you wanting the vols?

Another charming Botticelli I have got is a Virgin and Child, the Child is about to turn the leaf of the book lying before him being one of the prophets where his doom is foretold, and his mother interposes her hand to prevent him, while he looks round at her enquiringly. The same theme appears in M. Angelo's unfinished Holy Family in Nat. Gal. It was goodnatured of Murray to let me have this Sandro, as it belongs to a private collection and he doesn't know if he can get another. He says my portrait by Botticelli[3] is worth a great deal: he advises me to offer it to Nat. Gal. I forget whether I told you a funny story of Murray's American patron whom he reckons on to buy his own picture for 100£ and his Palma for 2000£. The story relates to the establishment of the Yankee's fortune. Did I tell it? Murray

Phyllis and Demophoon by Burne-Jones, Nos. 1 and 2

said this picture of his own had more subject than any he had hitherto done—I asked what it was, and was answered—Two lovers playing at Chess! I did not tell him that it hardly seemed to exhaust the Shaksperean cycle of humanity and that he had a subject or two still to fall back on.

This rambling has filled a few sheets but I fear is not worth your reading. I must ask Murray to show me his baby's photo. I dare say he thought it wd gnaw at the aching core of my babylessness, and would not therefore produce it. I fear seriously that his belief in his wife as a Venus will ruin his chances as a painter of beauty, though very amiable on his part.

Your most affectionate
Gabriel

I thought your handwriting rather better than the time before.

My housemaid has been home today to keep her Papa's birth *en famille*. I asked her what her Papa was, and she told me—A Gummer of Postage Stamps! Ye Heavens! Could it not be done in the Cradle? —and the man has 10 kids and presumably has kept them on this profession! So England seems to care for its own sometimes, whatever Top may say.

I think the Naworth[4] idea excellent—*if* no company.

PS This won't go in *one* of my envelopes so must go in *two* like the animal who came over in two ships.

[1] Fanny Keats married Valentin Llanos, author and member of the Spanish diplomatic service, in 1826, and settled in Madrid where she died in 1889, aged 86. Living in reduced circumstances in later years she was, through the initiation of H. Buxton Forman, granted a civil list pension by Lord Beaconsfield in recognition of her brother's world-wide renown. Rossetti was instrumental in obtaining signatures for Buxton Forman's petition.

[2] The picture was shown at the Old Watercolour Society exhibition in 1870, and complaints were made about the nude figure of Demophoon. Burne-Jones withdrew the picture and resigned his membership at the close of the exhibition. It was painted for Leyland, and is now in the Birmingham City Museum and Art Gallery. The Phyllis is Maria Zambaco. Burne-Jones made a larger and draped version entitled *The Tree of Forgiveness* in oil in 1881 and this is in the Lady Lever Art Gallery, Port Sunlight. It is not clear why Rossetti should make this unrelated comment in 1879.

[3] Portrait of Smeralda Bandinelli, half-length figure against architectural background. From the Pourtalès collection sold in Paris 1805, and bought by Rossetti from Colnaghi in 1867. Eventually sold by him to Constantine Ionides for £315 and is part of the Ionides bequest to the Victoria & Albert Museum. See Letter 112. It is now regarded as School of Botticelli. Rossetti noted the resemblance to the head of the central figure in the *Primavera*.

[4] Naworth Castle, Cumberland, home of George Howard, later 9th Earl of Carlisle.

Naworth Castle, Brampton, Cumberland.
Thursday

72 My dear Gabriel,

I am sending just a line to say that I have got here safely and am not feeling more fatigued than was to be expected after such a journey and so much previous weakness—one hopeful thing for me is that I sleep well here, both nights have been good. the weather is fine so that I can get in the garden, but I can't join in any of the excursions the rest of the party make to different places in the neighbourhood.

Do you know anything of a Signor Costa a painter from Rome? He is staying here with his wife, both seem pleasant, the wife an invalid like myself, so we spend some time together. Ned is expected tomorrow.

Always yours affectionately
Janey

Friday [15 August 1879]   **73**

My dear Janey,

I was very glad to hear from you in a harbour of rest as I hope it proves. You do not say how long the journey takes. I trust the next news of you may show real improvement, as the weather seems disposed to look up again.

Little Murray was here again yesterday evening, and brought with him one of Keats's sophistical fairified letters (the original M.S.) which he had bought, and which he read over to me while I worked, in the most practical tone imaginable. I am sure he *must* succeed— having no bent to fancies of any kind, except a great fancy for fruit tarts and I think babies so long as they are his own. He showed me the photos which I declared superior to those of all other Bambini, even in Botticelli's pictures. He brought me a most divine Botticelli Holy Family (photo) in which the Infant Christ is kissing the little St. John —really sweet beyond words. I have made a rhyme on Italian Art:—

    *   **   ***   ****
Mick and Lenny, Sandy and Vick,
of all Italian art are the pick:
   *****   ******
Tommy's a Stunner, but Raph's a stick.

      *   M. Angelo
     **   Leonardo da Vinci
    ***   Sandro Botticelli
   ****   Vittore Carpaccio
  *****   Masaccio (which is as one might say Blackguard Tom)
******   Raffaello Sanzio

Murray goes back in a few days. He has left his 2000 guinea Palma[1] with the National Gallery where he hopes to sell it.

I think I told you Mary Stillman is to sit to me, but whether that picture or any other will sell nowadays, heaven knows.

I wish I had any news of work. I get on rapidly with the 2 predella subjects for Graham, but dont know whether one's letters reach that weary old bloke or not, so when I shall get paid, heaven again knows.

I never heard of Signor Costa.[2] What style does he follow?

What did you do with the *very* condensed Greek drama? You might send it me someday if you dont wish to keep it.

I told you the price of the silhouette books for possible buyers. It is 25s. pr book. You dont say whether Jenny and May are with you, but I suppose they are. Ellis I hear is gone to Kelmscott so I suppose Top is tugging and blaspheming in a boat with him, while he indulges in sonorous British guffaws.

Let me hear again soon how you are.

Yours affectionately
Gabriel

Mrs William Morris
c/o Honble Geo: Howard
Naworth Castle
Brampton
Cumberland.

[1] Evidently rejected by Sir Wm. Burton the Director. See letter to Edmund Bates (D. and W. 2182).
[2] Giovanni Costa (1826–1903), Italian painter who developed a style of poetic landscape much influenced by his French and English contemporaries. Many of his artistic associates, for example Frederic Leighton, G. H. Mason, and George Howard, were English, as were the majority of his patrons. (His biographer records that 'only two small pictures by him were ever sold to Italians'.) Chief among his patrons was Lord Carlisle, who had been his pupil and remained his life-long friend. Costa visited England to stay with Lord and Lady Carlisle on more than one occasion. See Olivia Rossetti Agresti, *Giovanni Costa, his Life, Work and Times*, 1904.

                          c/o George Howard Esq M.P.
                 Naworth Castle, Brampton, Cumberland.

74 My dear Gabriel,

I was so glad to get your letter with all its pleasant anecdotes, and what a poem! I wish I had anything cheerful to write of in return, but alas, I have but relapses and recoveries to tell of, the rain comes with cold winds, and then I am confined to the house, then we get a day or two sunshine, and I get into the garden, that is my life here, I go on no expeditions—one great good I have gained by coming, that is good sleep which I think must tell presently if not just now, house garden and all surroundings are lovely, company pleasant. Jenny and May are with me and getting much good from the constant out-of-door life, the journey takes 10 hours, of course I had a sleeping-car. we shall stay till the end of this week when I believe Top will come to fetch us back.

I hear that Mr. Graham is likely to stay abroad all this winter, his daughter is in Town, and would surely know where letters of importance could be sent.

The Greek drama I have at home, and will return it on the first opportunity. I must finish, I have fainting-fits still if I sit up for more than a few minutes.

> Always your affect.
>
> Janey

Naworth Castle, Brampton, Cumberland. **75**

Monday

My dear Gabriel,

I have decided on staying here for a fortnight longer, the Howards being most kind, and refusing to let me start back to town in so weak a state, I continue in about the same way as when I wrote last, one day better, next day worse. Kelmscott is out of the question for me this year, I am too ill to manage an extra house and entertain visitors —I hear that there are sea-weed baths at Ramsgate for people of a delicate constitution, one is made into a kind of pie with the seaweed, when it is supposed that one absorbs vast quantities of Ozone by this means. Do you happen to know of them? I must find out something more, but I really think it seems a thing likely to be of use to me—I greatly fear that a journey South will be prescribed for this winter when I consult a doctor again, if so, would any of that money be got at for the purpose, supposing I could not raise any? Enough of my health—I am most glad that you have got M. Stillman to sit to you again, you will make a beautiful picture of her—Who would have thought a few years back (when I appeared so much the strongest woman of the two) that she would be sitting to you when I am becoming a mummy? So much has Happiness done for one and Misery for the other!

> Your loving Janey

Tuesday [26 August 1879] **76**

My dearest Janey,

I am full of regret that you should be returning after so short a stay between two such trying journeys, but perhaps you feel that you are better at home. Certainly your account of yourself is not very good, but this year has reduced many who started with excellent health.

I wish I had any news of an amusing kind. One thing I heard yesterday from Watts, is, that Whistler, after an incredible career of swindling quackery for some time past, is now 'bust up' altogether, though his late bankruptcy had somehow left him still stemming the tide. His last effort was to get the name of his street changed from

Tite-street to something else, since he said that the word Tite (tight) led to ambiguity and unpleasant reflexions. This was actually laid before the Chelsea Vestry, but they rejected his proposed names (which were Holbein-walk, Turner's-walk, or the Prince of Wales's Walk) and proposed a suggestion of Sir William Tite Street instead. This however was also thrown out on someone remarking that it wd certainly get cut down to Some-one-Tight Street. Since then the American Velasquez has weathered a few weeks, but now he is off for Venice, and his goods, such as they are, will be sold up by auction. Watts is of opinion that Yankeeland will soon get him again for good. One of his last feats was to introduce all his copper-plate etchings into his inventory as 'Copper at 3/6 a lb.' This however Leyland (who has much helped in flooring him) spotted and prevented; W. having made out such an inventory as he could evidently buy back himself if he could only get some one to lend him a few pounds for the purpose.

Howell has lately been several times seen with the eyes of Leyland and also of Watts. Leyland was at Pinti's[1] when H. walked in with a gentleman whom he introduced as his landlord Mr. Jenkins Jones. This gentleman wanted iron gates which he thought would look well at the end of his little 'garding'. However views differed as to price, Pinti asking £20 and Mr. J. J. offering £5 and consuming meanwhile about 2/6 worth of gin and water which was on the table. He was very explicit as to Pinti's having to look to 'Owell', for payment as 'O. owed him a lot'. However the negotiation fell through and Mr. J. J. left. Howell then began giving the most fearful account of Kitty's confinement. The baby was forty-eight hours with its head alone in the outer air, while Howell spent the whole time in administering chloroform to the lady who still contained the rest of the baby. Leyland could not help rolling on the ground with laughter at such a monstrous lie, while H. interrupted his narrative from time to time with animadversions on L.'s brutality. L. then tackled him on the subject of the forgeries[2] of my drawings but he said Attenborough wd give no explanation when he applied for one. He met every subject with his well known ability, and did the same when Watts lately brought the subject up to him on the top of an omnibus where they met. What he seemed most surprised at was that I did not wish in fairness to hear the explanation from his own mouth. However I understand he is most horribly hard up and will probably follow Whistler to America and show him them[?] with a long pole.[3]

Watts's sister must be even in a weaker state than yourself—a state into which she has fallen ever since having a child.[4] For many months she has never left the house—hardly her room—and is now yesterday gone to Brighton at last to try a change; the doctors recommended Margate strongly, but the additional 20 minutes of railway offered such a terrible prospect to her that she insisted on Brighton. She is constantly vomiting and fainting, and altogether must be in an even weaker state than you are; yet her spirits are excellent. I cannot bear to hear of these fainting-fits recurring in your case. Would not sea-air be the right thing to try. My mother and sister have lately returned from Seaford which they found cheap and invigorating—however it is so inconceivably dull. I certainly would try sea-air if I were you much rather than going to Kelmscott which cannot be the right place.

As to Graham, I heard from his daughter lately that he is to be in town towards end of October, but whether to stay or not, I do not know. I am in no mood to drop what is due to me from him on work in hand, about which he continues enquiry in letters, but without yet coming to this necessary point. I have finished one predella subject and well forwarded the other, so when he comes I shall be ready to tackle him.

I am still expecting Mrs. Stillman, to get about my new Desdemona picture from her. I have it all in my head and shall make it a good one. Every one is specially delighted with the Donna della Finestra done from your cartoon. It is certainly now my very best.

I have seen little Murray now and then and expect perhaps to see him once more before he returns to Italy about end of this week. He is very amusing—the development of the dealer through the artist is so very strong in him. He is leaving his Palma with the National Gallery where he hopes to sell it. I have seen a photo of it and it seems a fine thing.

I think I told you about Leyland having separated from his wife— or rather her having left him. It is a blundering sort of business. If you have not heard I can give you the particulars to fill another letter out.

Your affectionate
Gabriel

Mrs William Morris
c/o George Howard Esq MP
Naworth Castle
Brampton Cumberland

[1] According to Mrs. J. C. Troxell (*Three Rossettis*, p. 60 n.) there were two Italian artists of this name in London. More likely they were picture dealers. One Pinti was working with Howell in negotiations for the sale of Rossetti's Botticelli to the King of Italy, and Boyce records dining with 'Raffaelli Pinti the picture dealer', at 57 Wiltshire Road on 17 January 1874.

[2] Rossetti was perturbed about forged drawings which had appeared in Attenborough's shop in the Strand. He protested and gave warning in a letter to the *Athenaeum* in July 1878. Howell and Corder were probably responsible. See letters to Watts and to Marks (D. and W. 1937 and 1939). The letter to the *Athenaeum* is printed by D. and W. (1942), but wrongly assigned to *The Times*.

[3] i.e. Howell would act as Whistler's entrepreneur in America. Suggested meaning of doubtful reading in text.

[4] Bertie Mason, Watts's nephew, came with his parents to live at 'The Pines' where he was adored by Swinburne and he brightened the poet's life. Many of the late 'child poems' were written about 'my little Bertie'—'our little boy'. See Mollie Panter-Downes, *At the Pines*, 1971.

Kelmscott House, Upper Mall, Hammersmith.
Tuesday

77 My dear Gabriel,

This is grievous to hear of your being so very poorly. I have but ill news of myself. I find myself so much worse in London, that we all think it advisable for me to try what a month's sea-air will do before the weather gets too cold to try such a measure. Crom Price has offered me to go and stay with him and his sister, I hear it is healthy there and bracing without being too cold, so I think of trying it soon—I should not take either of the girls, they will go to Kelmscott with their father next week, unless the rain washes the place away meantime. I did not return alone from Naworth, they came with me.

I will see about the Clarissa and send it at once if found.

I was much amused at all your remarks on Ned, they are so perfectly true.

I will write a line on leaving London with exact address where you may write.

Your affectionate
Janey

Thursday [2 October 1879]

78 My dear Janey,

I fancy your present locality and surroundings must be conducive to improvement, only I wish the weather were more perfect. Nevertheless it might assuredly be worse than it is. I must not neglect your kind mindfulness in writing me, but otherwise have hardly any excuse for a letter as regards news.

Old Brown[1] has turned up once or twice lately. His Manchester work was a regular campaign, and really very creditable at his age

Found

and with his ailment of gout continually threatening. The draughts and disturbances of all kinds in this dreadful Town Hall where he is painting were arrayed against him like the foes of the Pilgrim's Progress, but he has got one picture done and is now designing another in London—As to gout, he has lately gone to one Oscar Clayton who is the great man now, having done the Prince of Wales a deal of good, and has got from him a medicine which acts most powerfully and rapidly.

As to work, I think I told you I was taking up the lifelong calf picture[2] again, so now I shall come to an end for sure, as it is plain that performance is never to reach completion. I am sending to an enthusiastic dealer in Leeds a few small things for disposal. He seems able to sell Smethams, so why not these?

With kind remembrances to Crom.

Yours affectionately
Gabriel

Write me again as to your health

Mrs William Morris
c/o Cormell Price Esq
United Services College
Westward Ho
North Devon

[1] See Letter 25.
[2] *Found*, begun in 1854, and unfinished at his death. See Letter 130.

Monday [6 October 1879]

79 My dear Janey,

I am writing you a line before hearing again from you, because I know you will be pleased to learn that Constantine Ionides looked in with his sister Aglaia[1] on Saturday and commissioned me to paint the drawing over the mantelpiece of you seated in a tree with a book in your lap—the one to which I put the hands last year.[2] This will be a considerable commission, though I must be moderate in these bad times. Terms are not yet settled exactly. Do you know whether Constantine has bought or is buying any pictures of Ned Jones? Of course that worthy need not know of this matter of mine.

I fancy Aglaia must somehow have quarrelled with Burton,[3] for she regularly roasted me for about 20 minutes with grins and guffaws because something led to my speaking in favour of a work of his. She wound up by saying—'I know some people assert that you say things you dont mean.' I answered—'No doubt many people say a great many things', and was on the point of adding 'I do not pretend

The Day Dream

to the monumental sincerity of E. Burne Jones.' But I refrained,—
no doubt he was the speaker quoted.

Hoping to hear how you are,

I am
affectionately yours
D. Gabriel R

Mrs. Stillman is to begin sitting to me on Wedy.
Constantine wanted to buy the 2 predella drawings, but I said they belonged to you. He was then for having replicas of them, but finally went off to the picture of you.

[1] Mrs. Coronio.
[2] The picture of Mrs. Morris seated in a tree, commissioned by Constantine Ionides from the drawing which hung in the studio, is referred to as *Vanna* and as *Monna Primavera*: when completed in 1880 finally named *The Day Dream*. Part of the Ionides bequest to the Victoria & Albert Museum. The drawing which inspired it was bequeathed by May Morris to the Ashmolean Museum in 1939 (S.259 and 259a).
[3] Sir Frederic William Burton, 1816–1900, Irish artist and portrait-painter. Director of National Gallery, London, 1874–94.

Thursday [9 October 1879]

80 My dearest Janey,

It is most cheering to hear of your getting nice drives in a beautiful country. I did not say, when you were with the Howards, how pained I was to be told that you joined in no excursions. I believe you were very much neglected there. I should be glad on the whole if you felt yourself able to get to Rome for the winter. Have you had any thoughts of trying it? Or would Florence answer? I am sure the Stillmans wd be most attentive, and you know others there too. Shall I ask Mrs. Stillman's views about it? Had I not better be sending you the interest on your money?

Constantine has behaved most handsomely abt the commission. I had to write him as to terms, and the bad times made me so funky that I named only 700 guineas. It is evident by his answer that he considers this low and wd have given more. But Pazienza! Perhaps he'll buy another when this is done. It is a pleasure to me to think that luck generally comes through the drawings of your dear face, and the sum is very convenient to turn round upon. I think of calling the picture Vanna Primavera,[1] making the tree a spring Sycamore, which is so beautiful in detail, but then I cannot well introduce a convolvulus.

I made a drawing of Mrs. Stillman, and have got the head on the canvas. She sits again on Saturday. Her gracious good nature is really inexhaustible. She told funny stories of little Murray, his dignity and independence, and complete refusal to be patted on the back or patronized. It seems he is going to sport a tail-coat for parties, in which he will be great. She says his family look on him with silent awe, and never speak much in his presence. It seems Stillman is subject to woful despondency and sits in complete collapse with his head and hands hanging. Just fancy, while a wife like that is at hand! He is now at Cadore, painting a large landscape, of which Marie does not seem interested in the details. His two daughters are with him.

Aglaia's attitude when here wd have amused you. The number of people she managed to be nasty about was surprising. Her hatred (as well as Constantine's) for Poynter, and scorn of his works, was very marked. Marie S. told me that Mary Z.[2] and her little pseudo-husband do nothing but work awfully hard at painting and produce Ned Joneses without number. They seem however to be very dejected, and the account rather recalled the end of M. de . . .[3] (if you ever read that horrid book) where the 2 lovers who have made all sorts of mistakes for each other's sake end by living in one house, walking about the grounds far apart, and never speaking to each other. I suppose it would be all right with the Greek lady if she had some kids by the connexion, but there are none.

Your affectionate
Gabriel

Mrs William Morris
c/o Cormell Price
United Services College
Westward Ho
North Devon

---

[1] With reference to the *Vita Nuova* where Guido Cavalcanti's love named Primavera goes before Beatrice as spring precedes summer. The title is rendered by Mrs. Angeli as *Janey in Springtime*.
[2] Mary Zambaco.
[3] Illegible and unidentified.

Kelmscott House, Upper Mall, Hammersmith.   81

My dear Gabriel, Wednesday

I am only writing a line to prevent your imagining that I am too unwell to do so. I have been very unwell, but since I saw a doctor about a fortnight ago, I am beginning to mend. I am taking cod-liver oil for the first time in my life with anything like success. You must let me come and see you one day next week if possible—unless the weather continues diabolical.

I should like to see Mary Stillman again, but suppose she is nowhere within my visiting distance.

Your affectionate
Janey

Wednesday [October 1879]

82 My dear Janey,
    Dont think of troubling about the flowers: I can get them quite easily, but if I need anemones, will ask if your garden has them later.

    I was so glad to see pen-and-ink—strong enough too. I hope you must really be feeling somewhat stronger.

    I have inserted some new stanzas to the old and grisly Sister Helen, developing a fresh incident! I dont know if you'd care to see anything so grim.

    Poor little Miss Moore.[1] If she does not pick and choose her artists, she will find it no lady's vocation. What *sort* of a looking girl is she? What height and what age? Of course she wouldn't sit for figure I suppose. Curiously enough I had a letter the other day from her Mamma, who sent me a printed paragraph about a portrait of Dante by Raffael belonging to her husband who appears to be the Raffael-ometer in General.[2] I could only recommend her to try the National Gallery. It seems the husband is dying.

    I have seen a lot of Holbein's in my time, (some very fine ones at Petworth)[3] but no such show as you speak of doubtless.

    It is very late. Good bye for the present.

Your affectionate
Gabriel

---

[1] See Letter 65.
[2] The reference here is obscure. There does not seem to be any record of a portrait of Dante attributed to Raphael nor of a Mr. Moore who owned it.
[3] According to Waagen, *Treasures of Art in Great Britain*, 1857, there were then five pictures attributed to Holbein at Petworth. One of these, *Derich Berck, Merchant of Cologne*, is now in the Metropolitan Museum, New York. See P. Ganz, *The Paintings of Hans Holbein*, 1950, No. 87.

Thursday[1]

83 My dear Janey,
    I enclose at last the new stanzas for *Sister Helen*. You see the tenor of the poem now shows that the witch began her spell on the wedding-morning of her false lover. Thus the 'alas for birth!' which was of course not probable. I think you will agree that the gain to

the subject is enormous—in fact, once thought of, I cannot think how I never did it before. Moreover the excess of her provocation (in spite of the height of her spite) humanizes her somewhat. I suppose you have the Tauchnitz edition which has several amendments. Of course I must have given you one.

I believe I shall confine myself to Snowdrops at last in the picture[2]. I have got two in the hand, and one serving as a mark in the centre of the open book. Some little jonquils given me were tempting but hardly so characteristic, and you had expressed yourself in favour of snowdrops. Of course the Member for Lechlade is only dallying with the fish tribe and angling for some much better kind of game.

I wish you had my vote which will remain a dummy.

I don't think the picture of Murray's you saw is the crack Palma which I believe is still with Burton. It is a girl looking as if she was playing on a mandolin, but she isn't—she's lifting her skirt as far as one can see and I suspect her of being a daughter of Lot cut out of some large picture; but a photo I have of it seems a fine thing. I judge this was not what you saw—I believe M. has two Palmas.

I hear from Mary Stillman that S[tillman] is off again for three months in the East. She writes as if rather weary of the world.

Your affectionate
Gabriel

On reflection I think I'll ask you to return the printed pages of *Athenaeum*,[3] as I am still wanting to sell the Blessed Blowed Damozel, and they might prove useful.

[*On another sheet, with preceding letter, to Mrs. Morris.*]

(To come after stanza beginning:

'The wind is loud but I hear him cry', etc.

'Three days ago, on his marriage-morn,
Sister Helen,
He sickened, and he's since then forlorn'
'He'll scarce be sick till a babe be born
Little brother'

O Mother, Mary Mother,
Alas for birth, between Hell and Heaven!
'Three days and nights he has lain abed,' etc.,

(the next six stanzas are to follow the stanza beginning
'He cries to you, kneeling on the road' etc.)

(To follow the stanza beginning
'They have raised the old man from his' . . . etc.)

'Flank to flank are the white steeds gone,
Sister Helen,
But the lady's dark steed goes alone.'
'And lonely her bridegroom's soul hath flown,
Little brother!'
(O Mother, Mary mother,
The lonely ghost between Hell and Heaven!)

---

1 This letter is from D. and W. 2142.
2 *The Day Dream.*
3 A description of *The Blessed Damozel* and other works, by F. G. Stephens in the *Athenaeum*, 1 Nov. 1879.
4 For textual history of the poem see *Rossetti's Sister Helen* edited by Janet Camp Troxell, New Haven, 1939.

Sunday [November]

84 My dear Gabriel,
I am again in tribulation as to your health, or is there any other reason for your not writing to me?
As to myself, I have been kept in for a fortnight, but am much stronger and can go out again just now.
Let me hear just a line from you soon if possible.
Always your affec.
Janey

Saturday [20 December 1879]

85 My dear Janey,
I cannot think how it is that so long a lapse has occurred since I last wrote: the reason must be simply that I have never anything to say: but it is too near Xmas not to require a line to greet you.
I have been reading Calderon—a dramatic poet of whom it wd be difficult to say that in several leading respects—plot, imagery, metaphor, dialogue, etc.—he is inferior even to Shakspere. The line of demarcation exists in Shakespere's invariable presenting of all the facets of individual character while Calderon is content to produce a clear main impression. The translator is Fitzgerald[1] who did Omar Kayam. I have also been reading an admirable Agamemnon

(Aeschylus) by him, and have by me another Persian thing of his which I have not yet read.

It is useless to speak of my work until some clear result is obtained. I hope you are faring no worse in this most provoking weather. I regretted after what you said that I did not seize on the photo: you offer me. I shall be very glad of it still if still to spare.

Your affectionate
Gabriel

Mrs William Morris
Kelmscott House
Upper Mall
Hammersmith

---

[1] Edward Fitzgerald (1809–83): *Six Dramas of Calderon freely translated*, 1853, *Rubáiyát of Omar Khayam*, 1859 (anon.), *Agamemnon, a tragedy taken from Aeschylus*, 1876, and *Salámán and Abdal: an Allegory freely translated from the Persian of Jámi*, 1856.
  Rossetti was one of the earliest admirers of Fitzgerald's *Rubáiyát*. He was introduced to it by Whitley Stokes, and for his enthusiasm see R. Glynn Grylls, *Portrait of Rossetti* (1964), Appendix D.

Xmas Eve   **86**
Wednesday [24 December 1879]

My dear Janey,

Our letters crossed: I am extremely sorry to have been so stupidly neglectful without thinking about it. The reason was, I suppose, that I had no immediate anxiety as to your health and had nothing to say on my own account. Tomorrow my mother and some of the family are to dine here weather permitting. I hope you on your part will have a Xmas not too unlike a merry one. I got a longish letter from Stillman yesterday. He writes from Florence where they seem quite settled. The baby boy seems to be an ideal, and Lisa has grown 2 inches taller than her stepmother! I don't believe it—she wd be as tall as her father.

I wish I had any more news—for instance such tidings as that Ruskin was hanged or something equally welcome. But I haven't, so its no use going on.

Your affectionate
Gabriel

I fear Constantine and his kith and kin may be thinking I am doing a little bit of Howell as to the picture. But I shall soon be in the thick of it to good purpose. Only I had to get Graham's horrid job quite out of hand and had made up my mind to alter the drawing of

Beatrice which has taken studies from nature, time to scratch out, time to re-lay, time to dry and heaven knows what.

Mrs Wm Morris
Kelmscott House
Upper Mall
Hammersmith

Saturday

87 My dear Gabriel,
I was glad to get your letter at last and to hear that you have found several interesting books to read, I did not know that Fitzgerald had ever done anything besides Omar Kayam translation—
As to the photograph of myself, I am sorry to say that I have sent away all the best, and the worst I will not send, for you would say 'Ah! I said so' I can get some more if worth while.
I should really like to see Lisa Stillman, I can imagine her having grown to be a splendid woman, but 2 inches taller than Mary Stillman seems impossible. My May is not very tall, though she looks very tall from being so slender, she is excessively delicate this winter, and I think will not drag through a long life. So much the better for her!
As bright a New-Year as is possible dear Gabriel, I wish you with all my heart.
Always your affectionate
Janey
I am cold and write hastily to catch this post.

Sunday [28 December 1879]

88 Dear kind Janey,
Your letter is true and tender as always. On Xmas Day, (when of course I had given up the idea of anyone coming here in such incredible weather, and meant to go to my mother's in the evening instead) my good mummy nevertheless turned up with one of my aunts (Christina and another aunt being not well enough to come) and spent the day very pleasantly looking at pictures and the evening in Xmas pudding etc.
I'll copy opposite a sonnet just made. It is in a different mood from

those of old, yet I have tried to sustain some beauty by natural images.

Your affectionate
Gabriel

Mrs Wm Morris
Kelmscott House
Upper Mall
Hammersmith

Sunday [4 January 1880] **89**

My dear Janey,

I am getting morbid about you, and wd like just one line. Of course there was nothing to answer in my last note, but I keep thinking whether you thought that sonnet extra dismal or something of the kind,—and then (as I say) I am morbid.

The other day an accident happened to the drawing of you from which I am doing the picture for Ionides. However the face and hands escaped completely, and it can be mended with certainty. But this has made me all the more morbid I dare say.

I can lend you the Calderon to read if you like, only perhaps I had better first get it bound as it is in a bad state—or at least one portion is so, for there are 2 vols at present.

Your affectionate
Gabriel

If by ill luck you are ill (O this pen!) write me a line in pencil

PPS. (Tuesday) I have kept this note over till now in the hope that a line might come in natural course without my worrying you, but I must now send it as I am anxious and troubled.

Tuesday **90**

My dear Gabriel,

I am again suffering from neuralgia, the last few days have been weary ones—today I am forced to stay in bed, but expect soon to be better, I got your note this morning and am much grieved to hear how low you are just now, we must all look forward to a change of weather, this constant black night is enough to sadden merrier lives than ours—

I should be very glad of the Calderon whenever you can conveniently spare it.

Always your affec:
Janey

Wednesday [7 January 1880]

91 Dear suffering Janey,

I have just kissed your handwriting, the most welcome thing in the world that I could have seen today. I am not *so very* low except on your account just now, but I had got so nervous and frightened about you that I dont know how I should have got through the night if I had not heard. My letter was posted quite early yesterday afternoon, and ought surely to have reached you before this morning. I had got to look on everything as an omen—having been working up again the dead Beatrice just at this moment and seeing the drawing's frame (which drawing I had to use in doing so) stand empty over my mantelpiece. Then there was the accident to the other drawing of you,—a tree fell in the garden—and altogether things looked ominous.

I really must tell you something that will make you laugh and I can laugh now myself. Hunt[1] told Scott the following marvellous tale. It seems he had suffered all inconceivable kinds of impediments in getting on with his present picture, and had often said to his wife that he believed the Devil (!) was trying to stop him at it. On Xmas day however he went down to his studio and set to work and felt himself freed in some way as to his progress with it—whereupon he ejaculated several times aloud—'I've conquered the Devil, I've conquered the Devil.' *And thereupon* ensued a tremendous explosion in the room itself (as it seemed) nothing however being visible. Hunt says (how can he know it?) that the whole block of studios of which his is one was perfectly empty that day. He looked out and saw nothing to account for it,—and so the Devil is bedevilled and no mistake, and the picture goes on swimmingly. I suppose it will be better not to repeat this, as H. may get into a madhouse if it gets wind—I dont yet know whether he is fool enough to tell it freely himself.

I heard only the other day of a case of neuralgia which I *know* was as bad as your own being cured at last by a certain medicine which I will get and send without delay. I will at once send the little vol. of Calderon (the one in a good state) and wait to get the 2 bound later. I value it very much (being impossible to get again) so I know you'll take care of it and not let Top send it astray, and let me have it again when done with. You will find the plays perfect masterpieces in their kind—the *Mayor of Zalamca* perhaps the most admirable—the next is *Three Judgements at a Blow*.

I have subscribed for a book called A Treasury of English Sonnets[2] (having been much plagued to do so) and just got it. I have found some interesting things in it however—especially some admirable sonnets by Chas: Tennyson,[3] whose work was not much known to me before. The living bards do not figure in the main collection, but turn up here in the notes, and among them

> Your ever affec:
> Gabriel

Mrs Wm Morris
Kelmscott House
Upper Mall
Hammersmith

[1] 'Holman Hunt all but saw the Devil on Xmas Day. He heard him halloa!! This is true.' Letter to Watts (D. and W. 2157).
[2] *A Treasury of English Sonnets edited by David Main*, 1880. The book was in Rossetti's library. He embodied his own sonnet on the Sonnet in a design which he inserted in a copy of Main's volume for his mother's birthday on 27 April 1880. The letter which accompanied the present is D. and W. 2246. See also S.258.
[3] Charles Tennyson Turner (1808–79) contributed with Alfred Tennyson, his elder brother, to *Poems by Two brothers*, 1827. His *Collected Sonnets Old and New* with preface by Hallam Tennyson was published in 1880.

Thursday [8 January 1880]   **92**

My dear Janey,

I sent the Calderon this morning by book post. No doubt you will receive it in due course, and I need not trouble you to acknowledge it if it comes to hand. I have not yet got the medicine I spoke of, but trust to do so tomorrow. It is *really* efficacious I *know*

> Your affectionate
> Gabriel

Mrs Wm Morris
Kelmscott House
Upper Mall
Hammersmith

Friday [9 January 1880]   **93**

My dear Janey,

I did not expect to find that the medicine recommended was so simple a thing as Chlorodyne.[1] Nevertheless, having heard of its undoubtedly proving very beneficial indeed, I send it on and advise you to use it when needed. I under[stand] that 30 drops in water may be taken about once in an hour or even more frequently.

I shall of course be very glad to hear from you when conveniently feasible, but shall be on my guard against getting alarmed to a degree likely to cause you anxiety in turn.

Your affec:
D Gabriel

Mrs Wm Morris
Kelmscott House
Upper Mall
Hammersmith

¹ A popular anodyne based on chloroform and morphia. Not to be confused with Rossetti's own drug, chloral.

Kelmscott House, Upper Mall, Hammersmith.
Sunday

94   My dear Gabriel,

Thanks for the Calderon, I am enjoying him immensely—the medicine I am glad to see shows your kind thought for me as ever, but indeed I will take nothing of the nature of an opiate.

I am better, I got a good night last night, but am still very weak, neuralgia leaves one prostrate, still I hope that before long I shall be about the same as usual.

Yours affectionately
Janey

Thursday [January 1880]

95 My dear Janey,

I did not write before as I wished to avoid hurrying you to answer again; but I did not fail to observe with immense satisfaction the vigorous writing of your note. I cannot but hope that by this time you are recovering a fair share of strength. I am glad you enjoy the Calderon. I think each of the plays a masterpiece of its kind: only I think the 'Painter of his own Dishonour' might have wound up more epically than by shooting 2 people through a grating with a brace of pistols!

I must tell you a funny story about Howell which I heard from Leyland. I must premise that there is a picture dealer named Brooks now retired, and who after being at one time a convict made a fortune in Bond Street but seems to be dealing still in a private way.

The beginning of the tale is that Leyland received a letter from Howell to the effect that something was on his mind. He had been assisting Whistler in disposing of some etchings made at one time by W from Leyland's daughters. He had felt all along that this was not right, and having all the proofs remaining in his own hands at present had resolved to transfer them to Leyland to whom they ought to belong. L. replied that, as they were from his daughters, he shd be willing to purchase them. To this H rejoined that he could not think of accepting money for them, but having to come to Liverpool on business on a certain day, wd then bring them down and meantime was mounting them suitably. The appointed day arrived, and Leyland was going down in the morning from his country house to the station on his way to the office at Liverpool, when he heard a hansom rattling after him. He turned round expecting to see Howell but instead saw a prize-fighting sort of character dressed very smartly who jumped out of the cab saying 'Mr Leyland I believe'. Being answered in the affirmative he went on—'My name is Brooks, and I should be much obliged Sir if you wd favour me with a call at my hotel in Liverpool to see a very fine Botticelli I have to dispose of.' Leyland assented, went, and after some bargaining, bought the Botticelli (a splendid Holy Family) for 1000 guineas. This being concluded, he asked Brooks if he knew a Mr Howell. 'Oh yes Sir' said Brooks 'a man of splendid talents, Sir, if he wd only keep square!' Leyland then intimated a suspicion that Howell was somehow connected with the present transaction and Brooks said 'O yes, Sir, Mr Howell wanted to bring this picture to show you, but in fact I couldn't trust him with it. I cant help admiring him though, and the other day he came down and wanted to borrow £10. I knew I should never see it again but I couldnt help lending it to him.' Of course the true story, as Leyland perceived, was that H. after failing to get B. to entrust him with the picture had extracted a £10 commission for the introduction. I need not say that of the etchings L. heard no more.

Your affectionate

Gabriel

Friday

96 My dear Gabriel,

I am writing you a line so that you may get it before another Sunday passes, that day without letters! I have no particular news of any kind, and none of a cheering nature of myself—I am advised to go to some warm place without delay, but think it unlikely that I shall stir from home; my doctor thought it most desirable for me to go, but not necessary, so perhaps I may pull round again without one of those gigantic efforts I have made so often to so little purpose.

Many thanks for your last most amusing letter—really Howell is a genius in his way, as Mr. Brooks said. I have not quite finished the Calderon, but can do so and send it whenever you say the word, or I will take care of it till I see you, if that should ever happen again.

Yours affectionately
Janey

Thursday [29 January 1880]

97 My dear Janey,

I was glad to hear that at any rate you are in about your usual state. To be well in this weather I should think must be impossible. How much longer we are to live in a region of toy-trees frosted to order, I don't know. It wouldnt matter if there was not so much fog with it. I should like to have the Calderon again when you can conveniently return it by book post—as for meeting at present that seems more than ever a dream. My view is that if the book remains with you, Top will no doubt send it heaven knows where irrecoverably, and I really dont want to lose it.

Const. Ionides was here a Sunday or two ago, with a daughter of his and her 'intended' as he called him on introduction. She is neither handsome nor the reverse, but rather the former—but I dare say you know her—she seems nice. I did not show him his own picture (a course which seemed quite to satisfy him) but he dwelt with rapture on the big one and I really think by what he said he wd buy it if he knew how to hang it—indeed he said as much. He asked me to make some monograms for him to be engraved on dinner plate, which of course I did prettily, and he is in the best of moods.

I never asked you at the time a question which I will just ask now, but hope not to displease you in any way. Is it conceivable that you put some *in*conceivable construction on that Sonnet I sent you? I ask because something of the sort happened with another sonnet years ago, and it is so unusual with you to make no sign whatever on receiving verse of mine. Of course I have no pique or vanity about so mere a trifle, but merely put the question, as I say, because of what happened (inconceivable to me) long ago.

I have been writing 3 'Beryl-Songs'[1] to go between the parts of Rose Mary and at the end.

I dont know whether you are familiar with Coleridge. I have been reading him again. 'The Three Graves'[2] is one of the finest poems in the world—possessing absolute invention and exquisite pathos: of course it begins in the middle and never finishes!

I wish I had more stories of Howell—there is nothing to match them except his own lies.

Ever your affectionate
Gabriel

I wont put another sonnet opposite—it might not be safe.

Mrs Wm Morris
Kelmscott House
Hammersmith

---

[1] Three songs written at this time were inserted in *Rose Mary* which had been written in 1871. The poem was published in *Ballads and Sonnets*, 1881.
[2] A ballad tale on the theme of a curse laid by a mother on her own daughter. Begun by Wordsworth and finished by Coleridge in 1798. Coleridge published Parts III and IV in *The Friend* in 1809. The complete poem was published in Coleridge, *Poetical Works*, ed. J. Dykes Campbell, 1893, when it was still unsuspected that Parts I and II were by Wordsworth. Rossetti valued the poem highly but in our eyes it has perhaps less poetic merit. See Moorman, *William Wordsworth; The Early Years 1770–1803*, pp. 388–90.

Kelmscott House, Upper Mall, Hammersmith.   **98**
Sunday night

My dear Gabriel,

I am quite grieved at my stupidity as regards the sonnet—the truth is, I was ill when I received it, and would not trust myself to make any remarks on what struck me most at first, its extremely woeful character, and afterwards on reflection it seemed to me that you must have written it when very ill, so very sad was its tone—that I resolved to say nothing about it, there is the truth of the matter. Forgive me if I caused you any uneasiness, I thought you would understand the reason of my silence, and question me no further.

It is odd, I too had been reading Coleridge lately, and was much struck by the poem, 'The Three Graves', the remark you make on it would apply to most of his things, his incompleteness must annoy you I think, but there are marvellous verses scattered all through his works.

Do send me the Songs you speak of for the Rose Mary poem, and anything else you are doing, you must feel sure how welcome your work always is to me—and there is little pleasure left one in this world. I am thinking of going to Hastings for a time, but I shall not start while it is so very foggy and wretched. May will go with me to take care of me, she is becoming a good nurse.

I think Euterpe Ionides[1] a very nice girl; I hear that she is not considered bright, but she seems to me particularly sympathetic and kind, and likely to make a good wife.

Always your affectionate
Janey

[1] Eldest daughter of Constantine Ionides, born 1861, married W. F. Craies of the Inner Temple, author of a standard treatise on statute law.

Graham Robertson, writing about her on 27 July 1937: 'She's a very interesting spirited old lady . . . She is eighty-two but still very handsome and sprightly, and declares that she enjoys old age much more than she enjoyed youth' (*Letters from Graham Robertson*, ed. Kerrison Preston, 1953).

Monday [2 February 1880]

99 My dear Janey,

I think Hastings may benefit you possibly, though I considered your doctor's counsel to go abroad a great mistake on his part after your experience of such efforts. I dare say you will let me have the Calderon again before you go, as otherwise the 4 winds will possess it.

Pardon my reverting one last time to that blessed sonnet. I never dreamed you wd not perceive that the tone adopted was only a contrasting framework for a set of natural images such as one does not put into relishing form if one is very ill! At least *I* am not at such times a sonnetteer.

If you are staying at all in town, perhaps you wd like me to send you a volume of sonnets just issued containing a great number of good ones by older and newer poets. The living ones do not appear in the text, but both Christina and myself figure in the notes. Only it is a very fat book, and I'm afraid might give you trouble in returning, and I've got to be more of a reader and referrer lately, so such books are useful.

William has been reading me this evening the 2nd of 2 lectures he has written on 'Poets' Wives',[1] bearing on the general opinion that the marriages of poets are unhappy. He proves however that after citing all available instances, English and foreign, the balance is considerably in favour of happiness!

A very fine piece of Coleridge (though with a very stodgy title) is 'Love Hope and Patience in Education.' He wrote it and a few other fine short ones just before he died.

I'll copy and send the 'Beryl-Songs' for Rose Mary. I have only written trifles besides and they are stodgyish. These songs of course are but trifles too.

Your affec:
Gabriel

Mrs Wm Morris
Kelmscott House
Hammersmith

---

[1] The two lectures on 'The Wives of Poets' were delivered at Newcastle, at Glasgow and at Birmingham. They were published in the *Atlantic Monthly*, Vol. XLVII, 1881.

My dear Janey,   Wednesday [February 1880] **100**

I send you the three songs. In copying them, I perceive them not to be merry; or if that quality is your present favourite in poetry, I fear they will find no favour. They are of course less songs than lyrical chaunts or choruses proceeding from the spirits of the Beryl. I thought them needed especially to elucidate the great transition of feeling between Parts I and II, and to explain the altered position of mother and daughter. The third song is also useful as giving some hint of the mother's finding the dead daughter. I dare say several things of a further explanatory kind have been done at intervals to the poem itself since you saw it, but all of a slight sort.

I have this minute finished reading Keats's *Endymion*, which I had never really read through in my life. It is a brilliant labyrinth—a sort of magic toy. The interview with Diana, however, in Book II is as human as it needs must be, but artfully interspersed with supernatural invocation, so as to give the unearthly element. The fourth Book is very groping and confused, but contains the finest piece of poetry in the work—the lyrical speech of Ariadne. I suppose you have read *Endymion*,—if not, it is worth your while, though not the easiest possible reading.

I refrained from noticing the pencil-writing of your last, lest you should charge me with preferring to see none at all!

I'll hope to hear from you soon again either in pen or pencil.

Your affectionate,
Gabriel

Beryl—Song I
(to follow Part I—)

We whose home is the Beryl
Fire-spirits of dread desire,
Who entered in
Fire-spirits of dread desire,
We whose home is the Beryl?

Beryl—Song II
(To follow Part II—)

We whose throne is the Beryl
Dire-gifted spirits of fire,
Who for a twin
Leash Sorrow to Sin,
Dire-gifted spirits of fire,
We whose throne is the Beryl?

[1] This letter is from D. and W. 2179. The third song is missing from the letter.

Sunday [15 February 1880]

101 My dear Janey,

I shall certainly adopt a snowdrop if possible after what Vanna herself has intimated as to her preference. My only question is, the poverty of the leaf, whereas the beautiful play of the convolvulus leaf and stem greatly aids the design of the hand and flower, and some spring bloom might possibly be found having the same quality. But I quite agree with you as to the unique charm of the snowdrop.

The tale of the humming bird is this. Shields went into a bird-stuffer's shop, who asked whether, as he was an artist, he wd kindly look at a drawing made by his son. This proved to be a drawing of the bird in question, whose identity at once superseded all consideration of artistic merits. The report was that one specimen had been found long ago, and that one more only had now been discovered from which the drawing had been made. This I think I told you. However some one who was astounded at the sight of the sketch I sent you on my table, after having examined it, said it recalled to him something he had heard of an old gentleman who devoted an ill spent old age to producing nondescripts in natural history—that his collection had been disposed of after his death, and that it seemed impossible to dissociate his memory from this specimen, as he was astoundingly ingenious. I think this must really be the solution.

Certainly a sea-beach so visited as you describe by wind and wave cannot be always an agreeable lounge. But nevertheless it is good to hear that you are sensible of improvement.

I have been reading a very funny book—Cottle's Early Recollections of Coleridge. Are you in want of further reading? When you are, I might send it you. By the bye, the Notes to the Sonnet Book are well worth reading through: they contain a great deal of interesting matter. I don't know whether it wd interest you to read a lecture on Politics and Art? Caine (who wrote what I sent you abt myself) has sent me a proof of such a thing (in the rough) which I'll enclose, as half your friends are named in it.

He proposed to dedicate it to me!!! but I simply told him in reply that I had never read a parliamentary debate in my life. It has excellent things in it, but is rather a hasty affair. The passage abt. Keats I think very fine—also what is said of the working man and Toryism is excellent. I did not know *I* was a Tory.

Your affectionate
Gabriel

I suppose a snowdrop does not absolutely disappear just yet, does it? Of course I mean to secure one in time.

Mrs Wm Morris
2 Carlisle Parade
Hastings

Friday [20 February 1880]   **102**

My dear Janey,

One word to say—so many thanks for the lovely snowdrops. I should like of all things to paint those of your sending, but am obliged to-day to go on with the hair which is in a state that will not wait. I have put the flowers in a cool place and hope they may be still good tomorrow—but there are no leaves. I know these are slight but some shd be there. I have just looked in Gerarde's Index[1] and the snowdrop is actually not to be found therein! I wanted to see how he drew the leaves.

Your affec:
Gabriel

Mrs Wm Morris
2 Carlisle Parade
Hastings

[1] John Gerard (1545–1612), author of the *Herball or generall Historie of Plantes*, 1597. Rossetti had a copy of the second edition, 1636.

Monday [23 February 1880]

103 I'm almost sorry
you came away

My dearest Janey,

I am so sorry the snowdrops were not yours. I certainly wd not have painted them in a hurry if I had known they came from any one else. As it is, I have done them, but may really have to re-do them, as having nothing but single stalks and no leaves I fancy they dont look growing rightly. Nevertheless the composition with the hand requires a certain arrangement and I *may* have to adopt another flower—probably primrose as simplest. Cowslips I think have no leaf to speak of.

Would you believe it that *Snowdrop* is not to be found in Gerarde's Index? This astounded me. I then turned up the Latin Dictionary— where I found *not* Snowdrop but *Snowdeep* which I suppose must be the real word. This was latinized as *Viola bulbosa*. This again was not in Gerarde's Latin Index! but being driven to desperation I sought Bulbed Violet in his Index, found it, and on turning to the page, there was an obvious snowdrop! It wd really seem as if the word was invented since his time, though one would have sworn it cd be found in Shakspere or I should have thought in Chaucer. There is a greater bulbed violet which seems to grow in clusters and might save my bacon as to arrangement; but I am uncertain as yet what to do. I shd be sorry to trouble you to get a pot, as I could get one from here if needed, so you had better put it out of your kind head.

You dont really consider me a Tory do you? I must write a line to Caine and tell him to do as he pleases abt the dedication, as I fear I may have hurt his feelings. I enclose you what I think a truly admirable paper of his on a very fine subject. Also his letter proposing dedication.

Your affectionate
Gabriel

P.S. I never looked at the postmark or handwriting of the Snowdrop package, making sure it must come from you. I now suppose Dunn who is away, sent it.

Mrs Wm Morris
Kelmscott House
Upper Mall
Hammersmith

Thursday [26 February 1880]   **104**

My dear Janey,

I have been meaning to write for some days. I hope you feel no worse now you are in London. I am just looking up an old tussore (if that is right) silk dress of yours to paint in the *Vanna*. I knew it wd be of use some day when you gave it me, and it is replete with your memory, empty as it is now.

I painted the Snowdrops in the picture but I dont think they'll do as I have got them. The design needs a bloom or leaf (leaf in the drawing) as a balancing value beyond the hand, and this the snowdrop cannot manage to give well. I think I shall use a snowdrop and primrose together. The leaves of the primrose, though not beautiful, may be made to do—particularly young ones. I wont ask you to trouble abt getting flowers unless I find them not easily obtainable (Dunn being still away); I know nursery-gardens abound in your neighbourhood. But as I shall probably begin the drapery tomorrow, I had better write again about this. I suppose primroses are hardly obtainable yet. Of the other flowers I have noted I suppose the Cowslip and Wood Anemone seem most promising, but the latter I judge wd be difficult to obtain, and the former not yet out. The head and hands are done and thoroughly successful. Should Aglaia happen to ask you anything abt the picture, it will be better to know nothing except that I say it is progressing rapidly and is my best.

Let me have a line from you when you can—I get fidgetty if I hear nothing. Shall I send you any book? The Vasari shall be returned as soon as Dunn comes to pack it, but it is ponderous. I can send Cottle's Coleridge and also Gillman's[1] Coleridge if you like—both amusing books. I have also a volume of Baldinucci's[2] Vite de' Pittori, containing the latter men,—Guido, Caravaggio etc.—about whom there is a lot of anecdote. Also I could send you shortly Donne's Poems if you liked to read them. They are quaint beyond everything —full of various merits and extremely funny. The first is called *The Flea*, and dwells on the touching community of life established between 2 lovers through a flea having sucked both of them and thus containing the blood of both together!! There is an excessively funny series of small pieces called the *Progress of a Soul*. The soul is supposed to enter vegetable as well as animal and human tenants, and begins its course in the apple which tempted Eve, winding it up as the animating principle of Cain's sister and wife. Meanwhile it inhabits animals of all sorts. All is full of picturesqueness and wisdom too in its way. The career of a rakish sparrow and the murder of a whale by a Thresherfish and a swordfish are specially racy. There are also many admirable devotional sonnets (though full of conceits) and many love-poems—a few admirable, especially one song,—and others very good on the rather naughty side of things for it seems Donne began life somewhat like his own rakish sparrow, though he afterwards became a model husband and parson. He is one of Wm's best instances among his married poets. I could also send you a very good book of ghost stories in small compass. I dare say you have found much to interest you in the Sonnet book. The notes are full of information.

Your affectionate
Gabriel

Mrs Wm Morris
Kelmscott House
Upper Mall
Hammersmith

---

[1] Coleridge lived with James Gillman and his wife at Highgate from 1816 till his death in 1834. *The Life of Coleridge* appeared in 1838; only the first volume was published.
[2] Filippo Baldinucci, *Notizie de' professori del disegno da Cimabue in qua*, 6 vols., Florence, 1681–1728. The book was in Rossetti's library.

Kelmscott House, Upper Mall, Hammersmith. **105**
Friday

My dear Gabriel,

I omitted to make any mention of the books you offered to lend me in my last letter, I should be very glad of them shortly if you will send them here, I am going down to Rottingdean today to spend a few days with Georgy and Phil.

Yours affectionately
Janey

Sunday [29 February 1880] **106**

P.S. I fear your
handwriting looks very weak

My dear Janey,

I am sending you Cottle's Coleridge and Gillman's ditto—the first belonging to Wm the second to Watts. When done with, please return, but no hurry.

Do not take any trouble about flowers. I am doing the drapery now, and when I need flowers will get pots from Cov: Garden and take care to be in time. The extreme usefulness of the dresses of yours which I have induces me to ask if you have any more 'Old Clo' of an artistic cut and material. If so you might make a bundle for this Hebrew. Mrs. Stillman has just sent all the way from Florence to borrow your old olive green velvet dress which I painted in that old fiddle picture.[1] She tells me that Stillman is on his legs again and instantly off somewhere to do some excavations. She seems to be worked *off* her legs herself, to judge by the account she gives.

I wish I had any news worth giving. Ned Jones looked in for a minute and a half the other day and told me that poor S.S. wrote to him from an hospital.[2] He did not answer, but wrote inquiries to his doctor and learned that S. had arrived at the hospital not only ragged but actually without shoes! I must say Ned's conduct as a correspondent is hardly consistent with the penultimate piece of news he gave me on the subject: viz: that he and his wife had judicially gone to view this Hebraic phenomenon at a friendly meeting planned for the purpose by Holiday and his wife![3]

P.S. You will recall the antique habit of waking the moon from her

Veronica Veronese

eclipse with music. Keats lies literally in the shadow of dead Rome—
i.e. in that of the pyramid of Caius Cestius.

I'll write you out my last Sonnet. Its only on Keats[4]—I wish it
were on Gladstone[5].

Your affectionate
Gabriel

Mrs Wm Morris
Kelmscott House
Upper Mall
Hammersmith

[1] *Veronica Veronese* painted in 1872 with Alexa Wilding as sitter (S.228), Bancroft Collection, Wilmington, U.S.A.
[2] Simeon Solomon (1840–1905), talented Jewish artist, one time friend of Swinburne, Rossetti, and Wilde. Painter of classical, scriptural, and Jewish subjects. His work was praised by Pater. After early success he was involved in homosexual scandal which ruined his career: he ceased to exhibit after 1872. For contemporary comment see Rossetti's letter to Madox Brown (D. and W. 1331). Lady Burne-Jones in the *Memorials* recalls their friendship with Solomon and sorrow at the tragedy of his broken career. See also Forrest Reid, *Illustrators of the Sixties*, 1928.
[3] Henry Holiday (1839–1927), painter and worker in stained-glass. His best-known picture *The meeting of Dante and Beatrice* is in the Walker Art Gallery, Liverpool. His wife, a skilled embroidress, worked for the Morris firm. See Henry Holiday, *Reminiscences of My Life*, 1914.
[4] One of Rossetti's sonnets on 'Five English Poets'. The others being Chatterton, Blake, Coleridge, and Shelley.
[5] Rossetti and his brother approved of the Gladstone Government's liberal policy in the Transvaal: and Lady Waterford had once told him at Penkill that Gladstone had repeated to her a poem of Christina's by heart.

Sunday [7 March 1880] **107**

My dear Janey,
I am now so far advanced with the drapery that I can pause to take
the flowers into consideration. I suppose what I shall introduce will
be a snowdrop and primrose in the hand: but these I need in *pots*, so
as to secure variety in the leaves such as may be needed, and to allow
time for failure. If I put a wood anemone it will probably be lying
separately on the lap or book. But the question rather presents itself
—are all these flowers consistent with a fairly advanced Spring
sycamore, such as the tree is to be? Would the Snowdrop necessarily
have disappeared by then? Not that correctness of literal kind is
imperative on this point. I dont *need* to trouble you about sending
the flowers in question, as I can get them in other ways; and if you
send them, it must absolutely be without inconvenience resulting to

yourself in your present weak state. I only mention it now on account of your sweet urgency in a former letter. There is no hurry, as I have plenty besides to attend to, but am ready for the flowers now at any moment.

I just write this line in a hurry and will soon write again.

Your affectionate
Gabriel

Mrs Wm Morris
Kelmscott House
Upper Mall
Hammersmith

Wednesday [10 March 1880]

108 My dear Janey,

Do not say that poetry is far from you. It shd be nearest to us when we need it most, though indeed I know how difficult it sometimes is to feel this. As to the flowers, I feel deeply how good it is of you to interest yourself about them, and the thought is very dear to me, for I am desolate enough, as you know,—indeed, without my work, should be lost altogether. It is a comfort to me to think that you on your side are not quite so companionless: I often hope that your daughters are worthy of you and devoted to you.

I expect a primrose and snowdrop[1] will be all I shall be able to introduce. They can only be in the hand or possibly though not probably just one near the book. So you see you must not take any *trouble* about it, though it wd be very sweet to me to use what came from you. I am very unlikely to want a wood anemone—still I *may* want it. At present I am getting rapidly on with the drapery, your old dress proving invaluable; but in a few days shall begin to think definitely about the flowers.

I dont know if you remember a drawing—under life-size—which I made of your head at Bognor.[2] I have since completed it by adapting hair and neck (which were unfinished but the face done) from other drawings of you; and the result is so good that everyone seems to think it the best I ever did. I mean to paint it very shortly as a Beatrice giving her salutation.[3] (Tanto gentile e tanto onesta pare etc.) and shall expect it to prove my very finest. I have not in the least forgotten the 2 Dante predella drawings for you, but the fact is I have made certain improvements in painting them which I wish to transfer to the original designs before framing and sending them and you know how little odd time one has in short days. But they shall be done soon.

I really almost fancy you ought to get away again. Your hand-writing looked so firm and hopeful when you were at Hastings, and the weather is warmer now. I shall soon send the dividend,[4] but, truth to say, am short till the next cheque comes which will be almost immediately.

I hear a good deal from young Caine[5] of Liverpool whose lecture I sent you. I will send it you again in a complete state. You need not return that article of his I last sent you, since I have another copy. He is a warm sympathiser with my doings—a thing worth meeting with when one's old friends care little or nothing whether one lives or dies.

However that is a morbid way of talking. Good old William moves along happily and often comes now to see me. Of course as usual I am expecting this house to tumble away from me. Do you know of any in your neighbourhood? The dirty Macdonald tribe[6] found old Brown's house (which they were in treaty for) even too dirty for them. Surely your tenancy following theirs must have required Augean labours of cleansing.

This letter spreads without any amusement for you I grieve to say. Howell has done nothing particular of late that I know of, except exhibiting Whistler's caricature of Leyland (called Portrait of a Creditor)[7] at a place in Chancery Lane. But a sadder fact in connec-tion with Leyland is, that I got a letter from him a few hours ago to say that his married daughter had just died in childbirth and that he was quite brokenhearted. Poor fellow! his affections are really most strong where they take root. His two remaining daughters are but slender plants, and if they were to go I verily believe he wd be soon gone too.

I have been asked by Mrs Gilchrist to take up my share of the Blake book for a new edition,[8] and have consented to do so. It will not give me much trouble. Her eldest son whom I remember as a boy about 10 must now I suppose be about 30! How the world wags! He is coming to see me on Saturday. William tells me he is an artist of some real promise.

I understand Hunt got Top, William, Ned and others to espouse his side at St James's Hall at a meeting about marrying one's wife's sister.[9] It is all very fine, but however reasonable the thing may be (and I think it quite so) calamities may follow it. Hunt's father-in-law has not only left all his money (90,000£ I hear!) away from Hunt's present wife but also from his son by the first wife who therefore remains sorely wronged through his father's act.

Cottle's Coleridge[10] will amuse you. In reading it I discovered a curious fact: viz: that Buchanan's attacks on me years ago were greatly plagiarized from 2 sources in this book: one being a most spiteful but most amusing letter of Lamb's to Coleridge, (towards end of Vol. 1) and the other Southey's attack on Byron which occurs in the Appendix (Vol. 2). No more of Gillman's Coleridge ever appeared than the one vol: I sent.

I never hear of poor Bessie now.[11] I hope she gets on all right. Has not Jenny become a bard or May painted a picture yet?

Your affectionate
Gabriel

[1] For the *Vanna* picture.
[2] Rossetti was at Aldwick Lodge, Bognor for nine months from mid-October 1875. Janey visited him there.
[3] One of Rossetti's last works, unfinished at his death. Purchased by Leyland and now in Toledo Museum, Ohio. The drawing is a study for this (S.260 and 260A).
[4] Rossetti's share of the capital in the Morris firm which he invested for the use of Mrs. Morris.
[5] See Letter 68.
[6] George Macdonald (1824–1905), the novelist and his family who lived in the house on Hammersmith Mall before the Morris's took it. For comments on their occupancy see Letter 29.
[7] One of three satirical portraits of Leyland which Whistler painted in revenge at the time of his bankruptcy. Originally called *The Gold Scab* it was renamed and appeared in the bankruptcy sale as 'Satirical portrait of a gentleman styled *The Creditor*'. It is a caricature of Leyland as a hideous peacock playing the piano and using his own White House as stool. It is now in a private collection in San Francisco.
    An account is given in the *Life of James McNeill Whistler* by E. R. and J. Pennell, 1908, Vol. I, pp. 256–9, and there is a reproduction in *James McNeill Whistler* by Denys Sutton, 1966, Fig. 15.
[8] Alexander Gilchrist, *Life of William Blake with Selections from his Writings*, 1863; second edition, edited by his widow and prefixed by a Memoir of Alexander Gilchrist, 1880. Rossetti helped to complete the book after Gilchrist's death, and assisted with the second edition.
    The eldest son Herbert H. Gilchrist exhibited regularly at the Royal Academy from 1876 onwards—landscapes, interiors, and historical subjects. He painted *Rossetti's Studio*, exhibited at the Burlington Fine Arts Club in 1883—its present whereabouts unknown. Also wrote 'Recollections of Rossetti' in *Lippincott's Magazine*, November 1901.
[9] After many futile attempts from 1850 onwards the Deceased Wife's Sister Marriage Bill finally became law in 1907. The topic was a matter of controversy throughout the century: it was of particular concern to Hunt who, after the death of his first wife, because of this restriction, was obliged to marry her sister in Switzerland. Cf. 'Queen and Peers' song in *Iolanthe* (1882)—
    Into Parliament he shall go . . .
    He shall prick that annual blister,
    Marriage with deceased wife's sister.
[10] *Early Recollections relating to the late S. T. Coleridge during his long residence in Bristol*, 1837. The second edition revised appeared as *Reminiscences of Samuel Taylor Coleridge and Robert Southey* in 1847. Rossetti is making ironic allusion to Cottle's revelations about Coleridge's opium addiction and breakdown.
[11] Janey's sister.

My dear Janey, Thursday [11 March 1880] **109**

I forgot to say yesterday that I must not yet let you be taking any trouble abt houses, though I shd like to hear of a really eligible one. I have not *yet* got notice as to the building which doubtless impends. Is Hamlet House an old or new house? I think you say it has a good garden. Do you know why Conway left it?[1]

This is but a P.S. to my yesterday's letter, so news it cannot contain. I think I did not tell you the sad circumstances of Mrs. Hamilton's (Leyland's daughter's) death. She married on 2nd July last a man double her age (she being 20) with 3 children. He was a Scotchman of some pretensions to family, and whose first wife had an estate contiguous to his own in Lanarkshire. I judge that the first wife's estate wd go to her children, and thus he wd provide himself with a 2nd *married* wife to fill up the deficiency. He has now got the dowry and can go in for a third wife and a third dowry. They had gone to Italy, whither Leyland escorted his 2 other daughters to join them, and I suppose the whole party were still there at the time of the death. As she died on 2nd March (8 months exactly after marriage) it would seem the birth was premature and she may possibly not have expected it and failed in getting proper medical attendance. It is a sad affair.

Your affectionate
Gabriel

I made for her a drawing of her father as a wedding present. This (through framing delays) was never sent to Scotland till she had gone to Italy, and now she is dead!

P.S. Did I ever send you an article from Athenaeum[2] on the 'Donna della Finestra etc.' (Nov: last)? Finding the page torn out and lying in a heap, I judge I may have laid one aside for you and never sent it.

Mrs Wm Morris
Kelmscott House
Upper Mall
Hammersmith

[1] Daniel Moncure Conway (1832–1907), pastor of the Unitarian Church in Washington. His strong anti-slavery views led to dismissal, and coming to England he became minister of the South Place Religious Society, Finsbury, an ultra liberal congregation, from 1863 to 1884. He and his wife were friends of the Pre-Raphaelite circle and he paid tribute to Mrs. Morris in his *Autobiography*. He delivered the address at the funerals of Oliver Madox Brown and of Ford Madox Brown.

Hamlet House, Hammersmith, a large handsome house where Conway lived and entertained liberally till 1878. See M. E. Burtis, *Moncure Conway*, 1952.

[2] See Letter 83.

Monday [12 April 1880]

110 My dear Janey,

I remember Friday was generally a day that suited you. Would Friday of this week suit? Of course I wd reckon on your staying the usual time—till abt 8.30 I think.

I am wanting to make drawings of your hands for the newly projected picture—'Tanto gentile e tanto onesta pare'. They wd take I suppose an hour and a half to make—hardly as much as 2 hours, and of course I wd manage to do them while you were lying down. I have made, with this view, slight sketches from nature, so that I could be sure of the action and not keep you changing. Were you to come on Friday at 3 instead of 4, there wd be more than time enough to make the sketches, or even after 4 it *could* be done but might be less comfortable.

The few who have seen this beginning think it will have a special charm for every one, and I think so too. You know I have but little work to show you—next to none indeed—so dont be disappointed. At any rate *I* shall see *you*.

Your affectionate
Gabriel

Dont look up any one else on the same day.
I dont like to be 'come on' to.
Let me know what you eat drink and avoid.
I suppose Friday doesn't happen to be a racing holiday or of that sort.

Mrs Wm Morris
Kelmscott House
Upper Mall
Hammersmith

Friday [30 April 1880]

111 My dear Janey,

I had half an idea that your silence must be owing to increase of illness, but was afraid to press your answer lest impracticability of writing on your part should awfully increase my anxiety. Truly if you live with open windows in this weather, what but influenza can ensue? Newsless, alas! am I. My good Mother wrote me a good and firmly indited letter on her birthday when the drawing (stuck in the book by Christina[1] to whom I had delivered it on the sly) had been revealed to her. Some one carried it off and photo'd it before it left me so I shall be able to endow you with one if worth your having. I think you look very like yourself now in the picture of Vanna, seated full length with a dangling foot, which, alas! I did from some one else.

A Birthday Sonnet

Murray has sent me some fine Italian street photos—chiefly from Siena—I wish I had always had them. He tells me that Mrs. Stillman had a sad fright about her youngest child whom the nurse carried off indefinitely, and Mrs. S. ran about half the night in the rain and was none the better for it. It seems the R.A. hangers have been making great havoc. Poor Arthur Hughes[2] his nephew son and daughter (certainly a gang of claimants for space) are all kicked out to solve the problem. I do so wish I had anything more to say, but I haven't, except that I shall be very glad as soon as it is possible for us to meet again.

> Your affectionate
> Gabriel

Let me know as soon as possible how you are again. Jenny puts Cheyne *Row* instead of *Walk*.

Mrs Wm Morris
Kelmscott House
Upper Mall Hammersmith

---

[1] i.e. in Main's *Sonnets*. See Letter 90.

[2] Arthur Hughes (1832–1915). Associated with the Pre-Raphaelites; he illustrated Christina Rossetti's *Sing Song*, 1872. *April Love* in the Tate Gallery and *Home from Sea* in the Ashmolean Museum are two of his best-known pictures.

Arthur F. Hughes (1878–1914), his son, exhibited landscape and domestic scenes at the R.A. and Watercolour Society. Arthur R. Hughes (1851–1914), his nephew, friend of Holman Hunt, was a Vice-President of the Royal Institute of Painters in Water Colour. He exhibited at the R.A. and in continental exhibitions.

Sunday [16 May 1880]

112 My dear Janey,

News, alas! is dearthly with me too, except the startling fact that I have turned dealer! i.e. to the extent of selling that Botticelli portrait[1] to Const. Ionides for 300 guineas. He fancied it much, so I didn't refuse. He was dining with me, and Aleco with him, on Tuesday last. He is a Briton and no mistake—his being Greek must be a matter of business. Aleco did not seem to me in the best of health, but both were extremely friendly. The idea of selling pictures you dont have to paint is certainly a very great one. If M Angelo had once smelt blood in that way, we should never have had the Sixtine Chapel!

Are you at all up in Chatterton? His life and works are both of absorbing interest, and his rank as a poet the very highest. I never went in for him much till just now. Watts is 'doing' him for a new Selection of Poets by Arnold and Ward[2], and I am contributing a sonnet on him to Watt's article—also helping with C's text which is a teaser—so much older than antiquity! I shall be sending you the dividend.

Your affec: D G R

P.S. I have got the frames for your 2 drawings. The picture is framed with the 2 predella subjects and looks fine.

Mrs Wm Morris
Kelmscott House
Upper Mall
Hammersmith

[1] See Letter 71.
[2] *The English Poets*, edited by T. H. Ward, 1880. Matthew Arnold contributed the General Introduction on 'The Study of Poetry' and the essay on Gray. The essay on Chatterton was written by W. Theodore Watts but it did not include the Rossetti sonnet. This appeared in the set on 'Five English Poets' in the *Collected Works*, ed. W. M. Rossetti in 1890.

Chatterton was a late enthusiasm of Rossetti's, and his later letters make clear how much he contributed to Watts's article in Ward's *Poets*.

Monday [14 June 1880]

113 My dear Janey,

I shall be glad when you can let me know how you are and what are your plans. I'm afraid I wrote disconsolately and stupidly last time. I still have the replica here, and must hope you will see it yet but am much impeded by the alteration in the Vanna, and the room most awfully blocked up. I enclose a letter from Mary Stillman showing what a Monster her William is. I have told her in reply that he ought to encounter Scylla and Charybdis, Polyphemus's Cave and everything else, and find no Penelope when he gets back. The swollen face she speaks of was caught in running after her baby in the rain all night. I told her I knew all about it. She really is too great a fool to him.

Lucy the Lovely[1] has just been here with William. Her Papa will have to pay some £100 to shore up his wall which is toppling over the Parish, and her Mamma has cut her hand very badly— in opening a bottle! The last I must say is not exact. Brown was opening the bottle and Emma seeing the corkscrew slip jumped forward lest he shd hurt himself and cut her hand, the bottle breaking. She is getting over it, but the cut was serious.

> Your affectionate
> Gabriel

Poor Mary S. does not mention that S. went wandering off with another Yankee, leaving said Yank's sick wife on her hands.

Mrs Wm Morris
Kelmscott House
Upper Mall
Hammersmith

---

[1] William Michael Rossetti married Lucy, daughter of Ford Madox Brown by his first wife, in 1874. A portrait drawing by Rossetti given as a wedding present is in the possession of her grand-daughter Mrs. Roderic O'Conor (S.454).

Thursday [8 July 1880]   **114**

My dearest Janey,

The account you give of yourself is not very brilliant, but then it might be worse. I dont understand *why* Richmond[1] is such a very funny dog. Does he tell many lies, or is it the stupidity of his pictures that makes you laugh? Davies is an honest fellow, and was smit of a heap when he first saw you in a gallery lately.

Will Wdy of next week suit you for coming here, *from* and *to* usual hours? I still have the large picture of Graham's—the replica I mean. The *Vanna* picture has quite a finished look now but is as yet unframed, nor is it really near a finish as to colour and tone. But I fear I shall have to change the name and call it perhaps *The Day Dream*, reserving the other title for another of the series. Since I painted the Spring leaves, the picture has undergone much remodelling; and though it is a fact that many of the largest leaves were on the tree together with the smallest, still it looks very full in leaf for a spring-tree, and I think the snow-drops will not do with it. I have removed them but not substituted another flower yet, and really almost think I may have to put off the flowers to the early part of next year—i.e. if I live (and the picture too, one may say I suppose if Hunt is to be trusted.) I don't know if Constantine is still in town. Do you? I have written him for another instalment, but not heard as yet.

Your affectionate

Gabriel

Mrs Wm Morris
Kelmscott House
Upper Mall
Hammersmith

[1] William Blake Richmond (1842–1921), painter of portraits and classical subjects. Friend and keen admirer of Ruskin and the Pre-Raphaelites. Executed decorative scheme in St. Paul's Cathedral. Slade Professor of Fine Art at Oxford in succession to Ruskin. K.C.B. 1897. See A. M. W. Stirling, *The Richmond Papers*, 1926.

Monday [19 July 1880]

115 My dearest Janey,

I have got the head in again safely, but must now defer further work on it for a week or two till it is quite dry. It has I am sure more vitality and importance than before.

I have come to the conclusion that a wild honeysuckle of the slight white and yellow order might stand for the flower. It seems to be longer in all the year round than anything else. Have you anything of the sort. If not, I think I know of a little boy who could be suborned to search for one.

I feel as if I did not get nearly enough of you last visit, though no doubt I seemed as dull as possible. Wont you come again. I saw you take a position while lying down which I think you could retain by intervals for me to make a drawing. Such a position as I last tried is apt to push the face out of shape with the pillows. When could you come again? Tuesday Wdy and Friday this week are engaged with me I believe.

Your most affec-
Gabriel

Mrs Wm Morris
Kelmscott House
Upper Mall
Hammersmith

Sunday [1 August 1880]   116

My dear Janey,

It was very sweet of you to send these sweet honeysuckles. I have painted one today, but dont know whether it's right yet. I have been a good deal out of sorts since I saw you and much troubled abt the head in the picture, but fancy it is at any rate better than the former one. As luck deserts one, one feels power may desert one too and that one may not be doing one's best as of old. I wish I had a shop and could put pictures in the window and price them lower every day till they sold for something.

I am expecting the frame of The Day Dream (for so I now call the ci-devant Vanna) in little more than a week now. You must come and see it framed when it will look quite another thing. I believe it is really equal to any work of mine, but I have never held back so much before, having altered the whole figure first and then repainted the head.

Your affectionate
Gabriel

Mrs Wm Morris
Kelmscott House
Upper Mall
Hammersmith

Friday [3 September 1880]   117

My dear Janey,

I will set about the ballad[1] copy as soon as may be.

In advising you to make 'tracks in time for Crom Price's' I merely meant that, as you had so pleasant an experience of his household before, you might (shd you want further change) go there again this year. In connection with what you say of the ballad you add 'I know that life wd be simply unendurable now if it were not for those who are merely friends.' Is this, dear Janey, the sweet shadow of reproach which you permit yourself less for my neglect of this trifling thing than for all the sorrow which I know that my isolation brings to you? I cannot fully explain the causes which make it impossible for me to act otherwise. One of them is the continual conviction that, if I make an appointment with you, I shall be far from being the only sufferer by my own gloom and blackness. If at your house, to all but you I shd be intolerable,—where, you have sometimes found it impossible to help telling me, however gently, of my unfitness for intercourse. However, I will trust at any rate to show you the picture, which Constantine asked me to retain till nigh the close of the year. I am now getting on with La Pia² which comes very well.

I wish I could create news. It wd be worse than useless to tell you that Gladstone had hanged himself: the river is too near at Kelmscott for such tidings to be safe. The only friend who besides Watts visits me steadily is Shields,³ and of him you know so little that tidings of him wd have no meaning. He has (as perhaps you know) married a girl young enough to be his daughter, with lots of golden hair but no brains under it and no wish to learn. The situation is a sad mistake. I have the satisfaction of returning the true friendship he has shown me for several years past by coaching him in systematic oil-painting which he now begins to understand for the first time, having hitherto done only water colour. I believe it will soon be likely to make quite a new career, as he already has buyers in view. He is painting here a very beautiful 'Mary Magdalene' looking into the empty sepulchre. Its companion picture is to be an admirably designed Lazarus bursting from the tomb and graveclothes. This figure is really as fine a thing as I have seen. He was telling me an inconceivable story of Guy Fawkes day in Lancashire. At one time he was renting about half of a magnificent but neglected mansion called Ordsall Hall at some distance from Manchester which afforded him a spacious studio. It appears that Harrison Ainsworth had chosen this house (quite without authority) as the abode of Guy Fawkes in his novel. This led to a showman renting the free part of the Hall and advertising it far and wide as the abode of Guy—although hordes of Lancashire roughs overran the premises from all quarters and were far from perceiving any distinction between Shields' part and the showman's. He had numerous skirmishes with them, generally resulting in an irresistable rain of brickbats, and on one occasion his wife fired off a gun at them

La Pia de' Tolomei

from the window and did succeed in scattering the foe. The district was out of police range, yet Shields was constantly going round to the chief constable of the neighbourhood who sent detectives from time to time but at last said half out of patience 'Sir, you are the most troublesome man in my district' to which S. replied 'Sir I am the most troubled man in your district.' He had long gone about with a bull-dog when at last Guy Fawkes day came round, and a special jollifica-tion was to be held, bonfire and all, by the showman and his friends outside the hall. The luckless S. thought he wd have a lark with them. The showman had spread a report that Guy's ghost haunted the place, and half believed it himself. Accordingly S. got himself up in the fullest fig for the character, having constructed a matchless mask, rolled himself hermetically in a railway rug, stuck on a comical hat, and gripped a lanthorn. In this figure, unknown to his wife, he sallied towards the bonfire. Unhappily he had forgotten that there was a well in the path uncovered save by a frail plank. The moment his foot touched this, in he went but fortunately it was not deeper than his own stature. However his costume became so saturated with water and the weight of it was such that extrication was impossible and he was soon fain to shriek his wife's name at the top of his voice. She heard and came to his assistance and eventually got him out without the showman's gang having twigged the incident. His drowned-rat condition you may imagine.

I am glad to hear for the first time a favouring account of Mrs Lewes.[4] She is a reminiscence of my earliest years, when I (a boy of 10 or so) knew her (a very handsome good-natured girl of some 17 or 18 I suppose) in the house of her father, Swynfen Jervis M.P. a radical member of those days and a very cultivated scholar. I remember Lewes also as tutor in the house. I still have a hapless recollection of my perturbed state of bashfulness when Agnes Jervis goodnaturedly tried to make me dance with her. I never could believe that she was likely to be quite in the wrong, when her husband was such a horrid fellow as I always thought Lewes. Why he shd have left her, doubtless still young and handsome, it is nevertheless difficult to understand. Of course you know the report was that she took up with the only man to be found who was uglier than Lewes—viz Thornton Hunt, whatever may be the case, my remembrances of her assure me that she is a good soul.

I had met Lewes in Bohemian Circles before the catastrophe, and always thought him a monster of physical ugliness and mental showiness in those days.

You remember my sending you a lecture on my poetry by a young Liverpool man named Caine. He has been in town for a few days and looked me up. I liked him much. It seems he is a henchman in some way of Top's Ancient Monument Society. He told me rather a good story of a meeting where some pretentious architect said that if the Society expostulated with him in some job of demolition he shd consider them worthy of less respect than if they dated from Colney Hatch. This being an objection to some speech of Caine's, it devolved on C to turn the laugh against the objector (who had raised one) and he did so by quoting from my poem[5] Dante's reply to Can

117. 3 SEPTEMBER 1880

Grande and saying that the speaker's view did not surprise him, as
　　'tis man's ancient whim
　　That still his like seems good to him.'
Caine is a great wellwisher to me, and told me he was going to
rewrite his lecture on my work and unite it with others under the
title

Ruskin Keats and Rossetti

I told him to do nothing of the kind as Ruskin wd be sure to be
roused into his nasty venomous state which anything will excite now.
　　I have not yet finished up with poor Poe, but his miseries even
deepen as the book goes on. His only real fault seems to have been
gloom, telling mostly against his own happiness, but also rousing him
to intolerance of folly and pretention to somewhat too dangerous an
extent. As to his drink, that never really set in till quite late—probably
not altogether till after his wife's death who wd have died on straw
(whereon she lay in her illness, warmed by hugging a large cat) but
for the goodness of a Samaritan lady who brought them bedding.
　　I'll put over a page a sonnet for The Day Dream.

　　　　　　　　　　　　　　　　Your affectionate
　　　　　　　　　　　　　　　　Gabriel

　　　　　　　The Day Dream[6]
　The thronged boughs of the shadowy sycamore
　　Still fledge young leaflets half the summer through;
　　From when the robin 'gainst the unhidden blue
　Perched dark, till now, deep in the leafy core,
　The embowered throstles' urgent clangours gore
　　The Summer silence. Still the leaves come new
　　Yet never rose-sheathed as those which drew
　Their spiral tongues from spring-buds heretofore.

　Within the branching shade of Reverie
　Dreams even may spring till Autumn; yet none be
　　Like woman's budding day-dream spirit-fann'd
　Lo! Tow'rd deep skies, not deeper than her look,
　She dreams; till now on her forgotten book
　　Drops the forgotten blossom from her hand.

PS. You seem by what you say about Carr[7] to think him well-
disposed towards my work. I assure you this is otherwise.

Mrs Wm Morris
Kelmscott Manor Lechlade

[1] 'The White Ship'.

[2] *La Pia de' Tolomei*: commissioned by Leyland, now in the Museum of Art, University of Kansas. Signed and dated 1868–80. It was started with Mrs. Morris as model in 1868, laid aside, and only resumed in 1880. The subject, taken from the *Purgatorio*, is the lady who was imprisoned without cause by her husband in a fortress in the Maremma where she pined away and died. F. G. Stephens described the picture in the *Athenaeum*, 26 Feb. 1881. There is a detailed account of it by Prof. W. D. Paden in *The Register of the Museum of Art*, University of Kansas, Vol. II, No. I, November 1958. (S.207.)

[3] He married his model Cissy aged 16 in 1874. He had gone to live at Ordsall Old Hall near Manchester in 1872. The novel is Harrison Ainsworth's *Guy Fawkes*, 1841.

[4] Agnes, daughter of Swynfen Jervis, M.P. for Bridport, married J. H. Lewes in 1840. Lewes had been tutor in the Jervis family, and Gabriele Rossetti had given instruction in Italian there. Christina had stayed with them, and Rossetti made an imaginary sketch of her taking dictation from Swynfen Jervis who was something of a poet (S.590). In 1854 Lewes left his wife and lived with George Eliot till his death in 1878. There was no divorce and his lawful wife lived on till 1880.

[5] 'Dante at Verona'.

[6] There are variations in the text from the later version published in *Ballads and Sonnets, 1881*.

[7] J. Comyns Carr, who succeeded W. M. Rossetti as art critic of the *Academy* in 1878.

Monday [13 September 1880]

118 My dear Janey,

Aglaia did come to see The Day Dream and seemed greatly delighted with it. She suggested however (what I had already suspected myself) that the shadow of the face against sky was rather heavy; and in this respect as well as in some others I have greatly improved the face since. It is now much to my satisfaction. The La Pia also draws to a conclusion somewhat, though of course the getting together will take some time. I fancy all the Ionides family are away now—Constantine certainly is. Aglaia was as kindly as ever, and really seemed bent on getting the picture hung to advantage which it seems she will have to see to. There is a white dado—a horrid thing of course for pictures, so I told her the best thing would be to hang a piece of the silk with which the walls are covered below the base of the picture somewhat like an altar-cloth, and this she said she wd do.

I wish I had any material in mind from far or near for a letter this evening, but wd not delay just writing a line to show I had got yours. My next step must be to copy the ballad in default of amusing news. I gave Aglaia a copy of the sonnet for which she expressed great liking.

An article has come out in the Contemporary Review on *The Sonnet in England* by one J. A. Noble,[1] who winds up with a long panegyric on my effusions. This is curious in the very Review which long ago brought out the pseudonymous attack.[2]

I dont know anything further of little Murray, or whether he went away about the time I saw him. I certainly think his proceedings appear scattered, but I fancy he is ready enough to do any work he can get.

Ned Jones has written again proposing to come down and wanting me to fix an evening. I suppose I shall do so. I hear he is having his works engraved.

I am unusually stupid this evening, but really believe there is nothing in the cells of my brain even if I could succeed in searching them thoroughly.

Your affectionate
Gabriel

Mrs. Wm Morris
Kelmscott Manor
Lechlade

1 James Ashcroft Noble, 'The Sonnet in England', *Contemporary Review*, Vol. XXXVIII, September 1880. Noble was a friend of Hall Caine.
2 Robert Buchanan's article on 'The Fleshly School of Poetry' in the *Contemporary Review*, October 1871, written under the nom de plume Thomas Maitland.

Sunday [19 September 1880]¹ **119**

My dear Janey,

I wish it were as easy to send you a string of lies about every one in prose as to put a little truth into verse. It would be much more amusing, but everyone's history seems barren of results as far as I know it. I will try if Shields has any more romances like the November one.

I send you the ballad² at last. You will remember every incident as being exact, and I have managed to realize that all is in one or another chronicle, even to the little boy at the end.

I don't know whether Aglaia is still in town but suppose not. However I have written to ask her to take another look at the *Day Dream* if she is—I have so much improved the head by last work since she saw it. The picture is now quite done.

Your affectionate
Gabriel

Ned wrote and I made an appointment but he said notice was too short—proposed another day which found me engaged.

1 The text of this letter is D. and W. 2330.
2 'The White Ship'.

Tuesday [9 November 1880]

120   My dear Janey,

You will have guessed there was nothing to say, or you would have heard from me again ere this. I have been a good deal shaky and still am so. The weather is really an outrage—I cannot imagine how you manage to bear up against it. The La Pia picture is to the wall just now, as I want the frame, but shall have doubtless to take the picture up before the frame comes in, as the delays are so great with framemakers. The picture will come well however.

Old Brown and Emma dined here on Sunday with Wm and Lucy. Emma had on a wonderful bonnet which had cost 8 guineas and a half—so it wd seem Manchester is not quite crippling her husband. There has been an epistolary explanation between Ned Jones and William (Lucy joining in too) on the subject of Brown's coolness towards Ned, which I must say seems to me natural enough on various accounts. I dont know if Brown is aware of the letters that passed. The matter took its rise in Ned's coming here one day accidentally while Lucy was in the room, and her cutting him dead on the spot. Since then he spent an evening here very pleasantly but seemed to have so bad a cold that I should think he has hardly got rid of it yet.

You have not been letting anyone see the Greek Drama,[1] have you? I was surprised the other day by Murray's seeming to know all about it. That youth is getting cocky again on some small successes he has had lately.

I am getting on with a Beatrice[2] from one of your cartoons, but hardly know what I think of it yet.

Your affectionate
Gabriel

Mrs Wm Morris
Kelmscott House
Upper Mall
Hammersmith

[1] He can hardly mean Fitzgerald's translation of the *Agamemnon* mentioned in Letter 83, 20 Dec. 1879. In Letter 73, 15 Aug. 1879, he asks what she has done with the 'very condensed Greek drama'. This may be what he is referring to, but there is no clue as to what it is, or why Murray should not see it.
[2] The later version of *The Salutation of Beatrice*, 1880–1, unfinished at his death. Acquired by Leyland. Now in Museum of Art, Toledo, Ohio (S.260).

My dear Janey,

I dare say I shall hear from you anon in answer to my last. Meanwhile I take up a pen, like the hook of the Parisian rag-picker, to grope for scraps of news.

I may first answer what you said about Ned and Brown. The grievance, I believe, is not at all as to the Greek matter, which wd now be ridiculous, but partly on account of the privation of income which B. suffered from loss of cartoon work, partly on account of the ridicule with which Ned has for years—not in the least maliciously but very pertinaciously and very thoughtlessly pursued Brown —and partly on account of the very marked indifference which poor Nolly's undoubted genius met with from the same quarter. I must say I cannot think the feeling quite causeless on Brown's part. As for Lucy, her feeling is merely on his account. However I hope matters may be somewhat mended by their correspondence. I may tell you a tale of a wonderful Yankee Poetess named Virginia Vaughan,[1] whose book Top I suppose must have received. It is (I am told by Wm who got it sent him) a Dramatic Trilogy relating to Italian patriotism. The first Act passes in Heaven, where a deceased Italian patriot is made a good deal of. The second is on Earth, where Mazzini during the siege of Rome, makes a good deal of that subject in Soliloquies etc. The third is in some sublimated sphere where everything goes right of itself.

The day before Wm told me all this, Leyland had looked in and informed me that he received a long letter from the same lady, saying that she forwarded him the work, and that her excuse for so doing was that she had once met him in the society of Mr Whistler, whom however she had since discovered to be a mass of egotism. She then went on to describe minutely the scope of her work, and to say it was deserving of the utmost attention. Leyland (who hates poetry more than anything) replied that he was then in Liverpool and that the work had no doubt arrived at his London address; and that it was equally certain that it would gratify him greatly to peruse it.

A day or two after, he got another letter of 16 pages, in which the lady proceeded to give an autobiography of herself, as having been nursed in the lap of luxury as the heiress of a South American[2] family whose possessions however were all swept away by the war so that she was now taking refuge under the pinions of poetry. She then continued:—'And now Mr Leyland, I must let you know what is the favour I have to ask of you.' This was that L. should lend her a large sum of money, the security being the copyright of her poem! She then gave various opinions of the Great (unknown however to Leyland) as to the vast merit of the work and its safety as an investment, concluding with that of some Great creature who said that he never thought much of Milton's sonnets, but that the one at the opening of her work was a masterpiece. Of course L. answered in 3 lines that he did not seem to see it. As for having met her, he says he does not believe he ever did so.

This is a long rigmarole which you may deem hardly worth the telling. I wish I had news nearer home.

Little Murray looks in now and then. He seems to have housed his sister with his wife in Italy, and is really a meritorious though cocky little cove. He told me an extraordinary story which you may perhaps have heard, but which seems to show both how he learned Italian and how he became a dealer. When at Siena, as yet unmarried and ignorant of Italian he was passing one of the gates and heard a man and woman go by talking English. He accosted the man thinking they were probably English servants, but found the man was an Italian and his wife English. Eventually the man came to him as a servant, leaving his wife on one side for the time it wd seem. The man's story was curious. He had been a mason at Certaldo, and wishing to better himself left his small native place and made his way to France where he worked as a mason and learned French. He then went on to England where he found the language very difficult, but managed to get a fellow workman who had learnt English to help him. He then read through the whole of Walker's pronouncing Dictionary and eventually (Murray says) spoke like a native. He then fell in with a woman who had a small annuity and married her. This man, seeing that Murray cared for nothing but pictures used, while M. was painting in the galleries, to hang about street corners and talk to passers-by, managing to turn the conversation on pictures. Thus he used to hear of wonderful bargains in corners and induced Murray to go and see some. Generally M. took a long walk which resulted in some old woman ushering him into her bedroom and showing him a vile daub; but eventually treasures began to turn up and he was the gainer by them.

Perhaps you may have seen in the papers the following tale of Howell the Great. It seems that a Miss Westbrook,[3] an amateur artist, brought an action against him for recovery of 3 pictures or their value which was stated as £50. Miss Westbrook was an eminent exhibitor and was in the habit of employing Miss Corder, at the rate of a guinea an hour, to touch up her pictures before they were sent in. She had lodged at Miss C's studio 3 pictures to be sent to the R.A. Howell called and said he would see about it, and took them off— doubtless to Attenborough's but this did not transpire. He then said they were accepted at the R.A. where however Miss. W. failed to find them. He then professed that 2 other exhibitions in succession had accepted them, but they never became visible on the walls. He then put in some books as part payment which he valued at 12 guineas but which the Judge said he could buy for 3s/9d. A frame was also claimed as an asset. The result I believe is that H. must either restore the pictures or pay the value claimed with costs. I suppose he will somehow fish them out of Attenborough's and deliver them. Neither he nor Corder put in an appearance but were represented by a lawyer on whom the Judge was rather severe.

I fear this is my last item of news, and it may be no news after all.

Your affectionate
Gabriel

I'll transcribe a Sonnet or two. I need not say who is the model of the 2nd.

Mrs. Wm Morris
Kelmscott House
Upper Mall
Hammersmith

---

[1] *The New Era.* A dramatic poem by Virginia Vaughan, 1880. A grandiloquent blank-verse drama which, she explains, is 'a link between two other unwritten dramas which will discuss questions of most deep and vital significance, casting a new light on the whole subject of a future life and others of equal significance'. She had previously published in Boston translations of several novels of George Sand.
[2] i.e. from the Southern States of U.S.A.
[3] Elizabeth T. Westbrook exhibited portraits regularly at the R.A. from 1873 to 1880.

Friday [26 November 1880]   **122**

My dear Janey,

I felt deeply the regard so deeply expressed in your last letter. I may claim to deserve it on the ground only of an equal regard—would I could say of any worthy result! The deep-seated basis of feeling, as expressed in that sonnet,[1] is as fresh and unchanged in me towards you as ever, though all else is withered and gone. This you wd never believe, but if life and fate had willed to link us together you wd have found true what you cannot think to be truth when—alas!—untried.

Ellis looked me up yesterday to talk of publishing. He thinks the best plan is to put the old and new together, and this is what I think. He seemed much inclined for picture buying but absolutely debarred by the hard times.

I have asked Watts to take a look at the Boltons, but think there must be some fag-end of lease or other inconvenience about it at such a rental. It is the house where Miss Herbert[2] (Mrs Crabb) lived for many years, and I had no idea she had left it. Perhaps she is dead.

Somebody said the other day that an exceptionally fine house with large garden is to let in your Mall. Is this so? What do you think they ask for any of those new red-brick houses (by no means of course equal to the large ones at the corner) along the embankment? Well, 700£ rent a year. Scott whose house[3] is likely to be pulled down looked at some and found this. And yet the old Scotchman boggles at a raised rent of 250£ or less on the Lawsons'[4] house which wd perfectly suit his needs. Of course if his present house comes down he will get great compensation, but this he professes to disdain, and says what he wants is his own house in his old age. No doubt he is sincere. The Lawsons are moving to Oakley Street.

I was extremely sorry to see lead pencil handwriting. But this weather is horribly changeable, and the warm worse than the cold. I myself have been by no means feeling well, and have made no great way with work.

Would you kindly send me back that *Contemporary*, as I believe I may have a need for it.

Your affectionate
Gabriel

Mrs. Wm Morris
Kelmscott House
Upper Mall
Hammersmith

---

[1] Probably the first sonnet entitled 'Herself' of the 'True Woman' group (Nos. 56, 57, 58), concluding the first part of *The House of Life*.

[2] Ruth Herbert, 'the beautiful Miss Herbert', first appeared at the Strand Theatre in 1855, then at the Olympic, and later at the St. James under her own management, where she played the heroine in *Lady Audley's Secret*. She was Rossetti's favourite 'stunner' between the period of Miss Siddal's failing health

and the dominance of Fanny Cornforth. He made many drawings of her in the year 1858–9, and she sat for the Magdalene in *Mary Magdalene at the Door of Simon the Pharisee*. She married Edward Crabb but separated from him. The house, No. 1 The Boltons, off the Brompton Road, was destroyed during World War II. See Virginia Surtees, 'Beauty and the Bird: a new Rossetti Drawing', *Burlington Magazine*, February 1973.

[3] Bellevue House where Bell Scott settled in 1870. It is still standing on Chelsea Embankment at the corner of Cheyne Walk and Beaufort Street.

[4] Cecil Gordon Lawson, landscape painter: he had for a time lived at 15 Cheyne Walk next door to Rossetti, and at other houses in Cheyne Walk. He is not recorded in Oakley Street.

Sunday **123**

My dear Gabriel,

I am sending you tomorrow an old blue cachemire gown, and a cloak that I thought might serve for the girl's dress in your picture, if not too dull in colour.

I want to hear from you again, I am feeling much stronger just now, and am getting quite excited about my journey. I start on Jan. 4. we go to Bordighiera on the Riviera, a place more sheltered than Oneglia was, I remember passing it, palm-trees grow out-of-doors.

Your affectionate

Janey

Monday [13 December 1880] **124**

My dear Janey,

It was most good of you to send the dress and cloak, but I ought to have mentioned when you first spoke of doing so, that I have been seeing to getting suitable things looked up, which shd be of a more festive character. I am succeeding in getting what I want, but your gift will come to be useful in some other way.

I was delighted to observe the revived tone of your letter and am sure the trip[1] must prove very beneficial. The Howards are good folk and I love them for being so careful of you.

I creep on with work, but nothing seems to get absolutely done, though several progress. Some day I must lend you the new edition of Blake's Life, which is really splendid in its get-up and illustrations, and of which I have just received a copy. William and I revised and augmented my share of the work.

As you were so kind in valuing the Sonnet I last sent, I send 2 more[2] on the same theme, forming a trio with which I intend to wind up the first part of the House of Life. This series now consists of 100 Sonnets (though I omit several of the M.S. ones) and forms 2 Parts viz:

> Part I   Youth and Change
> Part II   Change and Fate

I shall have nearly 50 Sonnets besides the House of Life ones.

Your affectionate
Gabriel

The *seer*[3] in the sonnet is Swedenborg, and the saying[4] a very fine one.

Mrs Wm Morris
Kelmscott House
Upper Mall
Hammersmith

[1] Mrs. Morris was leaving with the Howards to spend the winter months at Bordighera.
[2] Completing the 'True Woman' trio, Nos. LVI–LVIII.
[3] Emanuel Swedenborg (1688–1722), Swedish scientist and mystic. Gabriel Rossetti had used Swedenborg in his Dante studies and Dr. Garth Wilkinson the physician who had treated Lizzie Siddal in 1854 was a well-known Swedenborgian and translator of his works. Wilkinson also published a volume of poems, *Improvisations from the Spirit* (1857), which Rossetti in a letter to Watts called the 'bogy book'. A Life of Swedenborg was among Rossetti's books.
[4] 'If to grow old in Heaven is to grow young,
(As the Seer saw and said)'.
House of Life, LVIII.

Friday [17 December 1880][1]

125 My dear Janey,
    I hope you are not overworking as to preparation. This might bring on a breakdown.
    I am really going to get a new Volume out to be called *Poems Old and New*, but do not talk about it in the least, or there will be gossip paragraphs prematurely. Only I must get one long ballad[2] done—that on the death of James I of Scotland. Perhaps I told you that *The House of Life* now numbers 100 sonnets, and that I have forty-five besides as an extra series.
    I find to my bewilderment that the second half of No. II Sonnet had a repeated rhyme—*gave*. This made me alter the six lines, and I like them better now in every way.

> Lo! they are one. With wifely breast to breast
> And circling arms, she welcomes all command

Of love,—her soul to answering ardours fann'd:
Yet as morn springs or twilight sinks to rest,
Ah! who shall say she deems not loveliest
The hour of sisterly sweet hand-in-hand?

I haven't seen the poetic trash you speak of. I think you would do well not to look into such things at all.

Your affectionate
Gabriel

¹ This letter is from D. and W. 2362.
² 'The King's Tragedy'.

Kelmscott House, Upper Mall, Hammersmith. **126**
Saturday

My dear Gabriel,

It was most kind and thoughtful of you to write to prevent my anxiety, but I had not heard any reports of your illness. Aglaia had visited me the day before to wish me buon viaggio, but had not spoken of your being unwell. I hope and trust that you are better now than when you wrote last. As for me, I am in a state of excitement about my coming journey, so many things happen to delay it, I hear this morning that Mrs. Howard is very unwell, and consequently unable to leave so early as Tuesday, however I still expect to go some time next week—if not, I shall let you know when I know myself. Aglaia told me that Constantine was immensely proud of the picture.

Your affectionate
Janey

Kelmscott House, Upper Mall, Hammersmith. **127**
Tuesday

My dear Gabriel,

I have put off writing to you thinking that I should be able to state the exact day of my leaving, but really there are so many delays I begin to think that I shall not go at all—Mrs. Howard is still far from well, and has not yet fixed any day, so here I am still in an uncomfortable state of uncertainty.

Thanks for writing of yourself, I do not dare hope a very bright state of things for you during this horrible weather—I have not been out for days, and feel as if I never wish to go again, the talk of going to Italy has seemed a ghastly mockery the last few days—still I suppose that as soon as the sun shows itself, I shall show myself again.

I won't attempt to come, there would be no pleasure in meeting just now.

Your affectionate
Janey

P.S. I have just got a copy of Ebenezer Jones' poems—a different one it seems from the one you had.

Kelmscott House, Upper Mall, Hammersmith.
Saturday

128 My dear Gabriel,

I am really going on Monday to Dover, and shall cross next day—I should like to hear one word from you before then.

I heard more of Virginia Vaughan the other day, it seems that she has got to England and has fastened on to the Holidays. No doubt when they get her out of the house (they were complaining bitterly of her sticking qualities) she will try others.

Good bye once more I shall let you know how I get on as soon as possible.

Yours affectionately
Janey

Monday [24 January 1881]

129 My dear Janey,

I am rejoiced to hear of so favourable an outset to your journey. It is certainly a fact that the French are repulsively comfortable. That you have 3 separate rugs on your back it is also true that I can hardly believe, so sedulously uncomfortable are you in the habit of making yourself.

Whether you possess a progeny any longer I am not aware, as Stephens told me on Saturday that Jenny and May had taken Holly[1] to instruct him in the art of skating!

I wish I had any news of myself. I am snowed up and so is everyone else. There are but slight signs of a thaw as yet.

I write merely because I like to think your eye will rest on the writing. I can only hope that when I hear from you again and again write, I may have something to say.

Of what jumble respecting the localities of my native land my envelope may be guilty I do not venture to surmise.

Your affectionate
Gabriel.

Mrs William Morris
Poste Restante
Bordighera Riviera ponente
Italy

[1] Holman, son of F. G. Stephens, born 1868, godson of Holman Hunt.

My dear Janey,   4 Feb [1881] **130**

I have been getting anxious at not hearing from you since you wrote from Paris. This evening however Ned Jones tells me that he believes the news of you has been quite good all along. This has relieved me much, but I should like greatly to get a line.

You will be pleased to hear that I have sold that Blessed Damozel picture[1] to fair advantage, and that I am on my legs again in money matters. Now I can wait easily for other chances. The eternal *Found*[2] picture is really getting done!—the figures close upon finish. It reads like a tale of pre-existence.

Nothing happens to talk about. Nevertheless, in spite of my newslessness give me a word of your health and comfort.

Your affectionate
Gabriel

Poor O'Shaughnessy[3] has died almost suddenly. I dont know whether you knew him or not.

Mrs Morris
c/o the Honble George Howard
Bordighera Riviera del ponente
Italy

[1] 'The Blasted Damdozel' as he called it in a letter to Shields (D. and W. 2401). There are two versions. One commissioned by Wm. Graham in 1871 was finished in 1877, and is part of the Winthrop Bequest, Fogg Museum, Harvard. A replica, reduced in size and with some variation, begun at the same time remained unsold till 1881 when Leyland bought it. This is in the Lady Lever Art Gallery, Port Sunlight (S.244).
[2] 'I have really resolved to take up that Calf picture'—letter to Shields, Jan. 1881 (D. and W. 2375). Begun in 1853 for Francis MacCracken but laid aside; commissioned by James Leathart in 1859 but again abandoned; finally restarted for Wm. Graham in 1880 it passed into his possession still unfinished on Rossetti's death. Now in the Bancroft Collection, Wilmington, U.S.A. (S.64).
[3] Arthur O'Shaughnessy (1844–81), Irish poet. Author of *An Epic of Women*, 1870; *Lays of France*, 1872; *Music and Moonlight*, 1874.

Villa Margherita Bordighera
2 February 1881

131   Your letter reached
without delay.

My dear Gabriel,

I am at last settled where I suppose I shall be during my stay in
Italy in the Howards house—at first we were in an Hotel uncomfortable enough, and I seriously thought of coming straight back to
England—then comparing the accounts of your weather with ours
here as it was last week, I found that I had reason to be thankful, and
stayed on, accompanying the Howards to their Villa on Monday.
I can't say that I am very well as yet, but the weather is perfect,
bright sunny and not cold, so that I get out every day and must hope
to get acclimatised shortly. We are only a few minutes walk from the
sea—where there are most accommodating rocks forming splendid
places for rest with wraps and cushions.

You ask about Jenny and May, I have neither with me, the invitation was for me only, and they stay to keep house for their Father.—
they are becoming good housekeepers, and I think it does them good
to be made responsible beings sometimes, they have had a fine time
skating lately, and I have no doubt have enjoyed themselves finely.

My surroundings here are most beautiful, olives, lemons, oranges
everywhere, blue mountains—blue sea, and such sunsets! Everything
is a picture in itself—numberless date-palms growing all about
out-of-doors, just now these look very odd, they are all tied up to
keep the young shoots straight for Easter.

We have a garden facing the south in a stream of sunlight, olive-
trees on the hills all around. I can sit or lie out in the middle of the day
in perfect comfort without getting the least cold, the only thing is
to get in before sunset.

I made an excursion to San Remo, the old town there is most
interesting, I should like to live there, if it were not for the invalids,
there is a beautiful old large house in the old part with a garden and
orange-trees and palms hanging over in a most ravishing way—I
think I shall get great good here, I feel ashamed when I remember
that you are all snowed-up or frozen.

Your affectionate Janey

Please write again before long.

My dear Janey,

Such good news of you is thoroughly rejoicing. I wish I had any of myself, but there is just the daily driblet of work and nothing more. I am still going on with the *Found* of which the figures are now all but done. I may tell you privately that Graham is behaving very badly—indeed unaccountably so; and this troubled me a good deal as to prospects till lately but I am now all right, and shall take no notice of him whatever but make a replica of this *Found* at once and sell it to some one else, letting the original stand over till he comes to his senses. Watts says that in law he has not a leg to stand on, and this I can see for myself.

The Courtesy of Topsy will be getting into the Percy Anecdotes[1] when reprinted. The other day Valpy[2] wrote me that he was busying himself about the decoration of some schools at Bath and could Mr Morris be got to give suggestions? I did not like to say he couldn't so I wrote a line to Top as to a bear notorious for the sorest of heads; but to my perfect stupefaction got a reply to the effect that he had written to Valpy requesting plans of his schools, on receiving which he wd draw out a scheme of decoration gratuitously!!! What is happening to Top? His wrap-rascals[3] must for the future be made with a case for his wings.

Lo! I had to write again to Top, but my second missive, I misdoubt me was received less angelically. It accompanied a *memento* of O'Shaughnessy (being V. Hugo's longwinded poem *Le Pape*,) which was left here for Top by a cousin of O's. The conjunction of a brother bard, a French deity, and the call to write a note of sympathy, must I think have mingled a few strong expressions with the angelic strains now habitual.

O'Shaughnessy was certainly not inspiring, poor fellow, as a companion. He had a particular *Ah!* which served for recognition of most speeches addressed to him. It is related that Nettleship, (who has erected himself as that brother's keeper) once, at the close of an evening party, drew O'S aside and said to him 'When you were conversing with those ladies, did I hear you say *Ah!*?' The reply being that it might perhaps have been heard, N. rejoined, 'Will you tell me then *why* you said "Ah!"?' History goes no further.

Ned was here the other evening. His style in conversation is getting beyond the pussy-cat and attaining the dicky-bird. No doubt you know that he has bought a mansion near Brighton.[4] He appears to be culminating. I shall finish very soon, when I take it up, The *Salutation of Beatrice*,[5] which I began from one of your cartoons. It seems to enchant every one who sees it.

Affectionately yours
Gabriel

By the bye, my own memento of O'S is a huge folio of lithographed sketches from the *Raven*,[6] by a French idiot named Manet, who certainly must be the greatest and most conceited ass who ever lived. A copy shd be bought for every hypocondriacal Ward in Lunatic Asylums. To view it without a guffaw is impossible.

Mrs. Morris
c/o George Howard Esq.
Villa Margherita
Bordighera Italy

[1] *The Percy Anecdotes* by Sholto and Reuben Percy, 40 parts in 20 vols., London, 1820–3. The aim of this collection of moral anecdotes designed for family reading was 'to combine instruction with amusement'. During the four years of its publication it had a wide popular circulation. The pseudonymous authors were Joseph Clinton Robertson and Thomas Byerley. The title was taken from the Percy Coffee House in Rathbone Place where they met to discuss material.
[2] Valpy had retired to Bath in 1878 which was the occasion of his returning *Dante's Dream* to Rossetti.
[3] Archaic term for loose overcoat.
[4] From 1867 Burne-Jones lived at The Grange, North End Road, Fulham, a house once owned by the novelist Samuel Richardson. In 1880 he bought a small house at Rottingdean which he later enlarged. It became his favourite residence. It was called North End House. See Angela Thirkell, *Three Houses*, 1931.
[5] See Letter 120.
[6] *Edgar Allan Poe—Le Corbeau, traduction de Stéphan Mallarmé*, Paris 1875. Folio with text in French and English and four full-page lithographs by Edouard Manet. This memento was the presentation copy from Manet to O'Shaughnessy and was among the books at 16 Cheyne Walk sold after Rossetti's death.
   Rossetti's detestation of Manet and other artists 'of this incredible new French School' dates from his visit to Paris in 1864. A letter to his mother gives his impressions (D. and W. 563). Here he has perhaps not forgotten that he himself had made Poe's *Raven* the subject of an early drawing (S.19B).

Sunday [6 March 1881]

133 My dear Janey,

I have been rather expecting to hear since I last wrote you, but do not allow anxiety to get the better of me lest it shd become too serious as it is apt to do. I shd be very glad to know how you are, and suppose you cannot have returned or I must have heard of it.

Things have looked a little brighter lately in the picture world. Ionides seems disposed to buy again I think, and Tebbs[1] came here with the good merry Emily and bought 2 of your drawings—a larger one and a head (not the best) for 200 guineas jointly. I really was grieved to part with them, but times are serious. Constantine has bought at the Millais exhibition the old picture of *Isabella*.[2] I dont know what he gave, but I suppose nothing monstrous, as the much finer *Carpenter's Shop* sold at Christies lately for £450.

Top's view of the O'Shaughnessy bequest was so unnaturally courteous that I was compelled to address to him a serious remonstrance and warning. I hope he may yet return to his old Adam.

I have written a long ballad[3] on the murder of James the First of Scotland, which is probably the best thing I ever did.

Your affectionate
Gabriel

Mrs Morris
c/o George Howard Esq
Villa Margherita Bordighera Italy

[1] Henry Vertue Tebbs, solicitor and friend of Rossetti. With Howell he assisted at the disinterment in Highgate Cemetery in 1869. The drawings he bought were probably studies for *Astarte Syriaca* (S.249B) and for *La Donna della Finestra* (S.255A). Rossetti also did a portrait drawing of his wife: and he owned an early watercolour *Carlisle Wall* which, in accordance with his daughter's wish, is now in the Ashmolean Museum.
[2] *Lorenzo and Isabella*, painted in 1848 when Millais was 20. It passed through various hands till bought by Constantine Ionides. Sold by him 1883, and acquired by Walker Art Gallery, Liverpool, 1884.
[3] 'The King's Tragedy'.

Villa Margherita Bordighera **134**
5 March 1881

My dear Gabriel,

I have not been very well lately, and have put aside writing as much as possible, I got a slight attack of fever, as every one does I believe in Italy, it has passed away completely, but still I am weakened by it; our weather is damp just now which I never like, But why should I murmur to you of bad weather, who are in the most horrible surroundings of dirty snow in London: I expect to stay here about three weeks longer, and then I think I shall go on to Florence for about a fortnight before returning to England. Will you give me Mary Stillman's address? I should like to call on her and see her happy face in her Florentine home, I have never seen her children either.

I can't remember which of the cartoons you allude to as painting. Was it a profile? I knew that Ned had a little place at Brighton, and a very wise thing too, the sea-air is the only thing that braces up the nerves. I wish that I had such a place, and that Kelmscott was off my hands—but they are all obstinate and love it more than ever.

I am having a very pleasant time here, I like being among the babies, they are all nice and well-mannered and give me no trouble, Mary has a good notion of housekeeping, and only appeals to me from time to time, she is a sweet loveable girl and though only 16, has little of the child about her—Mrs. Howard comes back shortly now that they have gained the Election—but he will have to stay in London till the end of the Session.

I suppose if I go to Florence, I must have a look at little Murray, though I thought him more conceited than ever when he was in London last, and insufferably dirty—you might give me his address too when writing.

Your affectionate
Janey

Thursday [March 1881]

135   My dear Janey,

I was very glad to hear from you and to know that you are better again. I write a line only (having really no news) to give addresses

Mrs Stillman
14 Via Alfieri

Murray
108 Via de Serragli

I must tell you however that Murray has since moved, though his address wd doubtless be ascertainable as above.

I have had a photo taken from the larger drawing sold to Tebbs— also from the hands in the picture of La Pia and Mnemosyne[1] sold to Leyland.

Constantine was here and seemed quite in a mood to buy again— much disappointed that Mnemosyne was sold. I think Aglaia keeps him up to the mark, which is very good of her. He has bought Millais' early picture of Isabella out of the Exhibition now open in Bond Street.

Your affectionate
Gabriel

Mrs Morris
c/o George Howard Esq
Villa Margherita Bordighera

---

[1] In 1876 Rossetti was at work transforming a first version of the *Astarte* into 'a smaller and different thing which may bring grist to the mill'. It was offered to C. E. Fry as *Ricordanza* or *Memory* but remained unsold till purchased by Leyland in 1881. Now in the Bancroft Collection, Wilmington, U.S.A.

alutation of Beatrice

Mnemosyne

31 March [1881]

136 My dear Janey,

I write chiefly because you suggested it but also to say how glad I am you have benefited by your trip.

I have been a good deal put about and got little done. La Pia is still here and looks my best work. I have finished the figures in *Found*. The other day I received a deputation of the Town Council of Liverpool who are entertaining an idea of buying my large picture[1] for their permanent Gallery. At any rate they wd have room to hang it, but I dare say the affair will come to nothing, though the chairman, who was one of those who came, is certainly very appreciative and favorable.

I am printing my new vol. with Ellis,[2] who gives the same terms as formerly for it. After that, I shall reprint the old one—always if I live.

Your affectionate
Gabriel

Mrs Wm Morris
c/o Miss Cobden
18 Via Lamarmora
Florence
Italy

---

[1] *Dante's Dream* was first painted for Ellen Heaton in watercolour in 1856. This version was bequeathed by her descendants to the Tate Gallery.

The oil painting, Rossetti's largest picture ($83'' \times 125''$), was painted for Wm. Graham and finished in 1871. As it exceeded the dimensions he had indicated and was too large to hang advantageously in his house Graham returned it in exchange for a smaller replica. This is now in the Dundee City Art Gallery. The large picture was bought by Valpy in 1873 and he returned it for sale when he removed to Bath in 1878, with an arrangement to get equivalent value in smaller works. Finally through the efforts of Hall Caine it was acquired by the Corporation of Liverpool for £1,550 in 1881.

[2] Ellis published *Ballads and Sonnets*, 1881, and *Poems, New Edition*, 1881, a reprint of *Poems*, 1870, with some additions but omitting *The House of Life*.

13 April [1881]

137 My dear Janey,

I have received a letter of yours with the date of March 5. The postmark is Firenze 7-4-81. I dont know if an answer will reach you and indeed there is no special call to answer for the sake of my news.

I had my mother and sister staying here last week, and enjoyed their company much. My mother has been perfectly well through all the cold weather, and still is so. I have got nearly 100 pages of my new vol: in print, and the whole of it is ready. It will make about 300 pages, rather widely printed however.

Leyland has bought the Beatrice which I am painting from one of your cartoons, and this quite sets me going. Indeed things look well as far as the present goes. I am wanting much to begin a large picture, now that I am fairly in funds.

Your affectionate
Gabriel

Mrs Morris
c/o Mrs Stillman
14 Via Alfieri
Florence
Italy

16 Cheyne Walk **138**
28 April [1881]

My dear Janey,

I have been wondering why I have not heard from you, after writing to Mrs Stillman's address I should think 10 days ago. I try in such cases of delay to avoid being over-anxious, but it is not easy. I write again solely on this account, having no news. The Liverpool question as to the big picture is still pending. I have had a photo of it taken at their request and sent them one, but it is dark and blurry —still looks like a fine picture to any artist's eye.

I was very glad to hear so good an account from you of Mrs Stillman and her family. I always thought them extremely charming girls, and Lisa was almost grown up when last I saw her. Please give to all my very best regards, if you are still with them.

Yours affectionately
Gabriel

Mrs Morris
c/o Mrs Stillman
14 Via Alfieri
Florence Italy

Thursday [14 July 1881] **139**

My dear Janey,

After your former letter, I had naturally nourished some hopes of seeing you, and your last is therefore infinitely the more discouraging. I fear you will never get right in this heat,—it suffocates me absolutely.

In a recent letter of yours you said you felt that going abroad wd set you up at any moment. I am enclosing the dividend, and wish to tell you that there are about 300£ of your money still *immediately* available. More of what I owe you should come as soon as you needed it, unless my chances failed altogether, of which there seem to be no special signs now. I fancy some parts of Switzerland wd be delicious now; or you might take better advice than mine. What you would absolutely need wd be a travelling maid who spoke languages fairly. This it would not be very difficult to attain—perhaps Aglaia might know of one. Lucy has a housemaid just now who speaks French and Italian perfectly—having lived several years in Italy. I wish she could be nobbled, but I suppose that wd not be practicable. I will speak to Watts at once about getting at the money.

All is desolation around me. The old trees are all lying across the garden; and you may [be] sure that even minor causes wd prevent my being very merry. But far above all and all-absorbing is anxiety on your account.

Your affectionate
Gabriel

Do not suppose for a moment that *I* am needing the money in question. This is absolutely not the case. Please one line to say this reaches safely. Other points you can defer for consideration.

Mrs Wm Morris
Kelmscott House
Upper Mall
Hammersmith

140   Write me
something

Monday [18 July 1881]

My dearest Janey,

Watts relieved my mind last night after seeing you. I had feared you might be quite prostrate when I did not hear from you. He perceived, however, how weak you are at present. Watts was enraptured with the enormous democratic obesity of Top. O for that final Cabinet Ministry which is to succeed the Cabinet d'aisance[1] of his early years!

Did you ever read Hogg's Life of Shelley?[2] If not, I will send it you, and you *must* roar, in spite of the heat and the devil himself.

I lately bought Baldinucci's History of Painting.[3] This is full of interesting lives, though chiefly dependent on anecdotical interest—the men most treated of being those subsequent to Vasari and not very interesting as painters. It is in beautiful old Italian type. I can lend you a vol. if you like. It is in 6 quarto vols.

A book of Italian translations[4] has been sent me, containing some of my things. Also a very good review of me in an Italian journal.

You must have heard me speak of one Caine. I think he is coming to live with me, which will make my life less solitary, as he has talent and conversation. It is possible I may be going with him to the neighbourhood of Keswick where he has been lately staying. He says it is there now breezy and cool!

I cannot get on with anything. I dare say you suspended operations as to that drapery after I expressed a possible intention of using another instead.

I heard today from Aglaia who says that this lovely weather makes her long for all sorts of delightful things that of course she shan't get.

Your most affectionate
Gabriel

Mrs Wm Morris
Kelmscott House
Upper Mall
Hammersmith

[1] Probable allusion to the three-seated privy at Kelmscott Manor.
[2] Thomas Jefferson Hogg (1792–1862), sent down from Oxford after the publication of Shelley's pamphlet *The Necessity of Atheism* in 1811. Two volumes of his unfinished *Life of Shelley* appeared 1858.
[3] This was among the books in the sale at 16 Cheyne Walk after Rossetti's death.
[4] *Poeti inglesi e tedeschi*, Florence, 1881. The translations were by Luigi Gamberale. See Rossetti's letter to his mother (D. and W. 2525) and to William Michael Rossetti (D. and W. 2526).

I enclose postage envelope
which you may not have

[20 July 1881]   141

My dearest Janey,

Your cheerful view of my taking a housemate cheers me also. Caine is a particularly good fellow. He wrote to me as an utter stranger some 3 years ago, enclosing a printed lecture on my Poetry which he had delivered and which I think you must have seen at the time. He was then and till now settled in Liverpool, but now means to try his fortune in London. On two occasions within the last year he has paid flying visits to London and made my acquaintance, and I much like him. He is 26 now, and a thorough enthusiast.

I send you the Italian journal. Please let me have it again, as my mother wd like to see it. The book of translations is 'not without merit' but not so good I think as the article, which pleases me by noticing some of the less dramatic poems which are generally overlooked. Indeed the insight shown by a foreigner into this class of English verse is very remarkable.

I will send you Hogg's Shelley.

Your affectionate
Gabriel

Mrs Wm Morris
Kelmscott House
Upper Mall, Hammersmith

Tuesday [26 July 1881]

142 My dearest Janey,

I am glad the Italian notice pleased you, for I thought it good also. I cannot conceive what you are going to do with yourself while this water-party is coming off. Do tell me. Another thing I want to know is how poor Jenny is. I hope her illness is not of the old kind.

I heard yesterday something inconceivable—that is, that Ned had gone to spend a week at the countryhouse of Lewis[1] the Police lawyer! I shd as soon have thought of his applying for a lodging in Newgate.

I shall be very very glad if at some time I can make a study of your hands for the Desdemona[2] which I am now trying to tackle—not with much result as yet.

I have stupidly forgotten as yet to send on Vol. 1 of Hogg's Shelley, but will be doing so immediately.

I dont think Mrs Webster will be at all to your taste.

Your affectionate
Gabriel

Mrs Wm Morris
Kelmscott House
Upper Mall, Hammersmith

[1] Sir George Henry Lewis (1833–1911), well-known society solicitor whose firm of Lewis and Lewis was concerned in many *causes célèbres* of the period. Created baronet in 1902. An intimate friend of Burne-Jones whose *Letters to Katie* (1925) were written to his daughter.
[2] *Desdemona's Death-Song*. The design was finished and various studies survive, but little work was done on the canvas (S.254).

Desdemona's Death Song

Wednesday [10 August 1881]

143 My dear Janey,
   You were quite right in not coming, but I got your letter not at 4 but at 7. I do not judge that you think of coming tomorrow as you do not say so. I am very seriously in need of the sitting. Do not come on any account till you feel you can do so safely, but do give me a few hours.

Your affectionate
Gabriel

Fix your own day. If tomorrow, I can manage as all is ready.

Mrs Morris
Kelmscott House
Upper Mall
Hammersmith

Tuesday [16 August 1881]

144 My dear Janey,
   I was certainly surprised to see your address, and also bitterly disappointed. You say 'on reading your letter I see' etc. Then did my poor letter remain unread till now? The picture must thus be turned to the wall. Of course the question of your health is paramount; but would a reclining posture while I draw your hands have affected it more than the same posture at home?—surely not more than a sudden journey and stoppage to see the water-party. Up to your last stay in Italy, you evinced the old deeply-prized interest in me and my doings,—even up to our last interview. I have not the least claim on your consideration; but if you withdraw it, it is the only one of many withdrawals which will go to my heart. The rest passed by unheeded. If you read this letter, do not answer harshly, for I cannot bear it.

Your affectionate
Gabriel

P.S. Of course it did not fail to occur to me whether you would again pass this isolated interval in town here; but I did not venture to think it in the least likely, particularly as Caine is now with me.

Mrs Morris
Kelmscott Manor House
Lechlade

Thursday [18 August 1881] **145**

My dear Janey,

Your letter is a great comfort to me, as the removal of your long interest in me would be the only thing I could not bear at all. When you can, will you tell me what is likely to be the length of your stay at Kelmscott, and when there is any likelihood of your sitting to me for the hands. Till then, the picture can make but little progress if any. I always have a regular sequence in the parts of a picture, and cannot get on unless the next piece is out of hand.

It is not unlikely—indeed I trust it is likely—that I may be going with Caine to Cumberland,[1] which is a neighbourhood he knows well. I find him good company, as he never talks Politics.

In opening an old cabinet which had been long locked up, I found those groups of your family and Ned Jones's. There are only 3 containing yourself. Two are not quite satisfactory, but one is divine.

Your affectionate
Gabriel

I shall not be going away in any case till early September.

Mrs. Wm Morris
Kelmscott Manor House
Lechlade

[1] Rossetti accompanied by Hall Caine and Fanny Cornforth was in the Lake District from 20 September till 17 October in a state of deep melancholy.

Sunday [4 September 1881] **146**

My dearest Janey,

You will be glad to hear that the purchase at Liverpool is now complete. Fifteen hundred guineas tumbling out of the elements will turn me round I hope and enable me to do some good thing.

Your sitting was most valuable and I have got in the arms and hands of Desdemona to my satisfaction. I do not expect to do more than finish these and the hair before I go away for a change, for this I still trust may be possible.

I hope you are benefiting now, and finding some occupation for time. Would you like me to send you the 2nd vol. of Hogg and a book by the Cowden Clarkes on Keats etc.?[1] I am reading gradually again the ponderous Boswell which however never flags.

Watts is in torpor on the sofa as I write this, but rouses himself with kind remembrances. Caine I find very good company for

social purposes. He is doing a Sonnet collection[2] which is so good as
to Preface and Notes that it is sure to prove a great success. It is going
to be printed and brought out in the most superb manner.

Your affectionate
Gabriel

Mrs Wm Morris
Kelmscott Manor House
Lechlade

[1] *Recollections of Writers* by Charles and Mary Cowden Clarke, 1878.
[2] *Sonnets of Three Centuries*, 1882.

Wednesday [14 September 1881]

147   My dear Janey,
  I am sending you the 2 books by Parcels Compy. If you get them
in time to send me the remainder of Boswell before Monday next
please do so. On that day I am likely to be leaving town. I will write
you from my destination when I exactly know it.

Your affectionate
Gabriel

Mrs Wm Morris
Kelmscott House
Upper Mall Hammersmith

Thursday [22 September 1881]

148   My dear Janey,
  Thanks abt the books but there was no hurry. I shall be very glad
to get them however. Walks here are hitherto under pelting rain. I
need not describe the country, as you know it. However no doubt I
shall benefit. Kelmscott is absolutely populous as compared with this
district, and excitements are not many. I have brought some painting
materials with me to begin replicas for the desolate Valpy, and shall
skurry them off. Caine is at this moment reclining on the sofa, and
occupied in the exhilarating task of realizing in Petrarch a table of
sonnet-arrangements, counting the rhymes but not understanding
the language! This is for his Sonnet collection. 'Moo-cows' here are
few and far between though not undiscoverable. The lodgings are
convenient and moderate (a small farm house—£2 10/– a week) and
the fare good. There are some beautiful points of scenery, but I never
could write a landscape letter.

186

I have changed my housekeeper at Chelsea, and got an old woman who was the very first servant I had when I went to that house 20 years ago. She is at any rate trustworthy and frugal. There is no chance of having anything to say here, yet I will write again if I hear from you how you are.

Your affectionate
Gabriel

Mrs Wm Morris
Kelmscott Manor
Lechlade

Monday [26 September 1881]　**149**

My dear Janey,
　Please send the Boswell (when possible) to me
Fisher Place
Fisher Ghyll
Vale of St. John
near Keswick.
I shall be going there this evening

In great haste
Your affec G.

Fisher Place Vale of St. John Keswick　**150**
Saturday [1 October 1881]

My dear Janey,
　Thanks for the books which arrived safely. I should have written again before this, but have been hoping to give a better report of myself than I can as yet do. I still continue in a state of much bodily weakness and exhaustion, though of course I take walks daily and have even climbed a mountain here when first I arrived, 1200 ft high. Many of the mountains however are much higher than this. I am convinced that the air here is not bracing enough for me—indeed one can scarcely light a fire, and all is soothing sunshine. We have had but 2 days of rain all along. I am thinking of going elsewhere eventually. Do you know anything of Malvern or any other place suitable?
　A dozen copies of my new book have been sent me. Do you like me to send one, and to what address? Or two, for yourself and Top? Tell me just what you wd prefer.

I am not quite without work here, as I am doing a replica of Proserpine[1] which is one of the pictures I have to deliver to Valpy in exchange for the large Dante. I get on fast and well with it.

I continue to hear good reports of the picture from Liverpool and the people there have acted very well all along.

Your affectionate
Gabriel

I saw the wretched Oscar Wilde book,[2] and glanced at it enough to see clearly what trash it is. Did Georgie say that Ned really admired it? If so he must be gone drivelling.

Mrs Morris
Kelmscott Manor
Lechlade

[1] The eighth version of the *Proserpine*. Done on a reduced scale for Valpy and finished at Birchington just before Rossetti's death. Now in Birmingham City Museum and Art Gallery (S.233. R.3).
[2] *Poems*, 1881. Wilde's first book. Hall Caine gives a rather different impression: 'A young poet, who was just then attracting attention by certain peculiarities of personal behaviour and a series of cartoons in which he was caricatured by Du Maurier in *Punch* sent Rossetti his first book of poems. . . . This was Oscar Wilde, and I remember Rossetti's quick recognition of the gifts that underlay a good deal of amusing affectation' (*Recollections of Rossetti*, 1928, p. 148).

APPENDIX I

Letters of Mrs. Morris unplaced
in the Rossetti Series

Kelmscott House, Upper Mall, Hammersmith.
Friday[1]

My dear Gabriel,

I am grieved if any words of mine made you unhappy in any way, I cannot weigh the exact meaning of every word before writing, nor can any human being foresee what construction you will put on the most ordinary phrasing, surely you know as every one else does what a violent influenza cold does for one's appearance, you have sometimes refused to be seen under such circumstances, and you must pardon a woman if she has the same dislike of being seen with a red nose and the rest.

I am now better, thanks about the medicine, but I will not begin any new kind till I have given the present one a fair chance, it has really strengthened me to some extent.

Now pray do not worry about trifles, I am looking to seeing you soon, and shall not forgive you if you vex yourself for nothing at all.

Always your affectionate

Janey

[1] It is uncertain where this letter fits into the Rossetti sequence and it is therefore put with the unplaced group.

Tuesday[1]

My dear Gabriel,

I came back to town last Wednesday and found your letter awaiting me—I ought to have written a line of acknowledgement before, but Alas! I got so unwell that I was forced to lie idle. I get out again now, having got more or less used to the noise and dirt of London. You spoke of sending me the book last week, it has not reached me yet, I mention this fearing some miscarriage, but perhaps you put off sending till your return to town.

I have a letter from Mary Stillman this morning, she expresses great regret at not having seen you, she leaves for Florence tomorrow —her husband goes back to the East after he has seen his family safe to Florence, it does not seem cheerful for her.

Yours affectionately
Janey

[1] Placing doubtful—possibly after return from visit to Cormell Price, Oct. 1879.

Kelmscott House, Upper Mall, Hammersmith.
Sunday[1]

My dear Gabriel,

I am a little anxious at not hearing a word from you, though I am conscious of the dearth of news.

When will you like another sitting? I shall go away to the sea again before very long for about a fortnight, I feel myself sinking down gradually as usual.

I hope to get just a line from you tomorrow.

Your affectionate
Janey

[1] Possibly after the visit to Hastings in 1880.

Kelmscott House, Upper Mall, Hammersmith.
Dec: 7:

My dear Gabriel,

Here are my big babies who were so little and comic not long since, tell me what you think of the likenesses, I don't consider them good, but then you know I am no judge, being the mother of the originals.

I am really vexed that I came in yesterday, I shall never do such a thing again, but I did so want to see for myself how you were—and I have no means of finding out unless I come—for my own part, I should only be too glad to see a truly friendly face when I am too unwell to go out, I only wished to cheer you if possible; pray forgive me if I made any other impression on your mind.

Always your affectionate
Janey

My dear Gabriel,

I will come Tuesday at 3 or half past though you did write me such a NASTY LETTER.

Your affectionate
Janey

Kelmscott House, Upper Mall, Hammersmith.
Wednesday

My dear Gabriel,

I will come tomorrow about 4 o'clock, as I intend to stay till 9, if not too long for you. Pray make no trouble about dinner, I can eat anything now.

Your affectionate
Janey

My dear Gabriel,   Wednesday

I will come about 12 o'clock then, but I can't, won't wait beyond 1 for my dinner, I can eat anything at that hour, no dainties mind. I can stay all the evening till 9 about, I shall have to call at Ned's on my way back to take up Jenny where she will spend the day. As to the tapestry Mrs. Wieland[1] offers you, it was not my work, I had some hand in one of the figures, the other was Bessie's, the two were mounted on a piece of brick-red serge with a comic tree, and tufts of grass at the feet.—they were our first rough attempts at the kind of work, I should hate to see the thing about again, it is worth nothing at all, and I can't bear to think of your *buying* anything of needlework.

Your affectionate
Janey

[1] Widow of Warington Taylor, manager of the Morris firm. Shortly after her husband's death in 1870 she married Walter Wieland. W. M. Rossetti was a trustee and executor of Taylor's will. For light on the part played by Mrs. Wieland while still the wife of Taylor see 'Morris, Rossetti, and Warington Taylor' by L. Le Bourgeois, *Notes and Queries*, March 1975.

My dear Gabriel,

Do not please prepare dinner for me tomorrow, I could not possibly stay to show my powers of indigestion, I shall leave you about 7 o'clock, and I will tell my cab to return for me.

Yours affectionately
Janey

APPENDIX II

A Fragment

The following letter which commences abruptly and ends without signature was printed by T. J. Wise in the Ashley Catalogue, vol. VII, pp. 16–17 in 1925, and is now part of the Ashley collection in the British Library—B.L. Ashley A 1964. Wise claimed that it was addressed by Rossetti to Swinburne and obviously written in 1872.

. . . Unless you think me quite without feeling, you must know what I felt on reading the first of all your letters that had any bitterness for me. You will let me answer your question. I apprehend nothing whatever from criticism, and Watts who knows the press all along considered it out of the question. The poems attacked have now taken their place in the language, and the Review which attacked them had quite lately an article in emphatic praise of the Sonnets, which were far more open to criticism and special application than those now added. However, though I can be certain as to my own mood, it is intolerable to have any uncertainty as to yours, or to think you incensed against me. Every new piece that is not quite colourless will be withdrawn, and the book postponed. . . .

At your own house I could not speak as here with certainty of privacy.

In a letter to the *Times Literary Supplement*, 16 Dec. 1949, Mrs. Troxell pointed out that Rossetti and Swinburne had parted company for ever before June 1872, and that this document cannot be earlier than 1880–1, since it refers to J. A. Noble's article 'The Sonnet in England' in the *Contemporary Review* which appeared in September 1880. Mrs. Troxell gave other reasons too for the late dating. Mrs. Rossetti Angeli followed with a letter supporting Mrs. Troxell and suggesting that it was a draft submitted to Watts for his opinion.

It seems that this is the draft of a letter to Janey who had expressed anxiety about the tone of certain new sonnets to be added to *The House of Life* in the forthcoming *Ballads and Sonnets*, 1881. See Letter 118.

APPENDIX III

Two letters from
Mrs. Morris to Ford Madox Brown
and to William Michael Rossetti
written at the time of
D. G. Rossetti's breakdown in 1872,
from the Troxell collection

15 Marine Parade
Thursday [June 1872][1]

Dear Mr. Brown,

Have you any fresh news? I had a letter from Mr. Scott last Friday, but have heard nothing since although I have written to him twice. I had such dreadful dreams last night. I can't rest today without trying all means to get news. I am to come back to town on Friday.

You asked me about a ring—Gabriel had several of mine to paint from, but I don't know which he had just when he fell ill. I had one of about the date you say with a red stone but it had blue enamel round it and I think couldn't be the one you spoke of.

With affectionate regards to all yours affectionately

Jane Morris

[1] Rossetti's breakdown took place on 2 June 1872. Janey's letter dates from an early stage of the illness. Brown took charge of Rossetti at his own home in Fitzroy Square from 17 June till the move on 21 June to Urrard House, Scotland, lent by William Graham.

Manor House
Augst. 15th. [1872][1]

Dear Mr. Rossetti,

I am writing to you at Dr. Hake's request to tell you what I think of Gabriel's letter—it showed no sign whatever of his late distressing illness, no one could have told he had been ill, I am quite hopeful about him now. I believe he will get perfectly well, if only he can be kept in Scotland or at least away from his work a sufficiently long time. I must tell you too that his letter was not of a gloomy nature,

I have had many from his hand of a far more depressing kind. With my kindest and most affectionate remembrances to your sister.

Believe me

Yours very sincerely

Jane Morris

[1] Rossetti's letter, which has not survived, was written from Trowan, on 12 August. At the end of September he returned to Kelmscott. The circumstances are fully explained and documented by W. E. Fredeman in his article, 'Prelude to the last decade. Dante Gabriel Rossetti in the summer of 1872', *Bulletin of the John Rylands Library*, Vol. 53, 1970–71.

Rossetti and Morris Group

D. G. Rossetti, self-portrait, 1870

D. G. Rossetti by Charles Keene *c.* 1880

William Morris
attributed to C. Fairfax-Murray, *c.* 1870

Mrs. Morris by Burne-Jones

Janey reading, Scalands 1870

Janey in old age at Kelmscott Manor

Sitters and Friends

Marie Spartali (Mrs. Stillman)

Maria Zambaco

Mrs. Crabbe (Ruth Herbert)

Aglaia Coronio

James Smetham, self-portrait

Theodore Watts–Dunton

Charles Augustus Howell by Frederick Sandys

Rosa Corder by Whistler
(Arrangement in Black and Brown)

Frederick R. Leyland by Whistler

Settings

The sitting room at 16 Cheyne Walk by H. Treffry Dunn with D.G.R. and Watts–Dunton

The drawing room,
Kelmscott House,
Hammersmith Mall

Cabinet painted by Burne-Jones
in the drawing room

The library at Kelmscott House

Mrs. Morris's room at Kelmscott House

Mrs. Morris' bedroom at Kelmscott House

Hammersmith Mall from the river, showing Kelmscott House (centre left)

Kelmscott Manor, Lechlade

Index

Academy, The, 35 and n.1, 160 n.7

Agamemnon, a tragedy taken from Aeschylus (E. Fitzgerald), 126 and 127 n.1, 162 n.1

Agnew's, 30, 74

Ainsworth, Harrison, 156, 160 n.4

Aldwick Lodge, Bognor, 146, 148 n.2

Alice in Wonderland (L. Carroll), 33 n.1

Allen, George, 89 and n.1, 104 and n.3, 105

Angeli, Helen Rossetti, vii, 15 n.8, 43 n.4, 92 n.1 to l.54, 123 n.1, 192

Arnold, Matthew, 17, 55 n.6, 152 and n.2

Arundel House, Percy Cross, Fulham, 47, 62, 63, 64 n.1, 65

Ashmolean Museum, Oxford, xviii, 15 n.8, 23 n.2, 100 n.3, 122 n.2, 151 n.2, 175 n.1

Athenaeum, The, 49 n.8, 60 n.3, 78 n.2, 118 n.2, 125, 126 n.3, 149, 160 n.2

Attenborough's, 116, 118 n.2, 165

Auerbach, Berthold, 90, 91 n.1

Austin, Alfred, 17, 18 nn.4 and 5

autotypes, 47, 49 n.7, 52, 59, 70, 90

Bad Ems, Germany, visit of William and Janey Morris in 1869, xiv, xv, 8, 10, 11, 14, 18, 19, 21, 22, 23 and n.5, 25, 29, 30, 31 n.2

Baldinucci, Filippo, xvi, 142 and n.2, 181

Balfour, Arthur, 54, 55 n.4

Balliol College, Oxford, 26 n.3

Bancroft Collection, Wilmington, U.S.A., 9 n.9, 49 n.4, 102 n.3, 107 n.3, 145 n.1, 171 n.2, 176 n.1

Banting, William, 22, 23 n.9

Barker, Alexander, 97 and n.1

Barnaby Rudge, xv

Bates, Edmund, 114 n.1

Beerbohm, Max, xix

Bellevue House, Chelsea Embankment, 166, 167 n.3

Benson, A. C., 102 n.2

Birchington-on-Sea, Sussex, xx, 96 n.1, 188 n.1

Bird, Elfrida, 25, 26 n.4

Birmingham City Art Gallery, 67 n.4, 100 n.1, 112 n.2, 188 n.1

Blake, William, 53 n.7, 104, 145 n.4, 148 n.8, 167

Boccaccio, Giovanni, 40, 43 n.1, 97

Bodichon, Dr. Eugene and Mrs., 36 and n.4

Boltons, The, 166 and n.2

Bordighera, Italy, visit of Janey Morris with Mr. and Mrs. Howard in 1881, vi, xx, 167, 168 n.1, 171, 172, 174, 175, 176

Boswell, James, xvi, xx, 186, 187

Botticelli, Sandro, xviii, 9 n.9, 97–9, 110, 113, 118 n.1, 133, 152; paintings: *Smeralda Bandinelli*, 110, 112 n.3, 152; *The Story of Nastasio degli Onesti*, 97 and n.1, 98

Bowman, Sir William, 82 and n.1 to l.43

Boyce, George P., 5 n.2, 33 n.1, 82 n.1 to l.42, 118 n.1

Boyd, Miss Alice, visited by D. G. Rossetti in 1869, xiv, 4 n.1, 9 n.7, 25, 26 n.3, 30, 33 n.1

Briggs, R. C. H., v

British Library, The, 68 n., 192

British Museum, The, v, vi, 9 n.12, 15 n.13, 18 n.1, 23 n.8, 33 n.1, 55 n.3

Brooklyn Museum, New York, 70 n.1

Brown, Ford Madox, v, xviii, 15 n.8, 17, 20, 23 and n.6, 31 n.3, 33 n.1, 37 n.5, 52, 53 n.6, 55 n.2, 58 n.2, 78 n.2, 86, 87, 88 n.6, 91, 118, 145 n.2, 149 n.1, 153, 162, 163, 193 and n.1; paintings: *Chaucer at the Court of Edward III*, 23 n.6; *The Story of St. Edith*, 86, 87, 88 n.5

Brown, Mrs. F. Madox ('Emma'), 153, 162

Brown, Lucy Madox, *see* Rossetti, Mrs. W. M.

Brown, Oliver Madox ('Nolly'), xvi, 39 n.2, 78 and n.2, 149 n.1, 163

Browning, Robert, xvi, 9 n.2

Bruges, 14, 15 n.11

Buchanan, Robert ('Thomas Maitland'), attack on D. G. Rossetti in 1871, xvi, 148, 160, 161 n.2, to l.118

Burden, Elizabeth ('Bessie'), 1 and n.1, 8, 9 n.14, 17, 148 and n.11, 191
Burden, Jane ('Janey'), see Morris, Mrs. W.
Burlington Fine Arts Club, 148 n.8
Burlington Magazine, 166–7 n.2
Burne-Jones, Sir Edward Coley ('Ned'), xvi, xviii, 7, 9 nn.1, 3, and 9, 10, 21, 23 n.7, 36, 37 n.5, 40, 52, 54, 55 nn.2, 4, and 5, 56, 58, 67 and n.5, 85, 86, 92, 113, 118, 120, 122, 123, 143, 147, 161, 162, 163, 171, 173, 174 n.4, 175, 185, 188, 191, 195, 204; paintings: Beatrice, 12, 13, 15 n.5; Phyllis and Demophoon, 110, 111, 112 n.2; The Tree of Forgiveness, 112 n.2; Writings: Letters to Katie, 182 n.1
Burne-Jones, Lady ('Georgie'), 143, 145 n.2, 188
Burne-Jones, Philip, 67 n.5, 186
Burns, Robert, 21, 24, 25, 26 n.3
Burton, Sir Frederick William, 114 n.1, 120, 122 n.3, 125
Butler, Samuel, xvi, 78 and n.1
Byerley, Thomas ('Reuben Percy'), 174 n.1
Byron, George Gordon, Lord, 148

Calderón de la Barca, Pedro, xvi, 126, 129, 130, 131, 132, 134, 136
Caravaggio, 142
Carlyle, Thomas, 9 n.15
'Carroll, Lewis', see Dodgson, Charles Lutwidge
Cassavetti family, 9 n.4, 37 n.5, 86, 88 n.5
Cassavetti, Maria, see Zambaco, Mrs. D. T.
Cavalcaselle, G. B., see Crowe, J. A.
Chatterton, Thomas, xvi, 145 n.4, 152 and n.2
Chaucer, Geoffrey, 140
Cheyne Walk, Chelsea (No. 15), 167 n.4; see also Tudor House (No. 16)
Christie's sale rooms, 97, 175
Clarissa Harlowe, 107, 118
Clayton, Oscar, 119
Coleridge, Samuel Taylor, xvi, 108, 135 and n.2, 136, 137, 139, 142 n.1, 143, 145 n.4, 148 and n.10
Colonna, Vittoria, 54, 55 n.3
Cologne, visit by William and Janey Morris en route for Bad Ems, 1869, 8, 10, 14
Coming of Love, The (W. T. Watts-Dunton), 49 n.8

Comyns Carr, J., 159, 160 n.7
Contemporary Review, 160, 161 nn.1 and 2 to l.118, 166, 192
Conway, Daniel Moncure, 149 and n.1
Corder, Frederick, 92 n.1 to l.54
Corder, Rosa, xix, 15 n.8, 91, 92 n.1 to l.54, 118 n.2, 165, 202
Cornforth, Fanny, xx, 102 n.3, 166–7 n.2, 185 n.1
Coronio, Mrs. Aglaia, 25, 26 n.4, 35 n.1, 37 n.6, 56, 123, 141, 160, 161, 169, 180, 181, 199
Costa, Giovanni, xviii, 48 n.1, 112–13, 114 n.2
Cottle, Joseph, xvi, 108, 139, 142, 143, 148 and n.10,
Country Life, 26 n.2
Cousins, Samuel, R. A., 14, 15 n.13
Cowden Clarke, Charles and Mary, 185, 186 n.1
Cowper-Temple, Hon. William (later Lord Mount-Temple), 43 n.3, 54, 55 n.1, 56, 99
Cowper-Temple, Mrs., 40, 43 n.3, 99
Crabb, Edward, 166–7 n.2
Crabb, Mrs. E., 166 and n.2, 199
Craies, W. J. and Mrs., 136 and n.1
Crowe, J. A., and Cavalcaselle, G. B., xvi, 95, 96 n.3, 103
Culture and Anarchy, 55 n.6

Daily News, 85
Dalziel brothers (engravers), 49 n.5
Dante Alighieri, xvi, 75, 79, 80, 81, 94, 95, 124 and n.2, 158
Davies, William, of Liverpool, 53 n.7, 58 and n.4, 59, 88, 91 n.2, 153
Decameron, 97 n.1
Deceased Wife's Sister Marriage Act (1907), xix, 147, 148 n.9
Dickson (Dixon), Thomas, 104 and n.1 to l.67
Divina Commedia, 9 n.15
Dodgson, Charles Lutwidge ('Lewis Carroll'), xx
Donne, John, xvi, 142
Doughty, Oswald, v, xii, 14 n.1
Du Maurier, George Louis, 188 n.2
Dundee City Art Gallery, 178 n.1
Dunn, Henry Treffry, xx, 27, 29 n.2, 30, 31, 32, 39, 42, 62, 63, 69, 75, 76, 86, 99, 105, 107, 108, 141, 142, 203

Dürer, Albrecht, 24

Eliot, George, 160 n.4
Ellis, Frederick Startridge, 5 n.1, 8, 9
  n.13, 18 n.4, 28, 35, 53 n.4, 74, 75 n.1,
  81, 99, 100 n.1, 103, 105, 107 and n.3,
  114, 166, 178
Emerson, Ralph Waldo, 9 n.15
English Poets, The (ed. T. H. Ward, 1880),
  152 and n.2
Erewhon, xvi, 78 and n.1
Evans, W. H., 36 and n.2

Family Letters of Christina Rossetti (ed.
  W. M. Rossetti), 80 n.2
Faulkner, Charles, 9 n.14, 36 n.2
Faulkner, Lucy, 8, 9 n.14, 17
Fèret, J. J., 64 n.1
Fine Arts Company, Bond Street, 73–4
Fitzgerald, Edward, xvi, 126 and 127 n.1,
  128, 162 n.1
Fitzwilliam Museum, Cambridge, 23 n.2,
  55 n.3
Florence, 55 n.3, 85, 97 n.1, 99 n.1, 122,
  127, 143, 175, 176, 178, 179, 190; Casa
  Pucci, 97 and n.1
Fogg Museum, Harvard, 53 n.5, 60 n.2,
  101 n.1, 108 n.1, 171 n.1
Foord and Dickinson (picture-frame
  makers), 91
Forbes-Robertson, Johnston, 14, 67 n.2
forgeries of Rossetti drawings, 116, 118
  n.2
Forman, Henry Buxton, 17, 18 n.6, 27,
  29 n.3, 112 n.1
*Fors Clavigera. Letters to the Workmen and
  Labourers of Great Britain* (1871–84),
  55 n.2, 104 and n.3
Fortnightly Review, 17, 18 n.3
Fredeman, W. E., 26 n.3, 78 n.2, 194 n.1
Frere Gallery, Washington, 9 n.9
Frick Collection, New York, 92 n.1 to
  l.54
Friend, The, 135 n.2
Fry, Clarence E., 65, 67 n.3, 86, 176 n.1
Fry, Samuel, 85, 86, 88
Fulham, *see* Arundel House

Gamberale, Luigi, 181 and n.4
Gaskell, Charles Milne, 100 n.2

Gaskell, Lady Catherine, 99, 100 n.2
George III, 90, 91 n.3
Gerard, John, 140 and n.1
Germ, The, 29 n.5, 60 n.3
Ghent, 14, 30, 31
Gilbert, Sir John, 81, 82 n.2
Gilbert, W. S., 55 n.2
Gilchrist, Alexander, 148 n.8
Gilchrist, Mrs. A., 147, 148 n.8
Gilchrist, Herbert H., 147, 148 n.8;
  painting: *Rossetti's Studio*, 148 n.8
Gillman, James, xvi, 108, 142 and n.1, 143,
  148
Girton College, Cambridge, 36 n.4
Gladstone, William Ewart, 54, 95, 145
  and n.5, 156
Gloucester, William Frederick, Duke of,
  90, 91 n.3
Gloucester, William Henry, Duke of, 91
  n.3
Graham, John, 9 n.6
Graham, William, M.P., xvii, 4 nn.1 and
  3, 7, 9 nn.5 and 6, 11, 12, 26 n.6, 50, 53
  n.5, 56, 58 n.3, 60, 67 n.2, 69 and n.2,
  92, 93, 94, 104 n.1 to l.66, 108 n.1, 113,
  114, 117, 127, 153, 171 nn.1 and 2, 173,
  178 n.1, 193 n.1
Grange, The, North End Road, Fulham,
  174 n.4
Gray, Thomas, 152 n.2
Greville, Charles Cavendish Fulke, 90,
  91 n.2
Grimm, Hermann, 95, 96 n.4
Grosvenor Gallery, xiii, xviii, 9 n.2, 54,
  55 n.2, 56, 64, 65, 67 and n.5, 85
Grylls, R. Glynn, 127 n.1
Guido Reni, 142

Hake, George, 80 and n.1 to l.41
Hake, Dr. Thomas Gordon, 49 n.8, 80
  n.1 to l.41, 193
Hall Caine, Thomas Henry, v, xv, xvii,
  xx, 39 n.2, 58 n.4, 67 n.2, 104–5, 107
  n.1, 139, 141, 147, 158, 159, 161 n.1 to
  l.118, 178 n.1, 181, 184, 185 and n.1,
  186, 188 n.2
Hamilton, Mrs. (née Leyland), 102, 147,
  149
Hamlet House, Hammersmith, 149 and
  n.1
Hammersmith: The Mall, 166, 207; *see
  also* Kelmscott House; Hamlet House

Hastings, Sussex, 36 and n.4, 136, 139, 140, 147, 190 n.1
Heaton, Aldam, 71 n.1
Heaton, Ellen, 178 n.1
Henderson, Philip, 18 n.2
Herball or generall Historie of Plantes (1597) (J. Gerard), 140 and n.1
Herbert, Ruth, see Crabb, Mrs. Edward
History of Painting (F. Baldinucci), 181
History of painting in Italy from the second to the fourteenth century, A (J. A. Crowe and G. B. Cavalcaselle), 96 n.3, 103
Hogg, Thomas Jefferson, 180, 181 n.2, 182, 185
Holbein, Hans, 124 and n.3
Holiday, Henry and Mrs., 143, 145 n.3, 170
Horner, Frances, 9 n.5
Horrington House, Turnham Green, v, xviii, 39 and n.1 to l.20, 43 n.2, 65, 67 n.1, 69, 76, 83 n.1, 88
Howard, George James, M.P. (later Lord Carlisle), vi, xviii, xx, 43, 48 n.1, 52, 95, 112 n.4, 114 and n.2, 115, 117, 122, 167, 168 n.1, 171, 172, 174, 176
Howard, Mary, see Murray, Lady Mary
Howard, Mrs. Rosalind (later Lady Carlisle), 48 n.1, 68, 73, 115, 122, 167, 168 n.1, 169, 172, 176
Howell, Charles Augustus, xix, 5 n.2, 12, 14 n.2, 15 n.8, 29 n.6 37 n.5, 42, 43 n.4, 47–8, 67 nn.2 and 3, 74, 77, 91, 92 n.1 to l.54, 116, 118 nn.1, 2 and 3, 127, 133, 134, 147, 164, 165, 175 n.1, 201
Howell, Mrs. C. A. ('Kate'), 11, 14 n.2, 17, 116
Hughes, Arthur, 151 and n.2; paintings: April Love, 151 n.2; Home from Sea, 151 n.2
Hughes, Arthur F., 151 and n.2
Hughes, Arthur R., 151 and n.2
Hughes, Edward ('Ted'), 86
Hugo, Victor, 173
Hunt, Thornton, 158
Hunt, William Holman, xix, 25, 59, 62, 130, 131 and n.1, 147, 148 n.9, 151 n.2, 154, 171 n.1
Huntington Hartford Gallery, 55 n.4

Iceland, visits of William Morris, 36 n.2, 59, 104, 107
Illustrated London News, 82 n.1

Il Purgatorio, 160 n.2
International Association of Working Men, 55 n.6
Ion – a Grandfather's Tale (A. C. Ionides Jr.), 9 n.4
Ionides, Aglaia, see Coronio, Mrs.
Ionides, Aleco, 36, 37 n.6, 152
Ionides, Alexander, 26 n.4, 37 n.6, 93 n.1
Ionides, Alexander Constantine, Junior, 9 n.4
Ionides, Anthea Chariclea, 36, 37 n.6
Ionides, Constantine (patron of D. G. Rossetti), xvii, xviii, 37 n.6, 56, 92, 100 n.3, 112 n.3, 120, 122 and n.2, 123, 127, 129, 134, 136 n.1, 152, 154, 156, 160, 169, 174, 175 and n.2, 176
Ionides, Euterpe, see Craies, Mrs.
Ionides family, 7, 9 n.4, 160
Ionides, Luke, 25, 26 n.4, 37 n.6
Iolanthe, 148 n.9
Italy, visit of Mrs. Morris and her daughters 1877–8, 39 n.1, 40, 43, 58, 67 n.1 (see also Oneglia); D. G. Rossetti discusses photographs of frescoes, 110; visit there of C. Fairfax Murray, 117, 164; report of W. J. Stillman, 123; visit there of F. R. Leyland, 149; visit of Mrs. Morris with Mr. and Mrs. Howard, 170, 172, 175, 184 (see also Bordighera)

James, Henry, xx, 9 n.15
Jervis, Agnes, see Lewes, Mrs. J. H.
Jervis, Swynfen, M.P., 158, 160 n.4
Jones, Ebenezer, 77 and n.2, 170
Jones, Sumner, 77 n.2
Journal of the William Morris Society, v

Keats, Fanny, see Llanos, Mrs. V.
Keats, John, xv, 109, 112 n.1, 113, 137, 139, 145, 159, 185; Endymion, 137
Keene, Charles, 195
Kelmscott House (formerly The Retreat), The Mall, Hammersmith, v, vi, xviii, xx, 40, 43 n.2, 47, 56, 61, 62, 63, 64, 65, 83 and n.1, 84, 88, 148 n.6, 204, 205, 206
Kelmscott Manor, Lechlade, v, xv, xvi, xvii, xviii–xix, xx, 4 n.1, 9 n.13, 39 n.3, 42, 43 n.2, 46, 49 n.4, 55 n.3, 71, 76 n.1, 77, 79, 80 n.1, 114, 115, 117, 118, 156, 175, 181 n.1, 185, 186, 188, 194 n.1, 197, 207

Kelmscott Press, 9 n.13
Kemble, Fanny, xx
Keswick, Cumberland, visit of D. G.
    Rossetti in 1881, xx, 181, 187
Kingis Quair, The, 9 n.7, 26 n.3
Kipling, Rudyard, 23 n.7
Knewstub, W. J., 29 n.2

Lady Lever Art Gallery, Port Sunlight,
    9 n.8, 112 n.2, 171 n.1
Lake District, The, xvi, xx, 185 and n.1,
    187; *see also* Keswick
Lamb, Charles, 148
Landseer, Charles, R.A., 12, 15 n.4
Landseer, Sir Edwin, R.A., 15 n.4
Lawrence, Sir Thomas, R.A., 15 n.13
Lawrence Gallery, The (1853), 55 n.3
Lawson, Cecil Gordon, 166, 167 n.4
Leathart, James, xvii, 171 n.2
Le Bourgeois, L., 191 n.1
Legros, Alphonse, 48 n.1
Leigh-Smith, Barbara, *see* Bodichon,
    Mrs. E
Leighton, Frederick, 5, 15 n.7, 114 n.2
Letters of Dante Gabriel Rossetti, The (ed.
    O. Doughty and J. R. Wahl), *see* notes
    passim
Letters of D. G. Rossetti to his Publisher, The
    (ed. O. Doughty), 14 n.1
Letters of William Morris (ed. P. Henderson),
    18 nn.2 and 4
Lewes, Mr. J. H. and Mrs., 158, 160 n.4
Lewis, Sir George Henry, 182 and n.1
Leyland, Frederick R., xvii, xviii, 8, 9
    nn.8 and 9, 11, 12, 56, 69, 93, 97, 99 n.1,
    102, 112 n.2, 116, 117, 133, 147, 148
    nn.3 and 7, 149, 160 n.2, 163–4, 171 n.1,
    176 and n.1, 179, 202
Leys, Jean Auguste Henri, 2, 4 n.2
Leyton House, nr. Walthamstow, Essex,
    4 and n.5, 5
Life with Rossetti (G. Pedrick), 29 n.2
Lindsay, Sir Coutts, 55 n.2, 85
Lippincottts Magazine, 148 n.8
Little Holland House, Kensington, 5, 9
    n.1, 15 n.7
Liverpool, xvii, xx, 9 n.9, 67 nn.2 and 4,
    85, 133, 147, 163, 178 and n.1, 179, 181,
    185, 188; Corporation, 178 and n.1;
    see also Walker Art Gallery
*Lives of the most eminent painters, sculptors
    and architects* (G. Vasari, trans. J. Foster,

1855–64), 95, 96 n.2
Llanos, Valentin, 112 n.1
Llanos, Mrs. V., xv, 109, 112 n.1
London, xviii, xx, 2, 15, 21, 23, 28, 29,
    30, 31, 50, 60, 64, 68, 76, 93, 118, 141,
    163, 175, 176, 181, 182, 189
London Journal, The, 79 n.1, 81, 82 n.2
Losh, Miss, 24, 26 nn.1 and 2, 27, 33 n.1
Losh, Sara, 26 n.2
Lowell, James Russell, 9 n.15
Lushington, Godfrey, 55 n.5
Lushington, Rt. Hon. Stephen, M.P., 55
    n.5
Lushington, Vernon, 54, 55 n.5, 56

MacCracken, Francis, 171 n.2
Macdonald, George, xviii, 40, 43 n.2, 63,
    147, 148 n.6
Mackail, J. W., 23 n.7
Macmillan, Alexander, 8
Magazine of Art, The, 15 n.7
Magnusson, Eirik, 36 n.2
Main, David, 131 n.2, 151 n.1
'Maitland, Thomas', *see* Buchanan, Robert
Mallarmé, Stéphan, xviii, 174 n.6
Manchester, 45, 53 n.6, 56, 63, 65, 91, 118,
    156, 162; City Art Gallery, 67 n.3;
    Town Hall, 52, 54 n.6, 119; *see also*
    Whitworth Art Gallery
Manet, Edouard, xviii, 174 and n.6
Marillier, H. C. xii, 58 n.3
Marks, Murray, 107 n.3, 118 n.2
Marshall, Dr. John, xix, 21, 23 n.6, 59, 60,
    61
Marshall, Peter Paul, 14, 15 n.12, 21, 52
Marzials, Théophile, xix, 85, 88 and n.6
Mason, 'Bertie', 118 n.4
Mason, G. H., 114 n.2
May, Mrs., 62, 63
Mazzini, Giuseppi, 163
Memling, Hans, 14, 15 n.11
Memorials of Sir Edward Burne-Jones (Lady
    Burne-Jones), 145 n.2
Memories and Friends (A. C. Benson), 102
    n.2
Memories (L. Ionides), 26 n.4
Metropolitan Museum, New York, 124
    n.3
Michelangelo, 54, 55 n.3, 95, 96 n.4, 110,
    152, 197; paintings: *Holy Family*, 110;
    Ideal Head of a Woman, 55 n.3
Millais, Sir John Everett, 14, 15 n.13, 175

and n.2, 176; paintings: *The Carpenter's Shop*, 175; *Lorenzo and Isabella*, 175 and n.2, 176; *The Minuet*, 14, 15 n.13; *The Order of Release*, 15 n.13

Milton, John, 109, 164

Moore, Florence, xvii, 102 and n.1, 124

Morris, Marshall, Faulkner & Co., 1 n.1, 5 n.3, 9 n.14, 15 n.12, 37 n.6, 60 n.1, 82 n.2, 145 n.3, 148 n.4, 191 n.1

Morris, Jane, *see* Morris, Mrs.

Morris, Jane Alice ('Jenny'), v, xv, 1, 2, 4 n.4, 43, 48 n.2, 49, 52, 114, 148, 151, 170, 172, 182, 185, 190, 191

Morris, May, v, xv, 1, 2, 4 n.4, 42, 43, 49, 57, 71, 101 n.3, 109, 114, 122, 128, 136, 148, 170, 172, 185, 190

Morris, William ('Top', 'Topsy'), v, xiv, xv, xviii, xix, 1, 4, 5 n.2, 8, 9 n.13, 10, 11, 14, 15 and n.6, 17, 18 and nn.2 and 5, 19, 20, 21, 23 and nn.5 and 7, 24, 25, 26, 27, 29 and n.1, 30, 31, 33, 35 and n.1, 36 and n.2, 39 n.1 to l.20 and n.1 to l.21, 42, 43 n.2, 48 n.1, 50, 53 n.3, 55, 62, 64, 67 nn.1 and 6, 76, 77, 83, 85, 86, 88 n.3, 95, 96 n.5, 108, 109, 112, 114, 118, 130, 134, 147, 148 n.6, 158, 163, 172, 173, 175, 180, 187, 195; writings: *The Earthly Paradise*, xiv, 4, 5 n.1, 18 n.7, 23 nn.5 and 10, 29 and n.7, 30, 31 n.2

Morris, Mrs. W. ('Janey'), v, vi, vii, xiii, xiv–xx *passim*, 33, 34, 35, 36 n.4, 37, 68–71, 84–93 *passim*; Portraits, Frontispiece, 3, 195, 196; visits Bad Ems, 1869, 5–31; visits Oneglia, 1877–8, 39–67; moves from Turnham Green to Hammersmith, 61–83 *passim*; visits Naworth Castle, August 1879, 112–20; visits Bordighera 1880–1, 167–180; arranges return of D. G. Rossetti's belongings from Kelmscott, 71–82; exchanges views on books with D. G. Rossetti, 78–81 *passim*, 95–7 *passim*, 104–9 *passim*, 115–18 *passim*, 126–7, 128–52 *passim*, 173–5, 180–2, 185–8; D. G. Rossetti portraits and drawings of her, 1, 2, 3, 4 n.1, 7–8, 15–16, 45, 47, 50–2, 59, 64, 65, 69–73 *passim*, 89, 94–113 *passim*, 117–31 *passim*, 146–62 *passim*, 171–84 *passim*, 188, 190

Morris, Mrs. (mother of William Morris), 4 n.5

Moxon & Co., 49 n.5

Murray, Charles Fairfax, 49 n.4, 67 and n.4, 84, 85, 86, 88 n.3, 102 and n.2, 103, 105, 110, 111, 113, 117, 122–3, 125, 151, 160, 162 and n.1, 164, 176, 195

Murray, Mrs. C. Fairfax, 85, 86, 103, 112

Murray, Lady Mary, xx, 176

Museum of Art, Toledo, Ohio, 162 n.2

Museum of Art, University of Kansas, 160 n.2

Museum of Fine Arts, Boston, 23 n.2

National Gallery, London, 9 n.5, 110, 113, 117, 122 n.3, 124

National Liberal League, 96 n.5

Naworth Castle, Cumberland, vi, xviii, 49 n.1, 112 and n.4, 114, 115, 117, 118

Nettleship, Henry, 9 n.2

Nettleship, John Trivett, 5, 9 n.2, 12, 15 n.4, 20, 173

Nettleship, Richard Lewis, 9 n.2

New Monthly Magazine, 107 n.1

Noble, James Ashcroft, 160, 161 n.1 to l.118, 192

North American Review, 9 n.15

North End House, Rottingdean, 143, 173, 174 n.4, 175

Norton, Charles Eliot, 8, 9 n.15, 12, 20, 23 n.2

Norton, Mrs. C. E., 23 n.2

Notes and Queries, 77 n.2, 191 n.1

Notizie de' professori del disegno da Cimabue in qua (1681–1728) (F. Baldinucci), 142 and n.2

Oakley Street, London, 166, 167 n.4

O'Conor, Mrs. Roderic, 153 n.1

Odger, George, xv, 55 and n.6, 64

Old Water Colour Society, xviii, 112 n.2

Oneglia, Italy, visit by Janey Morris, 1877, xv, 39 n.1 to l.21, 42, 48 and n.1, 53, 55, 58, 60, 64, 67 and nn.1 and 5, 68, 167

Ordsall Old Hall, nr. Manchester, 156, 160 n.3

O'Shaughnessy, Arthur, xviii, 9 n.2, 171 and n.3, 173, 174 and n.6, 175

Oxford and Cambridge Magazine, 55 n.5

Oxford Union Debating Hall, 15 n.7

Paintings and Drawings of Dante Gabriel Rossetti (1828–1882), *The*, A Catalogue Raisonné (V. Surtees), vi, *see* notes *passim*

INDEX

Palma, Jacopo, 103, 110, 113, 114 n.1, 117, 125

Paris, xviii, 67 and n.5, 102, 171, 174 n.6

Pater, Walter, 145 n.2

Patience, 55 n.2

Payne, Burnett, 30, 31 n.3

Pedrick, Gale, 29 n.2

Penkill Castle, Ayrshire, xiv, 8, 9 n.7, 11, 18, 19, 20, 21, 22, 23, 26 and n.2, 29, 31 and n.3, 33, 145 n.5

Percy Anecdotes, The (Joseph Clinton Robertson and Thomas Byerley, alias Sholto and Reuben Percy), 173, 174 n.1

Petrarch, 186

Petworth House, Sussex, 124 and n.3

Pines, The, Putney Hill, 49 n.8, 118 n.4

Pinti, Raffaelli, 116, 118 n.1

Plint, Thomas E., xvii

Poe, Edgar Allen, xviii, 159, 174 and n.6

Polidori, Frances, *see* Rossetti, Mrs. Gabriele

Portrait of Rossetti (R. Glynn Grylls), 127 n.1

Poynter, Sir Edward, 123

Prado, The, Madrid, 99 n.1

Pre-Raphaelite Twilight (H. Rossetti Angeli), 15 n.8, 43 n.4, 92 n.1 to l.54

Price, Cormell ('Crom'), 21, 23 n.7, 67, 118, 120, 123, 155, 190 n.1

Prinsep, Henry Thoby, 9 n.1, 15 n.7

Prinsep, Mrs. H. T., 5, 9 n.1

Prinsep, Valentine Cameron, xv, 9 n.1, 12, 14, 15 nn.7 and 9; painting: *The Lion's Mouth*, 12, 15 n.9

Prinsep, Mrs. V. C., 15 n.7

Pucci family, xviii, 97–9

Punch, 188 n.2

Pusey House, Oxford, 92 n.1 to l.54

Quarterly Review, The, 58 n.4

Queen Square (No. 26), Bloomsbury, 2, 33, 34, 35, 36, 37, 39 n.1

Rae, George, of Birkenhead, xvii, 69 and n.2

Raphael, Sanzio, 124 and n.2

Recollections of Writers (C. and M. Cowden Clarke), 185, 186 n.1

Red House, Upton, 15 n.6

Reeves, Harry, 91 n.2

Reid, Forrest, 145 n.2

Reynolds, Sir Joshua, 15 n.13, 53 n.7

Richardson, Samuel, 174 n.4

Richmond, William Blake, 85 and n.1, 153, 154 n.1

Robertson, Graham, 136 n.1

Robertson, Joseph Clinton ('Sholto Percy'), 174 n.1

Rome, 58, 59, 90, 112, 122, 145

Rossetti, Christina, xvi, 17, 18 n.6, 27, 37 n.4, 80 and nn.1 and 2 to l.40, 104 n.1 to l.67, 117, 128, 136, 145 n.5, 150, 151 n.2, 160 n.4, 178; writings: *Collected Poems* (ed. W. M. Rossetti), 80 n.2 to l.40; *Early Italian Poets*, 80 n.1 to l.40; *Sing Song Poems*, xvi, 80 n.2, 81, 151 n.2

Rossetti, Dante Gabriel, v, vi, vii, xii–xx *passim*, 5, 9 nn.5, 7, 9, 11 and 13, 14 and n.2, 15 nn. 5, 7, 8 and 11, 23 nn.2 and 6, 55 nn.1, 2, 3 and 5, 67 and nn. 3, 4, and 5, 118 nn.1 and 2; portrait, 195; self-portrait, 195; visit to Penkill Castle, 1869, 8, 11, 15, 18, 19, 23–31; sittings by Janey Morris, 1, 2, 25, 33, 47, 69, 96, 150, 153–5, 184, 185; sends gift to Jane and May Morris, 1–4; dealings with patrons and buyers, 7, 11, 12, 30, 45, 56, 63, 65, 69, 74, 78, 82, 92, 93, 94, 97, 99, 100, 116, 117, 120, 122, 127–8, 134, 149, 152, 159, 160, 161, 171, 174, 176, 178, 179, 185; sittings by models other than Janey Morris, 8, 11, 12, 17, 20, 36, 40, 47, 93, 102, 117, 122, 124, concern for Janey Morris's health, 10, 18, 21, 23, 25, 26, 29, 31, 35, 39, 40, 49, 50, 57, 58–9, 60, 61, 68, 77, 81, 82, 88, 92, 95, 102, 104, 105, 115, 130, 131, 184; gives details of his writing, 17, 20, 25, 27–8, 30, 35, 39, 75, 113, 124, 125, 128, 134, 135, 136–7, 147, 149, 159, 161, 165, 167–9, 175, 178; details of domestic arrangements, 28, 40, 42, 47, 49, 50, 61–2, 63, 64, 65, 83, 90, 100, 102, 105, 112, 147, 149, 166, 187; details of artistic work, 37, 45, 47, 50–2, 54, 56, 59, 63, 64–5, 69, 71, 74, 89, 93, 94–5, 99, 103, 105, 113, 125, 129, 130, 138, 140–1, 143, 145, 146, 152, 153–5, 156, 159, 162, 171, 173, 179, 182, 186, 188; assists James Smetham, 52–63 *passim*; removes belongings from Kelmscott Manor, 71–82; breakdown, 1872, 193–4; discusses books with Janey Morris, 78, 79, 80, 81, 90, 95, 96, 97, 103, 105, 107,

108, 109, 114, 120, 126–7, 128, 129, 130, 131, 132, 134–5, 136, 139, 142, 143, 152, 159, 167, 180–1, 182, 185, 186, 187, 188; framing of pictures, 91; paintings and drawings: *Astarte Syriaca*, 65, 66, 175 n.1, 176 n.1; *Beata Beatrix*, xvii, 43 n.3; *Beatrice* (see also *Salutation of Beatrice*, The), 8, 9 n.10, 12, 128, 130, 146, 148 n.3; *Beatrice meeting Dante at a marriage feast denies him her Salutation*, 23 n.2; *Before the Battle*, 23 n.2; *The Blessed Damozel*, 50, 51, 53 n.5, 54, 56, 69 and n.1, 94, 103, 104 n.2, 125, 126 n.3, 171 and n.1; *Bruna Brunelleschi*, 54; *Carlisle Wall*, 175 n.1; *Dante's Dream*, xvii, 9 n.5, 25, 26 n.6, 58 n.3, 64, 65, 67 n.2, 78, 93 and n.1, 94–5, 96, 97, 103, 104 n.1, 107, 108 n.1, 113, 117, 174 n.2, 178 and n.1, 188; *The Day Dream* ('Vanna', 'Monna Primavera'), xvii, xviii, 93 n.1, 99, 101 n.3, 112 n.3, 120, 121, 122 and n.2, 123 n.1, 125, 126 n.2, 141, 146, 148 n.1, 150, 152, 153–4, 155, 159, 160, 161; *Desdemona's Death Song*, xvi–xvii, 117, 182 and n.2, 183, 185; *Domizia Scaligera*, 55 n.1; Drawing of Janey seated in a sycamore tree, xvii; *Fiammetta*, xvii, 43, n.1; *Found*, 119, 120 and n.2, 171 and n.2, 173, 178; *The German Lesson*, xiv, 15, 16, 18 n.1; *King Arthur and the Weeping Queens*, 49 n.5; *La Bella Mano*, 105, 106, 107 n.3; *La Donna della Finestra*, xvii, 9 n.13, 99, 100 n.1, 101, 103, 105, 107 n.2, 117, 149, 175 n.1; *The Lady of Shalott*, 49 n.5; *La Pia de Tolomei*, xvii, 156, 157, 160 and n.2, 162, 176, 178; *Mariana*, 4 n.1, 9 n.10; *Mariana in the South*, 49 n.5; *Mary Magdalene at the Door of Simon the Pharisee*, 166–7 n.2, 199; *Monna Primavera*, see *The Day Dream*; *The M's at Ems*, xiv, 8, 9 n.12, 16; *Pandora*, xvii, 6, 7, 9 n.6, 12, 17, 25, 46, 59, 60 n.2, 89; *Perlascura*, 70, 71 and n.3; Portrait of Jane Morris (1868), xvi, xvii, 2, 3, 4 n.1, 55 n.3; *Proserpine*, xvii, 9 n.13, 44, 45, 49 n.4, 50, 53 n.4, 59, 63, 64, 65, 74, 75 n.1, 89, 99, 188 and n.1; *The Sphinx of the Question* (*The Question*), 37, 38, 39 n.2; *Resolution; or The Infant Hercules*, 22, 23 n.8; *Reverie*, 11–12, 14 n.3, 73, 75 n.1; *Ricordanza* (*Memory*),

176 and n.1, 177; *Risen at Dawn* (or *Gretchen discovering the Jewels*), 47, 49 n.6; *The Roman Widow*, 76 and n.1; *Saint Cecilia*, 49 n.5; *The Salutation of Beatrice*, 162 and n.2, 174, 177, 179; *Sibylla Palmifera*, 7, 8, 9 n.8; *Silence*, 47, 49 n.7, 52, 70 and n.1, 72, 73; *Sir Galahad*, 49 n.5; Study for Llandaff altar-piece, xv; *Twilight*, 52, 59, 73; *Vanna*, see *The Day Dream*; *Venus Verticordia*, 2, 4 n.3; *Veronica Veronese*, 143, 144, 145 n.1; *A Vision of Fiammetta*; 40, 41, 43 n.1, 45, 49 n.4, 59, 63, 64, 69; *Washing Hands*, 15 n.8; *Water Willow*, 45, 46, 49 n.4; writings: 'Ave', 27; *Ballads and Sonnets* (1881), xv, 43 n.1, 134 n.2, 178 and n.2, 178–9, 192; 'Beryl Songs', xv, 135 and n.1, 136–7; 'A Birthday Sonnet', 150, 151; 'The Blessed Damozel', 27; 'The Burden of Nineveh', 27; 'The Card-Dealer', 27; 'The Cloud Confines', 39 and n.3; *Collected Works* (1890), 31 n.1, 152 n.2; 'Dante at Verona', 158, 160 n.5; 'The Day Dream', 159, 160 n.6; 'Dennis Shand', 28; *Early Italian Poets*, 15 n.5; 'Five English Poets', 145 and n.4, 152 n.2; 'Hand and Soul', 28, 29 n.5; *The House of Life*, xv, 9 n.8, 18 n.3, 28, 166 n.1, 168 and n.3, 178 n.2, 192; 'The King's Tragedy', xv, 168, 169 n.2, 175 and n.3; 'My Sister's Sleep', 27, 29 n.4; 'Nocturn', 27; 'Of Life, Love and Death', 18 n.3; 'The Orchard Pit', 30, 31 n.1; *Poems* (1870), xiv, xv, 9 n.13, 11, 14 n.1, 23 n.4, 25, 26 n.5, 31 n.1, 35 n.1, 36 and n.3, 178 n.2; *Poems*, New Edition (1881), 168, 178 and n.2; 'Rose Mary', xv, 135 and n.1, 136, 137; 'Sister Helen', 28, 124, 125 and n.4, 'Songs and Sonnets', 28; 'Sonnets on Pictures', and other sonnets, 28, 139, 142; 'Soul's Beauty', 9 n.8; 'The Staff and Scrip', 27; 'Stratton Water', 28; 'The Stream's Secret', 29 n.1; 'Trial Book', 20, 23 n.4, 25, 26 n.5; 'True Woman', 166 and n.1, 167, 168 n.2; 'Untimely Lost', 78 n.2; 'The White Ship', xv, 155, 160 n.1, 161 and n.2 to l.118

Rossetti, Gabriele, 160 n.4, 168 n.3
Rossetti, Mrs. Gabriele (Frances), xx, 26

n.2, 105, 117, 127, 128, 131 n.2, 150,
174 n.6, 178, 181 n.4, 182
Rossetti, William Michael, v, xix, 17, 18
n.6, 24, 27, 31 n.1, 33 n.1, 80 n.2, 104
n.1, 137, 142, 143, 145 n.5, 147, 153 and
n.1, 160 n.7, 162, 163, 167, 181 n.4,
191 n.1, 193
Rossetti, Mrs. W. M. (Lucy), 9 n.14, 17,
53, 153 and n.1, 162, 163, 180
Rowley, Charles, of Manchester, 49 n.7,
70 n.1, 88 n.6
Royal Academy, 5, 9 n.2, 12, 15 n.4, 23
n.6, 55 n.2, 65, 92 n.1 to l.54, 148 n.8,
151 and n.2, 165 and n.3
Royal Institute of Painters in Water
Colour, 151 n.2
Royal School of Art, 1 n.1
Royal Society, 23 n.6
Rubáiyát of Omar Khayam, xvi, 126
127 n.1, 128
Ruskin, John, 9 n.15, 15 n.8, 55 n.2, 56,
58 n.1, 59, 62, 74, 103–4, 104 n.1 to l.66
and n.7 to l.67, 127, 154 n.1, 159
Ruskin: Rossetti: Pre-Raphaelitism (ed.
W. M. Rossetti), 104 n.1 to l.67

Salome (Oscar Wilde), xvi
Sand, George, 165 n.1
Sandys, Frederick, 15 n.8, 201
San Remo, xx, 172
Scalands, Robertsbridge, nr. Hastings
(q.v.), 36 and n.4, 47, 59, 89, 90
Scotland, 70 n.1; see also Penkill Castle;
Trowan
Scott, David, 26 n.3
Scott, William Bell, xiv, 9 n.7, 24, 25,
26 n.3, 39 n.2, 92, 130, 166, 167 n.3,
193; writings: Albert Dürer: His Life
and Works, 26 n.3; Autobiographical
Notes, 26 n.3, 39 n.2; 'Rosabell',
26 n.3
Seasons: a Satire, The (A. Austin), 17, 18
n.5
Sewter, A. C., 88 n.5
Shakespeare, William, 109, 126, 140
Shelly, Percy Bysshe, 145 n.4, 180, 181
n.2, 182
Shields, Frederick, xviii, xix, 43 n.1, 49
n.7, 52, 53 n.6, 63, 81, 95, 96 n.1, 99
n.1, 102 n.1, 109–10, 138, 156–8, 160
n.3, 161, 171 nn.1 and 2; painting:
Mary Magdalene, 156

Shields, Mrs. F. ('Cissy'), 156, 158, 160 n.3
Siddal, Elizabeth ('Lizzie'), xvii, 20, 29
n.6, 36 n.4, 53, 78, 166 n.2, 168 n.3,
175 n.1; painting: Clerk Saunders,
23 n.2
Siena, 85, 151, 164
Sistine Chapel, 152
Slade School, The, 89 n.1
Smetham, James and Mrs., xviii, xix, 52,
53 n.7, 54, 56–7, 58 and n.4, 59, 62, 63,
89, 109, 120, 200
Smith, Ellen, 15 n.8
Society for the Protection of Ancient
Buildings, 15 n.6, 158
Solomon, Simeon, 143, 145 n.2
Sonnets of Three Centuries (ed. T. H. Hall
Caine), 58 n.4, 186 and n.2
Southey, Robert, 148 and n.10
South Place Religious Society, Finsbury,
149 n.1
Spartali family, 9 n.4
Spartali, Mary, see Stillman, Mrs. W. J.
Speke Hall, Liverpool, 9 n.9, 11
Staatsgalerie, Stuttgart, 55 n.4
Stained Glass of William Morris and his
Circle, The (A. C. Sewter), 88 n.5
Stalky & Co., 23 n.7
Stephens, F. G., 126 n.3, 160 n.2, 170,
171 n.1
Stephens, Frederick James, 59, 60 n.3, 62
Stephens, Holman, 170, 171 n.1
Steward & Brown (framemakers), 91
Stillman, Bella, 43, 48 n.3, 123
Stillman, Euphrosyne ('Effie'), 43, 48 n.3,
96
Stillman, Lisa, 43, 45, 48 n.3, 123, 127, 179
Stillman, Russie, 48 n.3
Stillman, William James, 9 n.11, 36 and
n.4, 40, 43, 53, 122, 123, 125, 127, 143,
153
Stillman, Mrs. W. J. (Mary), xvii, 8, 9
n.11, 12, 17, 20, 23 n.1, 40, 42, 43 and
n.1, 46, 47, 52, 53, 57, 91, 93, 96, 102,
103, 113, 115, 117, 122, 125, 127, 143,
151, 153, 175, 179, 190, 198
Stokes, Whitley, 127 n.1
Street, G. E., 15 n.6
Studies of Sensation and Event (E. Jones), 77
and n.2
Sumner, Mrs. Holme, 53, 55 n.1
Surtees, Virginia, vi, vii, xii, 9 n.10, 39
n.2, 166–7 n.2

Swedenborg, Emmanuel, 168 and n.3
Swinburne, Algernon Charles, xx, 26 n.3, 49 n.8, 55 n.3, 118 n.4, 145 n.2, 192
Switzerland, 21, 23, 26, 148 n.9, 180

Tate Gallery, London, 43 n.3, 69 n.3, 151 n.2, 178 n.1
Taylor, Warrington, 24, 82 and n.2, 191 n.1
Tebbs, Henry Vertue and Mrs. (Emily), 174, 175 n.1, 176
Temple Bar, 17, 18 n.4
Tennyson, Alfred, Lord, 46, 62, 131 n.3
Tennyson Turner, Charles, 131 and n.3
Tennyson, Hallam, 131 n.3
Thirkell, Angela, 174 n.4
Time and Tide, by Weare and Tyne (J. Ruskin), 104 n.1 to l.67
Time Remembered (Frances Horner), 9 n.5
Times, The, 118 n.2
Times Literary Supplement, The, 192
Tinsley's Magazine, 17, 18 n.6, 27, 30
Tite Street, Chelsea, 116
Toledo Museum, Ohio, 148 n.3
Tollemache, Georgiana, see Cowper-Temple, Mrs.
'Top', 'Topsy', see Morris, William
Treasury of English Sonnets, A (ed. D. Main), 131 and n.2, 150, 151 n.1
Trevelyan, Sir Walter, 26 n.3
Trowan, Scotland, 194 n.1
Troxell, Janet Camp, 26 n.1, 104 n.1 to l.67, 118 n.1, 126 n.4, 192, 193
Tudor House (16 Cheyne Walk), Chelsea, xviii, xix, xx, 1, 2, 4, 10, 21, 23 n.3, 31, 34, 37, 40, 49, 50, 53 n.1, 58, 61, 62, 64, 67 n.4, 68, 92 n.1 to l.55, 174 n.6, 179, 181 n.2, 187, 196, 203
Turner, W. A., of Manchester (patron of D. G. Rossetti), 43 n.1, 45, 48 n.4, 56, 63, 65, 69

Uberti, Fazio degli, 79, 80 n.1 to l.40
United Services College, Devon, 21, 23 n.7, 120, 123

Valpy, L. R. (patron of D. G. Rossetti), xvii, 54, 58 and n.3, 67 n.2, 77, 78, 82, 173, 174 n.2, 178 n.1, 186, 188 and n.1
Van Eyck, Jan, 14; painting: The Adoration of the Lamb, 15 n.11

Vasari, Giorgio, xvi, 95, 96 n.2, 97, 107, 108, 110, 142, 181
Vaughan, Virginia, 163, 165 n.1, 170
Venice, 39 n.1 to l.21, 53, 59, 64, 67 n.1, 116
Victoria and Albert Museum, London, 93 n.1 to l.56, 112 n.3, 122 n.2
Vita Nuova, xvi, 71 n.3, 75, 78, 79, 80, 81, 95, 123 n.1

Waagen, G. F., 124 n.3
Wahl, J. R., v, xii
Walker Art Gallery, Liverpool, xviii, 67 nn.2 and 4, 145 n.3, 175 n.2, 178
Wallop, Lady Catherine, see Gaskell, Lady
Ward, T. H., 152 and n.2
Waterford, Lady, 145 n.5
Waterhouse, Alfred, 53 n.6
Watney, Vernon, 99 n.1
Watts, George Frederic, 9 n.1, 99 n.1
Watts-Dunton, Walter Theodore, xx, 5, 12, 15 n.7, 39 n.2, 48, 49 n.8, 53 and n.1, 54, 59, 63, 71, 88, 115, 116, 117, 118 nn.2 and 4, 131 n.1, 143, 152 and n.2, 156, 166, 168 n.3, 173, 180, 185, 192, 201, 203
Webb, Philip, 12, 15 n.6, 18 n.2, 24, 28, 42, 67, 68, 145
Westbrook, Elizabeth T., 164–5, 165 n.3
Whistler, James McNeill, xvii, xviii, xix, 15 n.8, 47–8, 49 n.8, 55 n.2, 74, 115–16, 118 n.3, 133, 163; paintings: Arrangement in Black (portrait of F. R. Leyland), 9 n.9, 202; Arrangement in Black and Brown (portrait of R. Corder), 92 n.1, 202; Gold Scab, The, see Portrait of a Creditor; La Princesse du Pays de la Porcelaine, 9 n.11; Nocturne, 55 n.2; Portrait of a Creditor, 147, 148 n.7
Whitworth Art Gallery, Manchester, 88 n.6
Wieland, Walter, 191 n.1
Wieland, Mrs. W. (formerly Mrs. Warrington Taylor), 191 and n.1
Wilde, Oscar, xvi, 145 n.2, 188 and n.2
Wilding, Alexa, xvii, 9 n.8, 107 n.3, 145 n.1
Wilkinson, Dr. Garth, 168 n.3
Wise, T. J., 39 n.2, 192
Wood, Sir George, 91 and n.4
Wood, M. A., 26 n.2
Wordsworth, William, 135 n.2

INDEX

Working Men's College, 55 n.5
Wreay estate, Woodside, nr. Carlisle, 24, 26 n.2

Young, Miss, 20

Zambaco, Dr. Demetrius T., 37 n.5,
Zambaco, Mrs. D. T. (Maria), 15 n.5, 36, 37 n.5, 42, 86, 88 n.4, 112 n.2, 123 and n.2, 198